THE *ULYSSES* TRIALS
Beauty and Truth Meet the Law

THE *ULYSSES* TRIALS
Beauty and Truth Meet the Law

Joseph M. Hassett

THE LILLIPUT PRESS
DUBLIN

First published by
THE LILLIPUT PRESS
62–63 Sitric Road, Arbour Hill,
Dublin 7, Ireland
www.lilliputpress.ie

A CIP record for this title is available
from The British Library.

ISBN 978 1 84351 668 2

Set in 11 pt on 15 pt Garamond with
Akzidenz Grotesk titling by Marsha Swan
Index by Fergus Mulligan: www.publishing.ie
Printed in Navarre, Spain, by Castuera

Contents

Illustrations   vi

Foreword by Roy Foster   vii

Introduction   1

1. Margaret Anderson's Gospel of Beauty Meets John Quinn   7

2. Beauty and Truth Ignored: Quinn's Defence of 'Cantleman's Spring-Mate' and Early Skirmishes Over *Ulysses*   35

3. The Importance of Pairing Truth with Beauty in Defending *Ulysses*   71

4. John Quinn: The Advocate as Cynic   94

5. Between the Trials: *Ulysses* Wanders   116

6. Ernst, Woolsey and the Hands: *Ulysses* Unbound   125

7. The Impact of the *Ulysses* Decisions   166

8. Postscript: The Afterlives   189

Abbreviations   204

Acknowledgments   205

Bibliography   207

Index   215

Illustrations

Margaret Anderson	13
Jane Heap	14
Henri-Pierre Roché, Constantin Brâncuși and John Quinn, Paris 1921	21
Henri-Pierre Roché, Mme Picasso, Jeanne Robert Foster and John Quinn lunching at Picasso's summer home	21
Yeats at Petitpas' *by John Sloan*	25
John Quinn and W.B. Yeats	28
John Quinn *by John Butler Yeats, 1912*	43
The Little Review, *March, 1918*	54–5
John Sumner burning books	75
Seal of the New York Society for the Suppression of Vice	76
John Quinn and the Governor *by Jack B. Yeats*	89
Joyce's transcription of the New York Tribune *article from which he learned that Anderson and Heap had been convicted of obscenity for publishing an episode of* Ulysses	106
Sylvia Beach and James Joyce in front of Shakespeare and Company, 1921	107
Constantin Brâncuși greets Margaret Anderson and Jane Heap in his studio with Berenice Abbott and Mina Loy	112
Judge John Munro Woolsey	139
Judge Learned Hand	147
Ezra Pound, John Quinn, Ford Maddox Ford and James Joyce in Paris, 1923.	190
The opening of the Jockey Club in Montparnasse in 1923	194
Jane Heap, John Rodker, Martha Dennison, Tristan Tzara, and Margaret Anderson in Paris	195
Shakespeare and Company and Random House Ulysses *covers*	202–3

Foreword by Roy Foster

'Books register the ideas of an age; that is perhaps their chief claim to immortality.' The statement by one of the heroines of this book, Margaret Anderson, might also be applied to the law: which, in key confrontations, can exemplify and clarify a historical moment. This is what happened when James Joyce's great leviathan of a novel, destined to alter the course of literature, came up against the New York Society for the Suppression of Vice and the US Post Office, which literally consigned Joyce's text to the flames. The story has been told before, but never in the way it unfolds on these pages. This is because Joseph Hassett is both a gifted literary critic and a brilliant lawyer. In *The Ulysses Trials* he has succinctly and elegantly revised our understanding of what went wrong in the first trial of *Ulysses*, after Anderson and Jane Heap published extracts in their *Little Review*. And he also demonstrates, with forensic panache, the way it was put right.

Nor is this all. Hassett's previous books have dealt authoritatively with the life and work of W.B. Yeats, and this book provides an important addition to the biography of Yeats's friend and patron, the New York lawyer John Quinn. Subtle and often hilarious layers are added to the portrait of this irascible, talented, well-meaning but often obtuse Irish American, showing that his extraordinary ability to appreciate the coming vogue in art and literature was not always the same thing as understanding it. In this telling, Quinn's own oddly puritanical prejudices, and his 'complicated attitude to sex and secrecy', infused and derailed his attempted defence of Anderson, Heap and Joyce. Hassett's evaluation is in marked contrast to previous treatments, and is powerfully bolstered by the author's knowledge not only of the law, but of the social mores and practices of the contemporary world of lawyers (and of Irish-Americans).

Here we are led deftly and enlighteningly through the nuanced definition by Judge Learned Hand of obscenity, the aesthetic and moral arguments advanced by the advocate Morris Ernst in the later trial involving Random House, and the complicated issues of copyright following the first publication of *Ulysses* by the redoubtable Sylvia Beach. But these arguments never become abstract or obtuse; Hassett has the exceptional lawyer's gift of relating principles and precedents to real people and personal passions, and the astute literary critic's ability to seize the thought behind an author's words. This matters all the more when we are dealing with a writer who opens the English language, in Seamus Heaney's words, like a pack of cards in the hands of a magician. Key Joycean passages are illuminated here, and the elusive figure of Shem the Penman, 'piercing the barrier between private and public', shown in a new though characteristic light.

Above all, this is a story of remarkable people: Anderson and Heap, ecstatically engaged on their mission of truth and beauty; John Butler Yeats, living merrily in New York's Bohemia at Quinn's expense, while offering him – unrecognized – the key to arguing Joyce's case, and concluding regretfully that the lawyer had 'brains but no intellect'; his son, the poet W.B. Yeats, equally astutely noting his friend Quinn's shortcomings, and sharply intuiting the real importance of his one-time protégé Joyce's great novel. But above all, the lawyers steal the show: from puritanical servants of the New York Society for the Suppression of Vice and colourful and sometimes dubious Irish Americans, to perceptive interpreters of the intellectual zeitgeist such as Woolsey and the Hand cousins – 'judges of robust intellect and trenchant pen'. Robustness and trenchancy are evident in every page of this book. Looking back on the saga much later, Learned Hand reflected that for a judge to be 'literary' was 'a very dangerous thing': but danger could be averted if the judge in question was perceptive enough to 'exhibit a complete aptness for the occasion'. Joseph Hassett evinces exactly this combination of literary insight and legal dexterity, which is what makes his book such an original and subtly entertaining contribution to the history of modernist culture.

Roy Foster
Carroll Professor of Irish History,
Hertford College, Oxford

Introduction

The struggle of writers to free themselves from government control over the content of their writing is never-ending. It is at least as old as Plato, who banished poets from his Republic because he thought their seductive verbal pictures harmed society. Oscar Wilde flatly challenged this line of thinking in his famous pronouncement that 'There is no such thing as a moral or an immoral book. Books are well written, or badly written. That is all.'[1] Plato's ideas prevailed over Wilde's in this round of the long struggle. Wilde was imprisoned and effectively banished following a prosecution that started out as an attack on his aesthetic ideas.

The law of obscenity figures prominently in the war between law and literature. An obscenity trial, to borrow Arthur Miller's vivid metaphor, is a crucible for testing the relationship between these mighty cultural engines in which each confronts the other head-on. Literature, by its very existence, asserts a primal right to be heard. The law of obscenity seeks to silence a category of books and threatens to imprison their authors and publishers. Margaret

Anderson, founder of *The Little Review*, and her lover and co-editor Jane Heap, faced just such a threat in 1921 in the form of a criminal trial for publishing an episode of James Joyce's *Ulysses*. Heap saw the charges as an attack by the law on an eternal work of art. She maintained that 'Art is and always has been the supreme Order,' and thus is the only human activity 'that has an eternal quality'. Standing defiantly on this platform, she greeted her trial with the derisive exclamation: 'What legal genius to bring Law against Order!'[2] Heap and Anderson were convicted of a crime for being the first publishers of the immortal prose of what was ultimately recognized as the greatest English-language novel of the twentieth century.

Anderson and Heap urged their lawyer, John Quinn, to argue that Joyce's prose could not be obscene because it was beautiful literature, and Quinn's friend John Butler Yeats outlined an argument based on the societal value of Joyce's 'terrible veracity'.[3] Unfortunately, Quinn, a man of enormous ability and generosity, but hobbled by a mind filled with prejudice and closed to opinions that differed from his own, failed to advance these potentially winning arguments. Instead he made a series of unworthy and cynical points addressed to what he chose to call the 'ignorance' of the 'stupid judges'. After his clients were convicted, he failed to seek an appellate ruling on the important legal issues presented by the criminalization of an innovative piece of writing by a master stylist. Thus *Ulysses* was silenced after the serialization of fourteen of the eighteen episodes contemplated by Joyce.

Although the powerful ideas urged on Quinn about the value of literature's beauty and truth never even made it to court in the 1921 *Little Review* trial, they ultimately prevailed a dozen years later when the completed novel faced obscenity charges in federal court in New York. Responding to arguments by a new lawyer that were similar to those that Quinn ignored, United States District Judge John Munro Woolsey found that *Ulysses* was not obscene because the American public should not be denied exposure to 'an honest effort' by 'a great artist in words' to 'show exactly how the minds of his characters operate'.[4] In affirming Woolsey's decision on appeal, the United States Court of Appeals for the Second Circuit over-ruled a long-standing precedent barring publication of books that contained any passage tending to excite sexual desire. Persuaded by arguments grounded in the truth and beauty of Joyce's novel, the court decided that *Ulysses*, although sexually exciting, was not obscene because literature that was 'written with such evident truthfulness' that is relevant to the subject and 'executed with real art' was immune from the law of obscenity.[5] These federal decisions permanently altered the grounds of future obscenity trials in the United States and had significant repercussions elsewhere.

Ulysses is so much a product of its struggle to be born that many readers know it primarily as a once-banned book that reached the public only after a long voyage through the courts. Indeed, gener-ations of readers first encountered *Ulysses* through the prism of Judge Woolsey's decision, which was published as a preface to the Random House edition of *Ulysses* until 1986 and the Bodley Head edition until 1960. Moreover, as Joyce completed the novel with the result of the *Little Review* trial in mind, he both thumbed his nose at the legal process by incorporating incidents from the pros-ecution into the text, and helped shape the early critical response to the completed novel with an eye to impressing the courts with the book's literary pedigree. The judicial decisions involving *Ulysses* were not only essential to the novel finding its audience, but are also a part of the text and its reception.

In addition to their inherent historical significance, the two obscenity trials involving *Ulysses* are important because their differing approaches and results make them fertile sources of insight into how battles in the long war for freedom of expression are won or lost. There can be no doubt that the war is never over. The legal precedents that governed, and were changed by, the *Ulysses* cases could be changed again. Given the recurring appearance of political candidates who promise more prosecutions of literature, the emergence of misguided criticism of the bases for the *Ulysses* decisions, and the willingness of courts to overrule settled precedents, Judge Richard Posner's suggestion that 'maybe Joyce will be too bawdy for the second half of the twenty-first century' cannot be ignored.[6]

The long-standing need for a comparative study of the two *Ulysses* cases has been obscured by the fact that biographers of both Joyce and Quinn have erroneously and uncritically accepted Quinn's view that the *Little Review* case was unwinnable. The necessity of careful attention to the legal arguments and judicial rationales in the two cases has been brought into sharp focus by a recent book that goes beyond the traditional grudging approbation of Quinn's performance, and lauds it as 'sophisticated legal creativity' by a 'savvy' defence attorney.[7] Quinn, in fact, advanced arguments that were unworthy of Joyce and *Ulysses*, and failed to pursue a strategy that could have brought the novel to the American public a decade before it was finally published in the United States in 1934.

Another critical trend reinforces the timeliness of a comparative study of the two *Ulysses* cases. Proceeding from the erroneous premise that the winning arguments in federal court were based on a so-called 'esthetic theory' that literature has no effect on the reader, this critique argues that the courts have exonerated *Ulysses* at the cost of robbing literature of its power, and thereby failed to 'provide a lasting foundation for freedom of speech', and encouraged 'a dangerous indifferentism'.[8] This critique is based on a misunderstanding of what was actually decided in the federal *Ulysses* decisions, and the nature and context of the arguments that led to an important and enduring victory for freedom of expression.

This backdrop of misunderstanding about the legal decisions involving *Ulysses* invites a book that explores what can be learned from the process by which these epoch-transforming cases were decided. If, as Oliver Wendell Holmes said in the same year as the first *Ulysses* decision, 'a page of history is worth a volume of logic',[9] the important history here is biography – the life stories of the intriguing cast of characters involved in the struggle of *Ulysses* to find an audience. Those life stories show that the quality of the arguments and the subtlety and wisdom of the judicial decisions were heavily influenced by the personalities and educational backgrounds of the publishers, lawyers and judges. The seemingly quotidian experiences of the actors in these great dramas informed their devotion to great ideas like beauty and truth that can make law a profoundly humanizing cultural force.

NOTES

1   Oscar Wilde, *The Picture of Dorian Gray*, 1891, in Joseph Bristow, ed., *The Complete Works of Oscar Wilde* (Oxford: Oxford University Press, 2005) Vol. 3, 167.

2   Jane Heap, 'Art and the Law', *The Little Review* ('LR') (September–December 1920) ('Art and the Law') 5.

3   See Chapter 3.

4   *United States v. One Book Called "Ulysses"*, 5 F. Supp.182 (S.D.N.Y. 1933).

5   *United States v. One Book Entitled Ulysses By James Joyce*, 72 F.2d 705 (2d. Cir. 1934).

6   Richard A. Posner, *Law and Literature* (3rd edn, Cambridge: Harvard University Press, 2009) ('Posner') 505.

7   Kevin Birmingham, *The Most Dangerous Book: The Battle for James Joyce's Ulysses* (New York: Penguin, 2014) ('Birmingham') 168, 194.

8   John Vanderham, *James Joyce and Censorship* (New York: New York University Press, 1998) ('Vanderham') 11–12, 167.

9   *New York Trust Co. v. Eisner*, 256 U.S. 345 (1921).

Margaret Anderson's Gospel of Beauty Meets John Quinn

Margaret Anderson and Jane Heap were extraordinary women. Together they were the high-octane fuel that powered one of the early twentieth century's most influential journals for *avant-garde* literature and art. Anderson was hooked by the genius of *Ulysses* from the moment she read Joyce's description of the way Stephen Dedalus processes his view of Dublin Bay: 'Ineluctable modality of the visible ... Signatures of all things I am here to read, seaspawn and seawrack, the nearing tide.' She immediately told Heap, 'This is the most beautiful thing we'll ever have ... We'll print it if it's the last effort of our lives.'[1] Her comment was eerily prophetic. The effort would exhaust Anderson and Heap and drive them from publishing, largely because their lawyer, John Quinn, the Ohio-born son of Irish immigrants, did not believe in their enterprise and was unpardonably prejudiced against them.

There was nothing particularly literary or artistic about the circumstances into which Anderson was born in Indianapolis, Indiana, in 1886. Nonetheless, she was so thoroughly and instinctively committed to the importance of aesthetic experience, and believed so strongly in her own judgment, that at the age of five she refused to 'correct' her handwriting because she knew it was beautiful, and 'was glad to make a conversation', as she later wrote, 'in which I could use the word beautiful'.[2] After three years at Western College for Women in Oxford, Ohio, she departed for a brief stint at home before concluding, 'I really couldn't see this as my life, which was to be beautiful as no life had ever been.'[3] She moved to Chicago and employment as a book reviewer for a religious magazine founded by Cyrus McCormick, neatly transforming profit from the mechanical harvester into her words of appreciation for literature.

In 1914, at the age of twenty-seven, Anderson founded *The Little Review* in order to satisfy her need for what she described as 'inspired conversation'.[4] Conversation was no idle pastime for Anderson and her circle. Rather, it was exercise of the human mind at its creative heights. Anderson's description of how and why she conjured this remarkable magazine out of her own imagination tells much about her devotion to conversation. Awakening in the night feeling depressed because life was not satisfying her demand that it 'be inspired every moment', she divined the need to 'have inspired conversation every moment'. Most people, she felt, lacked the stamina and time for conversation. The solution came in a flash: 'If I had a magazine I could spend my time filling it up with the best conversation the world has to offer.' Her immediate decision to start such a magazine was rewarded with deep sleep.[5]

An essay she wrote a year later explained that the impetus to this almost mystical experience was a lecture at Maurice Browne's Little Theatre by John Cowper Powys, a British-born novelist, critic and lecturer, who was descended from the poet William Cowper. Powys's lecture drew Anderson's attention to the writings of Walter Pater, founder of the Aesthetic Movement that grew up around his famous dictum that 'success in life' is to achieve 'some mood of passion or insight or intellectual excitement that is irresistibly real and attractive' and 'to burn always with this hard, gem-like flame'.[6] Pater's ideas infused popular lectures in the United States by Oscar Wilde and William Butler Yeats, both of whom emphasized the role of the arts in inspiring a life lived consciously as a performance. Drawing on Wilde, Yeats proclaimed that 'Active virtue, as distinguished from the passive acceptance of a current code is … theatrical, consciously dramatic, the wearing of a mask.'[7] For Yeats, performance of an imagined self was 'the condition of arduous full life'. These ideas were alive in the creatively fertile atmosphere of Chicago as Anderson's concept of her magazine percolated. Her memoir tells of conversations about 'living like the hard gem-like flame' at soirées attended by Floyd Dell, later the influential editor of *The Masses*, Sherwood Anderson, Theodore Dreiser, and Powys himself.[8]

Her editorial in the debut issue of *The Little Review*, entitled 'Announcement', expressly invokes Pater as an exemplar of the creative character of criticism, and is itself an instance of Pater's aesthetic.[9] Addressing her reader as someone who has 'read poetry with a feeling that it was your religion, your very life', Anderson presents her magazine as an antidote to a materialistic society in which 'we live too swiftly to have time' to appreciate the 'glorious performance' of life. Anderson espouses the idea of life as a performance in which people can transform themselves if inspired to do so. She argues that 'everybody is given at least his chance to act', and we have the power to choose how to approach the role: we may do our simple best with the part we are assigned, or 'change our "lines" if we're inventive enough to think of something better', or even 'boldly accost the stage manager, hand back the part he'd cast for us, and prove our right to be starred'. The impetus to rewrite one's part in life, she says, is 'eager panting Art', which, 'treading on Life's heels … shows us the wonder of the way as we rush along'. Sounding the note that her publishing partner Jane Heap would later echo on the eve of their trial, Anderson declares that the magazine will find life-enhancing art in books because 'Books register the ideas of an age; that is perhaps their chief claim to immortality.' These foundational convictions will turn out to have real consequences: when Anderson and Heap risk jail to publish *Ulysses*, they will not be courting some ephemeral notion of beauty, but embracing art as the path to lives performed with depth and intensity.

Aware of the risks she was taking by publishing cutting-edge literature in a society still dominated by Victorian sexual mores, Anderson declares in her opening salvo that because the magazine 'is the personal enterprise of the editor, it shall enjoy that untrammeled liberty which is the life of Art'. Expressing pride in 'our youth', enthusiasm and courage, she proclaims an editorial philosophy 'that all beautiful things make a place for themselves sooner or later in the world', and hopes aloud that the magazine will 'be *very* beautiful!'

The spirit that marked the beginning of *The Little Review* was captured by one of the poets it published, Eunice Tietjens, who wrote that the 'adventure' in Chicago's art scene was Margaret Anderson:

> In her severe black suit and little black hat, under which her blonde hair swept like a shining bird's wing, she stood pouring out such a flood of high-hearted enthusiasm that we were all swept after her into some dream of a magazine where Art with a capital A and Beauty with a still bigger B were to reign supreme, where 'Life Itself' was to blossom into some fantastic shape of incredible warmth and vitality.[10]

Anderson was able to accept her own beauty unreservedly: 'It would be unbecoming of me', she later wrote, 'not to know that I was extravagantly pretty in those days ...'[11] She could recognize that her beauty was extravagant – even disgusting[12] – because she realized it was the outer garment of her inner resolve. Her friend Janet Flanner captured this dynamic years later in an elegiac *New Yorker* obituary, recalling:

> Her profile was delicious, her hair blonde and wavy, her laughter a soprano ripple, her gait undulating beneath her snug *tailleur.* The truth was that within her lay the mixture and mystery of her real consistence, in no way like her exterior. Her visible beauty enveloped a will of

tempered steel, specifically at its most resistant when she was involved in argument which was her favorite form of intellectual exercise ...[13]

This potent combination served Anderson well as she embarked on the daunting task of raising capital for a magazine that existed only in her nocturnal imagination. On a train trip to New York she improbably raised $450, securing ads from Houghton Mifflin and Scribner's, and enjoying a chance encounter at Scribner's with F. Scott Fitzgerald, who 'regretted with blushes that his stuff was too popular to be solicited by a magazine of the new prose'.[14] Back in Chicago she garnered a $100 contribution to the magazine from Frank Lloyd Wright.[15]

It was Anderson's signal achievement to raise sufficient money to fund a magazine that not only served as a vehicle for conversation about beauty in literature and art, but also had what she called in her initial editorial an 'ardent' commitment to feminism. An article in the inaugural issue insisted that 'we feel able to decide for ourselves what we most want and need' and will no longer let 'husbands, fathers and brothers decide for us just what it was best for us to do'.[16] In addition, Anderson, who had studied emerging literature about sexuality by Havelock Ellis and others, was an early advocate of equal rights for homosexuals and lesbians. Her review of a lecture by Ellis's lesbian wife Edith points out that, 'With us love is just as punishable as murder or robbery. Mrs. Ellis knows the workings of our courts; she knows of boys and girls, men and women, tortured or crucified every day *for their love* – because it is not expressed according to conventional morality.'[17] Anderson sharply contended that Mrs Ellis's failure to say this was a failure of responsibility.

Anderson's fundraising prowess was challenged when, in the magazine's third issue in May 1914, she praised 'the anarchist religion' after hearing a lecture by Emma Goldman.[18] True to her own religion of making her life a theatrical event, Anderson enacted the magazine's financial crisis by living in a tent on the shore of Lake Michigan from May to November with her friend and assistant

Harriet Dean, and Dean's divorced sister and her two young boys. A story in the *Chicago Tribune* about the 'Nietzsche colony' – *The Little Review* was then running an article about the philosopher – generated a stream of contributions.

A surge of unconventional energy flowed into the magazine in early 1916 when a friend of Anderson's brought Jane Heap to its offices. Born in Topeka, Kansas, in 1883, Heap, as Flanner put it, was 'an impressive-looking woman of Norwegian ancestry, whose father had been an alienist and the head of an asylum in the Middle West'. Heap found the company of the insane 'instructive' and was deeply interested in their 'irrationalities and imaginations'.[19] She had come to Chicago to enroll in the Art Institute, then taught at the Lewis Institute, and became a member of Browne's Little Theatre, another manifestation of the idea that amateurs pursuing their love of the arts could perform their lives more intensely and with a greater sense of fulfillment.[20] Heap was every bit as committed as Anderson to the idea of beauty as an essential component of a life well lived. 'I know that if everyone felt Beauty strongly,' she wrote to a lifelong friend, 'felt that everything beautiful was god [*sic*] and all things not beautiful not God. That woman was the nearest Symbol for Beauty. If one could see this – there would be no sin, or squalor, or unhappiness in the whole world.'[21]

The theme of 'conversation' that had engendered Anderson's magazine also served as a metaphor for her relationship with Heap, which she explained by saying she enjoyed one of Heap's caustic remarks so thoroughly that 'I felt that I could never henceforth dispense with Jane Heap's frivolity.'[22] They became partners in living and publishing, with Heap contributing idiosyncratic essays and trenchant reviews of books, plays and art under her distinctive and diminutive 'jh' by-line. Anderson later singled out the last lines of the first paragraph of Heap's review of Joyce's play *Exiles* as an example of Heap's lucidity, commenting that it showed an understanding of the play superior to Joyce's:

Margaret Anderson. (Attributed to E.O. Hoppé. Courtesy Curatorial Assistance, Inc./E.O. Hoppé Estate Collection and Professor Mathilda Hills for the Anderson Estate, University of Wisconsin-Milwaukee, Archives Department)

There are people, a few, always the artist I should say, who inspire such strong love in all who know them that these in turn become inspired by love for one another. The truth of the matter is that such a person is neither loved nor lover but in some way seems to be an incarnation of love, possessing an eternal element and because of it a brooding, a clairvoyance of life, and a disdain. In other people he breeds a longing akin to the longing for immortality. They do not love him: they *become* him. Richard is one of these.[23]

Jane Heap. (Copyright 2015 Curatorial Assistance, Inc./E.O. Hoppé Estate Collection, University of Wisconsin-Milwaukee, Archives Department)

Anderson explained the core of her relationship with Heap by saying that 'Jane and I began talking. We talked for days, months, years,' forming a 'consolidation that was to make us much loved and even more loathed.'[24] The magazine's pages were replete with conversation. One of its distinctive features was the written conversation Anderson and Heap carried on with each other. For example, the Winter 1922 issue, adorned with photographs of Anderson and Heap by Victor Georg and E.O. Hoppé, contained a 'Dialogue' between the editors that included Heap's insistence that ecstasy was not enough:

M.C.A. If we didn't waste so much time in good conversation we might at least be self-supporting!

jh. Be self-supporting – and take the conversation that goes with it.

M.C.A. Well … it might be called an impasse …

jh. (*allows her hand to droop from the wrist in the manner she is glad to know terrorizes her companion*)

M.C.A. But thank heaven I can still get some ecstasy out of life!

jh. Why limit me to ecstasy?[25]

In a section captioned 'The Reader Critic', the editors regularly opened the conversation to their readers, whose comments were often met with ripostes from the editors. For example, when a reader complained about the 'obs[cen]e commonplaces' of an episode of *Ulysses*, Heap responded that 'it is impossible for Joyce to be obscene. He is too concentrated on his work. He is too religious about life.'[26]

In the same issue, Heap delivered an uncompromising rebuff to a reader who, announcing that 'I consider myself fairly intelligent' and 'have read more than most', proclaimed, 'There are some few things I expect of a writer. One of them is coherence. Joyce will have to change his style if he wants to get on.' Heap's take-no-prisoners response began: 'You consider yourself an intelligent, "well-read" person. Did it ever occur to you to read anything on the nature of writers?' Such reading, she insisted, 'would help to remove from the mind of the reading public … some of its superstition of being able to put any compulsion upon an artist. All compulsion exists within the artist. … The only concern of the artist is to try in one short lifetime to meet these inner compulsions. He has no concern with audiences and their demands.'[27]

Anderson was equally uncompromising, but more politic than Heap, meeting an attack on the magazine's disparagement of 'all the things I like best' by inviting further dialogue with the observation that 'Art is a challenge to life.'[28] This craving for self-creation through the art of conversation explains Anderson's efflorescence into the creator of an immensely influential cultural force. Janet Flanner suggested in her *New Yorker* profile that Anderson was born 'a feministic romantic rebel with an appetite for Chopin and for indiscriminate reading', but that 'conversation was her real passion', and the impetus to her becoming an 'addicted listener' and gifted editor.[29]

Anderson's insistence on a superior level of conversation in the magazine led her to warn readers in August 1916 that publication of the journal would cease if there was no improvement in the quality of manuscripts submitted. Astonishingly, to illustrate the seriousness of her editorial dictum, the first thirteen pages of the September issue were left blank as a 'Want Ad', a stratagem that caught the eye of Ezra Pound. The expatriate poet, who had arrived in London in 1908 at age twenty-two, was acting as foreign editor for another Chicago-based magazine, Harriet Monroe's *Poetry*, as part of his goal of creating a new Renaissance by melding European and American culture. Pound had already taken note of the daring nature of *The Little Review*. He had asked Anderson in June to publish two long poems by the Belgian-French poet Jean de Bosschère because they were too long for Monroe and it would be 'very difficult to find anybody else sporting enough to print them in french [*sic*]'.³⁰ After reading the sporting Anderson's blank pages 'Want Ad', Pound, already one of the singular voices in modern poetry, was sufficiently impressed that he wrote Anderson asking whether there was any use in his trying to help *The Little Review*.³¹

Pound followed up with a specific proposal that arrived at about the same time that Anderson, Heap, and *The Little Review* moved their conversation to New York at the start of 1917. Presenting an opportunity whose extraordinary nature can be appreciated only in retrospect, Pound suggested that he be given 'a place where I and T.S. Eliot can appear once a month (or once an issue) and where James Joyce can appear when he likes, and where Wyndham Lewis can appear if he comes back from the war'.³² Stirring beneath the surface of this letter are two extraordinary aspects of Pound's personality: he was one of the first to recognize the genius of Joyce and Eliot, and he selflessly devoted his tremendous energy to promoting their work and the work of other emerging writers, often to the detriment of his own. Joyce's work had come to Pound's attention at the instigation of W.B. Yeats. While the young Pound was staying with the older poet in Sussex during the winter of 1913, and the 31-year-old Joyce was teaching English in Trieste, Yeats recommended a poem from Joyce's *Chamber Music* for inclusion in Pound's anthology *Des Imagistes*.³³ Pound promptly became so vigorous a supporter and promoter of Joyce that even the self-focused Joyce recognized that Pound was a 'large bundle of unpredictable electricity', and 'a miracle of ebulliency, gusto and help.'³⁴

These qualities prompted Pound's letter to Anderson seeking a place to showcase the work of the writers he was promoting. In exchange for Anderson's providing such a forum, Pound offered a 'prospective guarantor', a 'Mr X' who would donate money to pay the contributors that Pound would secure. Mr X was John Quinn, who had offered to pay Pound $750 a year to support himself and pay for manuscripts of writers whose work he sought to promote.³⁵ Quinn was an Ohio-born baker's son who, after a year at the University of

Michigan and law studies at Georgetown and Harvard, became a successful New York attorney with a high-powered corporate and finance practice. Quinn's progress to the bar navigated a period of great change in American legal education. When he left the University of Michigan to go to Washington as private secretary to President Harrison's Secretary of the Treasury, a former Ohio governor and family friend, a college degree was not required for admission to most law schools, which functioned primarily as alternatives to apprenticeship for practical training in legal skills.[36] Thus Quinn was able to enroll in Georgetown's two-year night school while employed in the Treasury Department.[37] When he arrived at Harvard for additional legal studies after earning a law degree at Georgetown in 1893, he found an institution that had been leading the reform of American legal education since 1869, when the university's new president, Charles W. Eliot, set out to transform Harvard Law School into an academically rigorous part of the university.[38] The dean appointed by Eliot in 1870, Christopher Columbus Langdell, did just that.[39] By the time of Quinn's matriculation, the standard Harvard Law School education consisted of a three-year programme, for which a college degree was a prerequisite, although admission by examination could be permitted.[40] Perhaps because he already held a law degree, Quinn, who was admitted in 1893, graduated two years later.[41]

He quickly developed a successful practice in New York. The most formative experience in the eleven years he spent working for others was his six years as an associate with the firm of Alexander & Colby from 1900 to 1906, during which time he developed a reputation as an able practitioner in corporate, finance, insurance and banking law. He took maximum advantage of an opportunity that presented itself in 1905 as adviser to financier Thomas Fortune Ryan in a contest for control of The Equitable Life Assurance Society of America, whose senior officers included members of the Alexander family. Ryan obtained control of Equitable, and Quinn acquired a lifelong client.[42] Quinn struck out on his own the following year, and by 1910 was Ryan's chief counsel, and counted the National Bank of Commerce, which Ryan controlled, among his clients.

Although Quinn had a number of colleagues over the years, his office was essentially a one-man band. He often had somewhere between one and three colleagues – variously denominated associates or partners – who served at his pleasure. As his biographer put it, Quinn was 'reluctant to delegate labor or trust, and almost never satisfied by the way a job was done by anyone but himself'.[43] As a result, his office remained small and its composition was constantly changing. He was famous for having fired five partners in a single year. [44]

While making his way in the legal community, Quinn also established himself as a force in New York Democratic politics, particularly within a circle of successful Irish Americans, including, for example, Judges Daniel Colahan and Martin Keough.[45] He was an elected delegate to the Democratic National Convention in 1908 and again in 1912. Although Quinn distanced himself from the taint of corruption sometimes associated with the New York's Democratic Tammany Hall political machine, his biographer describes him as a 'Tammany stalwart', and he certainly was in the good graces of politicians and judges associated with Tammany Hall.[46] This was, of course, natural for an Irish-American Democrat in New York, and there has never been any suggestion of corrupt activity by Quinn himself.

By temperament unable or unwilling to build a large organization around his many talents, Quinn never amassed anything like the large fortunes built by contemporaries in the business world, and had no source of income other than his law practice and the return on invested earnings.[47] He devoted the bulk of his income to building an amazing collection of cultural artefacts, including most of Joseph Conrad's manuscripts, many of W.B. Yeats's, the draft of Eliot's *The Waste Land* bearing Pound's shape-changing emendations and, not least, the manuscript of *Ulysses*. Quinn's cultural interests were not limited to literature. After being introduced to French art by Augustus John during a 1909 visit to Europe, and with his curiosity piqued by reports of Roger Fry's groundbreaking exhibition of *Manet and the Post-Impressionists* in London in 1910, Quinn became a major art collector and patron. He bought more than 2500 paintings, drawings, and sculptures, including twelve Picassos, twenty Matisses, and works by Brâncuşi, Cezanne, Braque, Rouault, Dufy and Van Gogh. He lunched with Picasso, dined on meals prepared by Brâncuşi in his studio, visited Derain, Dufy, and Matisse, and went motoring with Braque. In the judgment of the organizer of the Hirshhorn Museum's 1978 partial re-constitution of his collection, Quinn had assembled 'one of the greatest modern art collections of the twentieth century'.[48] Because he was buying the new while it was new, and had an astonishing eye for recognizing the promise of modern art in its infancy, Quinn acquired this impressive collection solely with the income from his own work as a lawyer. The cost of his collection was comparable to the approximately $600,000 ($8.1 million in today's dollars) for which it was sold following his death.[49]

Quinn was also, as scholar Stanley Sultan put it, 'an industrious and highly talented sponsor, promoter, unpaid lawyer, agent, and editor' for a distinguished roster of writers and artists.[50] Merging his persuasive powers with his collector's impulse, he successfully lobbied Congress to eliminate customs duties on contemporary works of art, thereby according them the same duty-free status as old masters. Energetic and connected, he was widely recognized as 'a moving spirit' of the New York Armory Show of 1913, technically known as the International Exhibition of Modern Art.[51] He was counsel to the organizers of the exhibition, and was 'the single biggest lender to and buyer from' the show.[52] He was 'in the thick' of the organizers' plans, 'gave interviews and speeches, sponsored a dinner, [and] stopped by the show almost daily ...'[53]

*Henri-Pierre Roché, Constantin Brâncuşi and
John Quinn, Paris 1921. (Archives of American Art,
Smithsonian Institution, Aline Saarinen papers)*

*Henri-Pierre Roché, Mme Picasso, Jeanne Robert Foster, and John
Quinn lunching at Picasso's summer home. (Archives of American
Art, Smithsonian Institution, Aline Saarinen papers)*

Introducing such experimental forms of painting as cubism, fauvism and futurism, the Armory Show was a transformative event that, as art critic Aline Saarinen put it, 'jolted the American public as no other artistic event has before or since'.[54] When the show moved to Chicago, Margaret Anderson's mentor Floyd Dell captured its effect on the circle that included Anderson by writing in the *Chicago Evening Post* that it 'exploded like a bombshell' that was not only an aesthetic experience, but 'an emotional experience which led to a philosophical and moral revaluation of life'.[55] Quinn's enthusiastic involvement with the Armory Show is particularly interesting because of his later ambivalent reaction to Joyce's innovative prose, which was part of the same modern revolt against Victorianism. The affinity between Joyce's stylistic revolution and the Armory Show is apparent in both negative and positive comment on the show. On the negative side, the *New York Times'* editorial about the exhibition no doubt had in mind the movement in which Joyce would feature prominently when it placed modern art in a 'general movement, discernible all over the world, to disrupt and degrade, if not to destroy, not only art, but literature and society too'.[56] On the positive side, proponents of the show praised it in terms similar to Anderson's view of the role of art and literature in fostering a life lived with greater understanding and satisfaction. Hutchins Hapgood, a journalist and anarchist, wrote that the virtue of the Armory Show was that it 'makes us live more abundantly' and thus 'will help us all to understand more deeply what happens to us in life – to understand our love and our work, our ambitions and our antipathies, and our ideals in politics and society'.[57]

Significantly, Quinn's interest in the artefacts of modernism was that of a collector and patron rather than as a proponent of the personal and social transformation sought by Anderson. He matched perfectly the title of the book that identified him as a pioneering American collector, Aline Saarinen's *The Proud Possessors*. Whereas Anderson felt that viewing art or reading literature led to a more intensely lived life, Quinn found that it was as a patron and collector that 'he could enlarge and intensify his existence'.⁵⁸ Quinn revealed how strongly his desire for ownership was embedded in his identity when he wrote Joseph Conrad that the 'passion for having things and collecting things and doing things and being something is a cursed, damnable passion …'⁵⁹

The path that led Quinn to Pound opened from the point at which Quinn's interest in his Irish ancestry converged with his passion for collecting. He had made an inquiry in November 1901 about buying paintings by John Butler Yeats ('JBY') and one of his sons, Jack Yeats, younger brother of the poet William Butler Yeats ('WBY').⁶⁰ This incipient connection with the Yeats family opened doors to a lively Irish artistic and literary world and, incidentally, to brief sexual relationships between Quinn and two talented women who were captivated by his energetic and effective support of their artistic endeavours. Within months of his initial inquiry, Quinn had met Jack Yeats in London with results so cheering that JBY wrote to his elder son (who was already on his way to fame as a Nobel Prize-winning poet) that 'John Quinn is the nearest approach to an angel in my experience – he has bought ten of Jack's [paintings] and given me several commissions.'⁶¹ Before the summer was over, Quinn had visited WBY and his colleague in establishing and managing the Abbey Theatre, Lady Augusta Gregory, at Gregory's estate Coole Park in the west of Ireland, not far from the birthplace of Quinn's father in County Limerick. Friendship with Gregory broadened and strengthened Quinn's ties to the revival taking place in Irish literature because Gregory's ideas, powerful personality, and success as a dramatist, essayist and popularizer of Irish mythology made her a major cultural force.

On a return visit to Ireland the following summer, Quinn suggested that WBY undertake an extended lecture tour in America, and followed up with characteristic reliability and efficiency, orga-nizing more than thirty lectures for the successful eight-month tour that began in November 1903. Quinn's involvement in the Irish literary revival also provided opportunities to deepen friendships with powerful figures in the United States. During WBY's tour, for example, Quinn arranged for him to visit President Theodore Roosevelt, who took pride in his mother's Irish ancestry, was a founder of The American Irish Historical Society, and had a keen interest in Irish history, literature and myth.[62]

The relationship between Quinn and WBY deepened when the poet, like many other Irish visitors, stayed with Quinn during his time in New York, where his tour began and ended. Quinn's next involvement with WBY as lecturer manifested the peculiar combination of public prudery and private license that characterized Quinn's approach to sexual matters. In response to WBY's 1906 proposal to undertake a joint American tour with his sometime lover Florence Farr, who recited poems while accompanying herself on a stringed instrument called a psaltery, Quinn wrote that, 'It wouldn't do for you and Miss Farr to come here together. This is after all a provincial people.'[63] Quinn explained that WBY was known in a most dignified way in America 'and can lecture here again, especially at the Women's Colleges. But coming here with a woman it would be entirely different'. Following Quinn's rebuff of Yeats's proposal, Farr toured America on her own for four months in 1907, lecturing on 'Speaking to the Psaltery'. Yeats implicitly warned Quinn away from Farr early in her tour, noting that 'she & Lady Gregory are my closest friends, and I have seen a good deal of her, of late especially ...'[64] Nonetheless, Quinn became Farr's lover during the tour on which, as Quinn had insisted, she was unaccompanied by Yeats.[65]

Nothing if not efficient, Quinn simultaneously found time to help WBY's father settle into New York when the *pater familias* gradually extended a visit into a fourteen-year stay that lasted until his death. Quinn contributed mightily to JBY's support through commissions and by paying his rent at the Petitpas sisters' boarding house in return for manuscripts of WBY's work. Quinn and JBY were in frequent communication in person and by letter, with Quinn sometimes visiting the restaurant at Petitpas', where JBY held court with a lively group of artists that included John Sloan, whose painting *Yeats at Petitpas'* memorializes the prevailing camaraderie. In August 1910 in what turned out to be a momentous occasion in the history of *The Little Review* and the publication of *Ulysses*, JBY invited his son's friend Ezra Pound to dinner at Petitpas', where he introduced Pound to Quinn, who, six years later, would be the Mr X that Pound would offer to Anderson to support her magazine in publishing Joyce. Pound had cultivated Quinn's potential as a patron in his creative response to the lawyer's letter complaining about Pound's article in *The New Age* that Quinn read as criticizing him for collecting older (and fake) art and manuscripts rather than supporting new artists and writers.[66]

Yeats at Petitpas' *by John Sloan. John Butler Yeats* (second from the left) *is depicted at the restaurant where he met Ezra Pound, setting in motion the chain of events that brought* Ulysses *to* The Little Review. *(National Gallery of Art, Washington, DC)*

Responding to Quinn's vigorous defence of his collecting practices, Pound seductively stoked Quinn with an idea that exalted the patron to the status of co-creator: 'My whole drive,' Pound wrote on 8 March 1915, 'is that if a patron buys from an artist who needs money (needs money to buy tools, time and food), the patron then makes himself equal to the artist: he is building art into the world; he creates ...' Pound urged Quinn that he could 'bring on another cinquecento.'[67] The imperiousness Quinn would later exhibit in dealing with *Ulysses* may be traced to this notion of the patron as a co-creator.

Quinn's involvement in Irish cultural affairs was far from idle in the interim between meeting Pound and agreeing to back Pound's stable of writers. A burst of his typically energetic support awaited Lady Gregory when she accompanied the Abbey Theatre Company in bringing John Synge's *Playboy of the Western World* to the United States in late 1911 and early 1912. Quinn correctly anticipated that rabid self-styled Irish-American patriots would stage a repeat of the public protests that had greeted the play's Dublin production in 1907 on the claimed ground that it maligned the Irish people by showing sympathy for parricide and referring to Irish women wearing only an undergarment called a 'shift'. Despite considerable disorder at the opening night in New York, Quinn found time to accept Gregory's invitation to dine before the next evening's performance with herself and former President Theodore Roosevelt, who had corresponded with Gregory about her book of Irish mythology, *Cuchulain of Muirthemne*, and written an article on Irish myth for *Century Magazine*.[68] Roosevelt graciously supported the Abbey players by attending and vigorously applauding the play.[69] Later in the tour, when the company was arrested on charges of putting on a sacrilegious and immoral performance in Philadelphia, Quinn travelled there twice for periods of several days and secured their release after a vigorous cross-examination of the prosecution's witnesses, which he summarized by saying, 'I skinned them alive.'[70]

Before her return to Ireland, the sixty-year-old Gregory, who had dressed in black 'widow's weeds' since her (considerably older) husband's death fifteen years previously, and had a forbidding reputation for insisting on public propriety by the Abbey company, added a brief affair with Quinn to their years of shared efforts in political and cultural causes.[71] Gregory's passionate letter two days after her return to Ireland reflects the intensity of the experience from her standpoint: 'My John, my dear John, my own John, not other people's John. I love you. I care for you. I know you. I want you. I believe in you. I see you always … Don't think I am fretting. I am proud. I am glad.'[72] With characteristic intuition, she put her finger on the nature of Quinn's attraction in a follow-on letter: it was not 'all the piled up goodness of the years' but rather 'It is the call that came in a moment. Something impetuous and masterful about you that satisfies me. This gives me perfect rest …'[73] Quinn was less emotional. When he learned that the ancient seal ring Gregory sent him had gone down with the *Titanic,* he commented to Augustus John, 'Perhaps I am as well off without the ring.'[74]

The connection between Quinn's sexual relationships and his practice of collecting cultural artefacts lies in the murky depths beneath his 'considerable … reputation as a pursuer and conqueror of women'[75] and his grating insistence that he 'succeeded in remaining a bachelor by great foresight, courage and iron determination'.[76] In addition to his more sporadic pursuits and conquests, Quinn had sustained relationships with a succession of companions, including Ada Smith, May Morris, Dorothy Coates and Jeanne Foster, the last of whom stated that by the time their relationship began, probably when Quinn was forty-eight, he was no longer able to function sexually.[77] The fact that Quinn introduced Foster to Pound as his travelling secretary[78] emphasizes his penchant for secrecy about sexual matters, a personal instance of the societal impulse that motivated the censorship of *Ulysses.* That same predilection for secrecy had led Quinn to break with

W.B. Yeats for five years beginning in 1909 because of his belief that his erstwhile boon companion had been gossiping about his relationship with Dorothy Coates (while simultaneously, Quinn suspected, trying to emulate it).[79] Although Coates engineered a reconciliation between Quinn and WBY in 1914,[80] Quinn continued to cloak his sexual life in secrecy.

John Quinn and W.B. Yeats. (Arnold Genthe 1914)

In short, the 'Mr X' that Pound offered as a patron to Anderson brought a complicated attitude toward sex and secrecy to the relationship that began in May 1917 when she accepted his support by appointing Pound foreign editor of *The Little Review*. Pound delivered. In addition to bringing *Ulysses* to the magazine, he secured twenty-one poems from W.B. Yeats and eight from T.S. Eliot.

Shortly after Pound's appointment, Quinn invited Anderson and Heap to dinner with the artists Walt Kuhn and Arthur B. Davies, whose energy and *avant-garde* ideas were driving forces behind the Armory Show. The dinner took place in Quinn's apartment on Central Park West at 66th Street, a sumptuous residence where ninth-floor drawing rooms looked out over Central Park, and a long high corridor was stacked from floor to ceiling with some of his six- or seven-thousand books. Anderson noted that the rooms were also filled with modern paintings and sculpture, Brâncuşi's *Child in the World* forming a vivid image in her memory. Over dinner, Quinn offered a great deal of unsolicited advice, 'telling us how we ought to run *The Little Review*', advice that Anderson wryly characterized as 'excellent – anyone with a fortune could have followed it'.[81]

Failing to register Anderson's lesbianism, Quinn initially seems to have fancied himself the object of her romantic interest. His early epistolary comments frequently dwell on her looks, even as they betray a persistent interest in her relationship with Heap. On 2 June 1917, for example, following the dinner with Anderson and Heap at his apartment, he commented to Pound that 'Miss Anderson is a woman of taste and refinement and good looking' and 'has got associated with her a woman named Miss Heep [*sic*], of about her own age, who is a typical Washington Squareite'. Unused to dealing with women who had ideas of their own, he comments that Anderson and Heap, whom he had just smothered with advice, 'are both wilful women, not bad tempered, but just wilful, and I don't think they are very receptive to ideas'.[82] Quinn liked women to be listeners. Nonetheless, Anderson had taken the opportunity over dinner to describe the dire financial circumstances of the magazine. Two days later Quinn sent a letter announcing that he was arranging to endow *The Little Review* to the extent of $1600, contributing $400 himself, and obtaining similar commitments from three other patrons.[83] The support for *The Little Review* was in addition to Quinn's commitment to contribute $750 to Pound for himself and writers he designated.[84]

A revealing letter the following October suggests that Quinn saw himself as an attractive Lancelot to a vulnerable maiden who desperately needed his assistance. The letter crudely, if indirectly, portrays the potential of their relationship in sexual terms, observing that, 'Miss A is a very beautiful woman ... [who] could get a good "backer" if she was ready to have him be a "fronter" first or simultaneously.'[85]

Acting out his fantasy, Quinn rode to Anderson's rescue by acting as her lawyer when the Post Office barred the October 1917 issue of *The Little Review* from the mails because of the alleged obscenity of a story, 'Cantleman's Spring-Mate', by one of Pound's protégées, the English writer and painter Wyndham Lewis, who is perhaps best known as a pioneer of the geometric abstract style of painting Pound called 'Vorticism'. Quinn's role as Anderson's counsel would bring to the fore their differing ideas as to the proper relationship between law and literature.

NOTES

1 Margaret Anderson, *My Thirty Years' War* (1930; New York: Horizon Press, 1969) ('TYW') 174–5.
2 *Id.* at 5.
3 *Id.* at 9.
4 *Id.* at 35.
5 *Id.*
6 Walter Pater, *The Renaissance* (1873; New York: Modern Library, 1919) 196–7.
7 W.B. Yeats, *Autobiographies* (London: Macmillan, 1955) 469.
8 TYW 38.

9   Margaret Anderson, 'Announcement', LR (March 1914) 1–2.

10 Eunice Tietjens, *The World at My Shoulder* (New York: Macmillan, 1938) 64.

11 TYW 15.

12 *Id.*

13 Janet Flanner, 'A Life on a Cloud', *The New Yorker* (3 June 1974) ('Flanner') 44.

14 TYW 43–4.

15 *Id.* at 69.

16 M.H. Partridge, 'The Feminist Discussions', LR (March 1914) 21–2.

17 Margaret Anderson, 'Mrs. Ellis's Failure', LR (March 1915) 19.

18 TYW 54–5.

19 Flanner 46.

20 Holly A. Baggett, *Dear Tiny Heart: The Letters of Jane Heap and Florence Reynolds* (New York: New York University Press, 2000) ('Dear Tiny Heart') 2.

21 Letter of 20 July 1909 to Florence Reynolds, Dear Tiny Heart 38. The significance of Heap's inconsistent capitalization of god is unclear.

22 TYW 107.

23 Margaret Anderson, *The Strange Necessity* (New York: Horizon Press, 1969) ('TSN') 146.

24 TYW 107.

25 LR (Winter 1922) 25.

26 LR (June 1918) 56.

27 *Id.* at 54.

28 LR (March 1920) 60–62.

29 Flanner 44.

30 Letter of 30 June 1916, Thomas L. Scott *et al.*, eds, *The Letters of Ezra Pound to Margaret Anderson: The Little Review Correspondence* (New York: New Directions, 1988) ('EP/LR') 1. The lower case f in french is Pound's.

31 Letter of 29 November 1916, EP/LR 4.

32 Pound to Anderson, 26 January 1917, EP/LR 6.

33 Patricia Cockram, *James Joyce & Ezra Pound: A More Than Literary Friendship* (Dublin: National Library of Ireland, 2004) 1–2; Letter of 26 December 1913 from Pound to Joyce, Forrest Read, ed., *The Letters of Ezra Pound to James Joyce* (New York: New Directions, 1965) ('Pound/Joyce') 18–19.

34 Herbert Gorman, *James Joyce* (New York: Farrar & Rinehart, 1939) ('Gorman') 272.

35 B.L. Reid, *The Man from New York: John Quinn and His Friends* (New York: Oxford University Press, 1968) ('MNY') 284–5.

36 William P. LaPiana, *Logic and Experience: The Origin of Modern American Legal Education* (New York: Oxford University Press, 1994) ('LaPiana') 7–28.

37 www.law.georgetown.edu/about/history

38 LaPiana 7–28.

39 *Id.*

40 *Id.* at 17, 88–9.

41 Harvard Law School, *Quinquennial Catalogue of the Law School of Harvard University 1817–1899* (Cambridge: Harvard Law School, 1900) ('HLS Quinquennial') 111.

42 MNY 33–5.

43 *Id.* at 153.

44 *Id.* at 402.

45 *Id.* at 17, 64, 91, 110.

46 *Id.* at 63; 573–4.

47 See *id.* at 153.

48 Judith Zilczer, *'The Noble Buyer': John Quinn, Patron of the Avant-Garde*, Exh. Cat. Hirshhorn Museum (Washington, 1978) ('Noble Buyer') 57.

49 Judith Zilczer, 'The Dispersal of The John Quinn Collection', *Archives of American Art Journal*, Vol. 30, No. 3 (1979) 15 ('Zilczer').

50 Stanley Sultan, *Eliot, Joyce and Company* (New York: Oxford University Press, 1987) 125.

51 Avis Berman, '"Creating a New Epoch": American Collectors and Dealers and the Armory Show', in Marilyn Satin Kushner *et al.*, *The Armory Show at 100: Modernism and Revolution* (New York: New York Historical Society, 2013) ('Berman') 413, 416.

52 Noble Buyer 27.

53 Berman 416.

54 Aline B. Saarinen, *The Proud Possessors* (New York: Random House, 1958) ('Proud Possessors') 206.

55 Floyd Dell, *Homecoming: An Autobiography* (1933; Port Washington: Kennikat Press, 1969) 238.

56 *New York Times* (16 March 1913) 59.

57 Hutchins Hapgood, 'Life at the Armory,' *New York Globe and Commercial Advertiser* (17 February 1918) 8.

58 Proud Possessors 211–12.

59 Letter of 14 February 1919 in John Quinn Papers, Manuscripts and Archives Division, The New York Public Library, Astor, Lenox, and Tilden Foundations ('QC'). See MNY 152–3.

60 MNY at 8.

61 Letter of 31 July 1902, in Joseph Hone, ed., *John Butler Yeats: Letters to His Son W.B. Yeats and Others* (London: Faber & Faber, 1944) ('JBY Letters') 73.

62 MNY 18 (visit with Roosevelt); Wayne Andrews, ed., *The Autobiography of Theodore Roosevelt* (New York: Scribners, 1958) 4 (Irish ancestry); http://aihs.org/ (founder of American Irish Historical Society); http://www.irishtimes.com/news/letters-reveal-roosevelt-s-fascination-with-celtic-mythology-1.606083 (interest in Irish literature and myth) ('TR Letters').

63 Letter of 13 July 1906, quoted in John Kelly and Ronald Schuchard, eds, *The Collected Letters of W.B. Yeats, Vol. 4* (Oxford: Oxford University Press, 2005) ('CL4') 237 n. 2.

64 Letter of 18 February 1907, CL4, 630.

65 *Id.* at n. 14.

66 Timothy Materer, ed., *The Selected Letters of Ezra Pound to John Quinn 1914–1924* (Durham: Duke University Press, 1991) ('Pound/Quinn Letters') 4.

67 QC; see also Pound/Quinn Letters 20–24.

68 Augusta Gregory, *Our Irish Theatre* (1913; New York: Capricorn Books, 1965) ('Our Irish Theatre') 204–5; TR Letters; Theodore Roosevelt, 'The Ancient Irish Sagas', *The Century Magazine*, Vol. LXXIII (January 1907) No. 3; http://www.theodorerooseveltcenter.org/Blog/2010/September/20-A-Letter-from-Lady-Gregory.aspx

69 Our Irish Theatre 204–5: see MNY 116–17.

70 Letter of 8 March 1912 (QC); MNY 118.

71 Mary Lou Kohfeldt, *Lady Gregory* (New York: Atheneum, 1985) ('Kohfeldt') 232–3.

72 Letter of 12 March 1912, The Henry W. and Albert A. Berg Collection, New York Public Library (Berg) (quoted in Kohfeldt at 232).

73 Letter of 2 April 1912 (Berg) (quoted in Kohlfeldt 232–3).

74 Letter of 24 May 1912, MNY 121.

75 MNY x.

76 Letter to Arthur B. Davies, 10 October 1917 (QC).

77 MNY 21, 80–84, 639–40; William M. Murphy, *Prodigal Father* (Ithaca: Cornell University Press, 1978) ('PF') 307; Richard Londraville and Janice Londraville, *Dear Yeats, Dear Pound, Dear Ford: Jeanne Robert Foster and Her Circle of Friends* (Syracuse: Syracuse University Press, 2001) xxvii.

78 PF 527.

79 MNY 74–5.

80 MNY 176.

81 TYW 208.

82 QC.

83 TYW 208.

84 See Quinn letter of 3 December 1918 to Anderson (QC).

85 Letter of 31 October 1917 to Ezra Pound (QC).

Beauty and Truth Ignored: Quinn's Defence of 'Cantleman's Spring-Mate' and Early Skirmishes Over *Ulysses*

Quinn's role as the attorney defending 'Cantleman's Spring-Mate' from obscenity charges revealed a tendency to force the ideas of his clients and colleagues into a predetermined structure that defended books charged with obscenity on the ground that they deterred rather than encouraged desire. This same predilection had already manifested itself in the interesting conjunction of law and literature that came about when Quinn took on the mantle of literary critic by publishing a review of Joyce's *Dubliners* and *A Portrait of the Artist as a Young Man* in the May 1917 issue of *Vanity Fair*. His review repeatedly asserted that Joyce and his work were 'sincere' without explaining what was meant by an amorphous adjective that carried no more meaning in 1917 than it would later in the century when Lionel Trilling observed that, 'To praise a work of literature by calling it sincere is now at best a way of saying that although it need be given no aesthetic or intellectual admiration, it was at least conceived in innocence of heart.'[1]

Beyond his iterative assertion of Joyce's sincerity, Quinn addressed the fact that *Portrait* had been, as he wrote, 'refused by publisher after publisher in London ostensibly because of the frankness with which certain episodes in the life of a young man were treated'.[2] Exhibiting an attitude that would later dominate his approach to *Ulysses*, Quinn neglected the book's quality as literature in favour of a discussion of its assumed effect on the reader's conduct. Quinn dressed his views in a critical vocabulary that sanctioned fictional depiction of sexual matters so long as the writing is 'hard' rather than 'soft'. Neither term is defined, but Joyce's prose is declared 'hard' in contrast to the 'soft' language of an H.G. Wells novel about a young Edwardian woman's sexual and political awakening that had been denounced by the London *Spectator* as 'capable of poisoning the minds of those who read it'.[3] Quinn opined that, although *Portrait* is perhaps not 'a book for all young women, ... yet no young man or young woman of the right fibre would be harmed by it' because, unlike 'such a soft and false and dangerous book as *Ann Veronica* by H.G. Wells, for example, not to speak of similar American trash that reeks and smells of sex, Joyce's book is bracing and hard and clean'. Quinn likely borrowed the word 'hard' from Pound's review of *Portrait* in the February 1917 *Egoist*, but Pound had made clear what he meant – 'hard, clear-cut, with no waste of words, no bundling up of useless phrases, no filling in with pages of slosh' – and said nothing about cleanliness or sexual mores.[4]

By the time Quinn brought these critical theories to his representation of Anderson in the Cantleman case, he had already given them a trial run in court. They had informed his defence of Mitchell Kennerley in a 1914 obscenity trial in federal court in New York arising out of Kennerley's publication of Daniel Carson Goodman's novel *Hagar Revelly*. Kennerley was charged with violating a federal obscenity statute that barred use of the mails to 'every obscene, lewd or lascivious, and every filthy book, pamphlet ... writing ... or other publication of an indecent character ...' and made it a crime to deposit such material in the mails. The statute – known as the Comstock Act after its proponent, anti-obscenity crusader Anthony Comstock – was first adopted in 1865 in the wake of a report by the Postmaster General that great numbers of obscene books and pictures were being sent by the mails to Civil War soldiers.[5] Previously, Congress had perceived a federal interest in obscenity only in terms of books being imported from outside the country, a threat addressed in the Tariff Act of 1842, which barred and criminalized the importation of obscene material. Apart from these two statutes regulating federal mail and customs functions, obscenity was a matter for state law, with states, beginning with Vermont in 1821, adopting their own obscenity statutes, which criminalized distribution of obscene materials without requiring the government to establish use of the mails or importation across the national borders, as would have been required for federal jurisdiction.

Goodman, the author of the allegedly obscene novel published by Kennerley, was a St Louis physician and social hygienist who wrote his novel in order to teach the 'innocent youth of the land ... the wiles of vice'. It tells the story of two sisters in New York City, one of whom, Thatah, voices Goodman's ideas. The other, Hagar, is seduced by her employer. Although the statute did not itself define the term 'obscene', the United States Court of Appeals for the Second Circuit (which includes New York, Connecticut and Vermont) had, in a case called *United States v. Bennett*,[6] adopted the test for obscenity articulated in an 1868 English decision, *Regina v. Hicklin*. Elaborating on the undefined term 'obscene' in the British Obscene Publications Act of 1857, the court in *Hicklin* stated that 'the test of obscenity is ... whether the tendency of the matter charged as obscenity is to deprave and corrupt those whose minds are open to such immoral influences', and added that the suggestion of 'impure and libidinous' thoughts constituted just such a tendency.[7] Seemingly oblivious to the fact that sexual desire is necessary to perpetuation of the species, *Hicklin* loomed on the horizon like some fraught but still potent Leviathan, its impact exacerbated by two subsidiary rulings. The first was that the obscenity of a work is to be measured, not by its effect on the hypothetical reasonable reader, but on the most susceptible – specifically 'those whose minds are open to such immoral influences and who might come in contact with it'. The second rule was that *any* obscenity in a book violated the statute, no matter how beautifully written the book might be as a whole. As one New York court put it:

> Charm of language, subtlety of thought, faultless style, even distinction of authorship, may all have their lure for the literary critic, yet these qualities may all be present and the book be unfit for dissemination to the reading public.[8]

Under this approach, the better the writing, the more dangerous the obscenity. This line of thinking has ancient roots. Indeed, it was the very beauty of Homer and Sophocles that convinced Plato of the danger of their language and imagery. For example, Plato insisted that 'Homer and the other poets' should not be 'angry if we strike out' certain passages that might discourage courage in battle, 'not because they are unpoetical, or unattractive to the popular ear, but because the greater the poetical charm of them, the less are they meet for the ears of boys and men who are meant to be free, and who should fear slavery more than death.'[9]

Quinn moved to dismiss the indictment, but the trial judge, Learned Hand, whom we shall meet again, ruled that under the prevailing judicial definition of obscenity in the Second Circuit, where he sat in a lower court as a District Court judge, one passage of the novel could be found to be obscene, and thus the case had to be tried by a jury. Because it did not finally resolve the case, Hand's ruling was not appealable. The arguably offending passage in *Hagar Revelly*, which Hand identified by page number but did not quote, simply described Hagar's heart 'pounding unmercifully' as her employer 'forced her close to him' and 'took her head between his hands and drew her face to his lips'.[10] At trial, Quinn stressed

Goodman's reformist intent, arguing to the jury that 'the object of the book was to portray the evil influences to which girl workers were subjected, the reward of virtue, and the penalty usually paid by those women who attempt to defy the laws of nature and of society'.[11] He read to the jury a supportive letter from the muckraking journalist Ida Tarbell – already well known for her 1904 *History of the Standard Oil Company*. Tarbell 'commended the novel as teaching a moral lesson'. In commenting on the passage that Hand had identified as arguably obscene, Quinn urged the jury that 'it tells the old, old story. It is a scene which could not be left out: it cannot be said that it was used for the purposes of corruption.' Kennerley was acquitted.[12] There was thus no occasion to seek appellate review of Hand's pre-trial ruling declining to dismiss the indictment.

Quinn's approach to the Cantleman case was shaped by his experience in *Kennerley*. Shortly after the October 1917 issue of *The Little Review* containing Lewis's story was suppressed, Quinn wrote to the Solicitor of the Post Office Department, W.H. Lamar, urging that the suppression be lifted on the ground that the story 'does not come within gunshot of violating the statute or any Federal statute'.[13] When Lamar declined, Quinn, armed with his precepts of literary criticism favouring the 'hard' and the 'clean', and buoyed by his successful hygienist defence in *Kennerley*, filed suit on behalf of Anderson in federal court in New York seeking judicial review of the Post Office determination that 'Cantleman's Spring-Mate' fell within the federal bar on mailing obscene material.

Even under *Hicklin*'s sweeping definition of obscenity, the Postmaster's determination was questionable. Lewis's story was far from lascivious. Cantleman, a soldier undergoing training in an English camp before dispatch to the front, experiences thoughts darkened by 'the prospect of death'. His attitude to a young woman named Stella from the neighbouring village is coloured by his belief that 'all women were contaminated with Nature's hostile power

39

and might be treated as spies or enemies'.[14] He thus approached her 'with as much falsity as he could master' and regarded their single sexual experience as a 'devouring of his mate'.[15] The description of that experience is more tepid than torrid:

> On the warm earth consent flowed up into her body from all the veins of the landscape. The nightingale sang ceaselessly in the small wood at the top of the field where they lay. He grinned up towards it, and once more turned to the devouring of his mate. He felt that he was raiding the bowels of Nature: not fecundating the Aspasias of our flimsy flesh, or assuaging, or competing with, the nightingale. Cantleman was proud that he could remain deliberate and aloof, and gaze bravely, like a minute insect, up at the immense and melancholy night, with all its mad nightingales, piously folded small brown wings in a million nests, night-working stars, and misty useless watchmen. They got up at last: she went furtively back to her home. Cantleman on his way to camp had a smile of severe satisfaction on his face.

Cantleman departs for France, where he ignores a letter from Stella telling him of her pregnancy, 'and when he beat a German's brains out it was with the same impartial malignity that he had displayed in the English night with his Spring-mate'.[16]

However questionable the Postmaster's determination, existing case law provided that it was entitled to deference and could be overturned only by convincing the court that it was 'clearly wrong'.[17] The case was heard by Learned Hand's cousin, then District Judge Augustus Hand, who had been appointed by President Woodrow Wilson in 1914 and served in that capacity until 1927, and then as a judge of the United States Court of Appeals for the Second Circuit until his death in 1954. Despite the generally forbidding judicial landscape dominated by the Victorian *Hicklin* case, the twin paths to overturning the Postmaster's determination had been suggested by Learned Hand when he reluctantly felt unable to dismiss the indictment against Kennerley. Both Hands had educational backgrounds that were likely to produce minds open to considering the law of obscenity in terms of the societal value of beauty and truth in literature. Both graduated from Harvard Law School after attending Harvard College in the era of President Charles W. Eliot, a profoundly influential educator, whose inaugural address had defined the college's mission as the education of graduates with 'an open mind, trained to careful thinking, instructed in the methods of philosophic investigation, acquainted ... with the accumulated thought of past generations, and penetrated with humility'.[18] Learned Hand, in particular, was known for a commitment to freedom of expression developed in college courses taught by such pioneering giants of American philosophy as George Santayana, William James and Josiah Royce.[19] Appointed to the federal district court in New York by President William Howard Taft in 1909, and to the Second Circuit Court of Appeals by President Coolidge in 1924, his judicial career lasted until his death in 1961. He is widely regarded as the preeminent American jurist in the first half of the twentieth century.

Learned Hand's opinion in the *Kennerley* case, while recognizing that the *Hicklin* definition of obscenity prevented a trial court judge like himself from dismissing the indictment, had focused on the harm to society of judge-made law that barred literature from distribution simply because some part of a great achievement in writing sounded an erotic chord. In a subtle turn of thought, Hand characterized *Hicklin* as reflective of 'mid-Victorian morals', and questioned 'whether in the end men will regard that as obscene which is honestly relevant to the adequate expression of innocent ideas, and whether they will not believe that truth and beauty are too precious to society at large to be mutilated in the interests of those most likely to pervert them to base uses'.[20] Hand's opinion was an open invitation to lawyers to use the ideas of beauty and truth to reshape the law of obscenity so that, as Hand suggested, 'shame ... [would not] for long prevent us from adequate portrayal of some of the most serious and beautiful sides of human nature'. In typically stylish prose, Hand also encouraged lawyers to challenge the

Hicklin notion that the standard for measuring obscenity was not the reasonable or average reader but one most susceptible to corruption: 'To put thought in leash to the average conscience of the time', he wrote, 'is perhaps tolerable, but to fetter it by the necessities of the lowest and least capable seems a fatal policy.' Hand's open invitation was available to Quinn as he undertook to attack the Postmaster's determination that Lewis's story was obscene. Quinn failed to grasp the opportunity.

An argument made to order for Hand's invitation to challenge the law of obscenity on the basis of the importance of literature's beauty and truth was presented to Quinn in one of his many exchanges with John Butler Yeats. The elder Yeats, a brilliant stylist and inveterate letter-writer, had the potential to be a great asset to Quinn. Initially, JBY wrote Quinn outlining an argument perfectly suited to one of the two paths that Hand had identified as the route around – or over – the roadblock of *Hicklin*. JBY's letter emphasized the essential truthfulness of Lewis's story. His offence, according to JBY, was that, 'He has told too much. It is not good social form.'[21] JBY observed wryly that, although he liked hypocrisy, 'I am not so utterly abandoned as to help it destroy truth and honesty.'

Elaborating on this theory, JBY wrote:

> 'Respectability' and 'social order' do not like this kind of art because of the shock. It is horrible for us to be stripped naked. Swift did it in his day. Such writers are without pity, but are of enormous value in breaking up the strength of hypocrisy and sentimental decency.[22]

Unfortunately, JBY's follow-up letter of 15 November 1917, perhaps influenced by his frequent conversations with Quinn, shifted his emphasis from the story's value as truthful literature to its deterrent effect in the moral realm. Echoing Quinn's defence of *Hagar Revelly*, JBY argued that the reader of Lewis's story 'will receive a most salutary shock' and 'will watch his steps lest he fall into the horrible abyss of loathsomeness of which that article is a revelation'.[23]

John Quinn *by John Butler Yeats, 1912. (Hirshhorn Museum and
Sculpture Garden, Smithsonian Institution, Washington DC)*

Although *Hicklin* referred to a work's 'tendency to deprave or corrupt those whose minds are open to … immoral influences', the federal 'Comstock statute' barring obscene material from the mails did not include language about a tendency to corrupt. It was thus open to Quinn to argue that the court should not apply *Hicklin*'s language, but instead hold that Lewis's story was not obscene because it was beautiful and truthful literature. Faced with a powerful and direct argument along these lines, Judge Hand might have ruled that the story was not obscene under the *Hicklin–Bennett* test. If he did not, his order would have opened a path to asking the Second Circuit to overrule *Bennett's* adoption of *Hicklin*.

Instead, Quinn pursued the 'moral warning' argument that he had employed successfully in the different circumstances of the case involving *Hagar Revelly*. The affidavit Quinn prepared for Anderson to submit in support of the motion to overturn the postal bar, while asserting that the story told 'the stern truth', used verbatim JBY's above-quoted language about the story's salutary effect in the moral realm.[24] Quinn wrote to JBY that he 'used your ideas and almost your very words in my brief'.[25] A letter that Quinn wrote to Anderson after his oral argument before Judge Hand suggests that his argument emphasized that the story was 'hostile to vice and selfishness', but ignored JBY's insistence on its value as honest and truthful literature. Quinn sought to justify this approach to Anderson, insisting that he 'took the only possible line on which a Court could have decided in your favor, namely, that the story made vice unattractive and contained a moral warning'.[26]

Hand's short opinion shows that he was attentive to, but not persuaded by, this line of argument. Early in his discussion of the story, Hand specifically notes that it 'may be urged that this story points various morals', including that it 'shows the wickedness of selfishness and indulgence', the 'degradation of camp life and the demoralizing character of war'. The ensuing discussion gives the impression of a judge searching for a basis for overturning the bar order but not finding it in Quinn's argument. Reflecting an antipathy to postal bar orders, Hand emphasized the need for the postal authorities to exercise judgment and circumspection 'to avoid interference with a justifiable freedom of expression and literary development'. Nonetheless, Hand stressed the need for a powerful argument against suppression, pointing out that, given the deference owed the Postmaster, he could overturn the order only if it was clearly wrong. Unfortunately Hand's discussion of Cantleman focused so intently on Quinn's line of argument, which he characterized as exhibiting 'unusual ingenuity and ability', that he relegated the judicial definition of obscenity to secondary importance. Focusing first on Quinn's argument that the story taught a valuable moral lesson, he concluded that:

> The young girl and the relations of the man with her are described with a degree of detail that does not appear necessary to teach the desired lesson, whatever it may be, or to tell a story which would possess artistic merit or arouse any worthy emotion. On the contrary, it is at least reasonably arguable, I think, that the details of the sex relations are set forth to attract readers to the story because of their salacious character.[27]

Approaching the case from the standpoint of whether it taught a moral lesson led Hand to a negative answer, from which it was a short step to the conclusion that 'there is ground for holding that portions of the short story in question have a tendency to excite lust and if this is so, it falls within the prohibition of the statute'. It may fairly be asked whether the result would have been different had Quinn urged forcefully that the description of the relations between Cantleman and his lover was indeed necessary to tell the story, rather than to teach a lesson, and that the story was valuable for its artistic merit. No doubt the United States' entry into World War I just months prior to the suppression of Lewis's story clouded the atmosphere. The prevailing climate is apparent from the fact that Learned Hand's decision in *Masses Publishing Co. v. Patten*,

244 Fed. 535 (S.D.N.Y.1917), was reversed, 246 Fed. 24, for being overly protective of free speech to the detriment of the government's power to regulate criticism of its war policy. Quinn thought *The Little Review*'s earlier support of anarchist Emma Goldman had attracted the government's attention,[28] and Paul Vanderham's diligent research shows concern within the Post Office over the possible subversive influence of the Cantleman story.[29] Nonetheless, the case arose under the obscenity statute, and an opportunity to challenge the statute's application to literature was lost.

Quinn advised Anderson that there was no point in an appeal because Judge Hand, although wrong on the merits, was right 'on the technicalities', explaining to both Anderson and JBY that Hand was correct that the Post Office was entitled to deference.[30] Quinn's purported distinction between Hand being wrong on the substance but right on the technicality as to the standard of review missed the point that any deference that might have been accorded to the Post Office could be overcome by a strong showing that the Post Office was wrong to treat literature as obscenity – the very argument that Anderson wanted to make. Anderson made clear in print that she would have seized the opportunity that Quinn ignored. Although generously observing in her commentary in the December issue of *The Little Review* that the magazine 'was brilliantly and, because of the irony of the situation, humorously defended', she disagreed 'even with the best arguments that could be presented in a contemporary court-room about the merits' of a story like Cantleman. Apparently accepting Quinn's dictate as to what was possible to achieve in court, Anderson lamented that the only legal argument that can be made today 'is that the story is a brutal one containing a lesson and a terrible warning, and therefore salutary in its effect'.[31]

Anderson preferred an aesthetic argument to a moral one. Moreover, of the two values of truth and beauty identified by Learned Hand in *Kennerley*, she would have substituted an emphasis on beauty for JBY's focus on truth. Perhaps she was too polite to quote Théophile Gautier, who, in the course of articulating the doctrine of 'art for art's sake' in 1835, rejected arguments of the kind that Quinn would make in defence of Lewis. 'Books follow morals,' Gautier insisted, and whoever said 'literature and the arts influence morals ... was undoubtedly a great fool'.[32] Without quoting the arch Gautier, Anderson made a similar point. In the spirit of Gautier and Oscar Wilde, she insisted that the story had a right to be heard because it is literature, a status it enjoys because its author 'is master of the mysterious laws by which words are made into patterns or rhythms'. '"Good" and "bad" in literature', she insisted, 'have no other connotation than this.'[33] Anderson saw the thinness of Quinn's distinction between Judge Hand being right on the procedure but wrong on the substance. Her editorial explained to her foreign readers that, in America, 'our Postoffice [sic] is the supreme authority on all matters of intellectual interest.'[34] Had Quinn expressed Anderson's powerful ideas in the vocabulary of the advocate, he would have argued that the Post Office Department was entitled to no deference on the question whether literature should be suppressed because it had no competence to assess literature, and that Lewis's prose was not obscene.

Quinn's failure to make the argument Anderson wanted was driven by his reluctance, which will become increasingly apparent, to be publicly identified as a 'free smut, free sex advocate', a fate against which he warned Ezra Pound.[35] His timidity, cynicism, and lack of conviction as an advocate are apparent from his 2 December 1917 letter to Pound in which he echoes Anderson's praise of the 'rhythm' of Lewis's prose, but adds revealingly, 'Of course, I didn't believe in that part of my argument and brief where I spoke of the "terrible moral lesson".'[36]

Quinn's public persona as advocate played Plato to Anderson's Wilde. His insistence that an effective legal argument required a showing that the story had a salutary moral effect echoed Plato's argument that poets and other writers were welcome in the state only insofar as they told stories that inculcated good behaviour. Indeed, Plato began his discussion of the role of the poet by justifying the practise of telling fictitious children's stories calculated to have a good effect on conduct. Such stories are desirable, he maintains, 'in the case of a young and tender thing; for that is the time at which the character is being formed and the desired impression is more readily taken'.[37] Similarly, stories conducive to undesirable conduct should not be allowed. From this beginning, Plato moves to the corollary that it will also be necessary 'to establish a censorship of the writers of fiction', letting the censors approve passages with good effect and reject the bad, 'and we will desire mothers and nurses to tell their children the authorized ones only'. Even the great poet Hesiod, Plato declares, should be censored. His accounts of the struggle between Cronus and Uranus, 'even if they were true, ought certainly not to be lightly told' to young people because a young person 'should not be told that in committing the worst of crimes he is far from doing anything outrageous; and that even if he chastises his father when he does wrong, in whatever manner, he will only be following the example of the first and greatest among the gods'.[38] Having built his case on the need to instruct the young in their formative years, Plato jumps to the conclusion that 'the poets should also be told to compose for [adults] in a similar spirit'.[39]

Plato's insistence that literature promote good behaviour leads him to censor Homer's depiction of Achilles' grief at the death of Patroclus because he fears it will teach the lesson that death makes even a good man grieve and thus would diminish courage in the face of danger. 'Our principle', he explains, 'is that the good man will not consider death terrible to any other good man who is his comrade.'[40] Plato cannot accept the idea that poets should be permitted to depict good people being affected by adversity because good people, by definition, are happy in their knowledge of ultimate and transcendent union with the Good.[41] Thus Plato declares that poets are guilty of making the gravest misstatements when they tell us that wicked men are often happy, and the good miserable; and that injustice is profitable when undetected, but that justice is a man's own loss and another's gain – these things we shall forbid [poets] to utter, and command them to sing and say the opposite.[42]

Ultimately, after extensive discourse, Plato bars poets from the Republic, emphasizing that their appeal to the non-rational part of the soul threatens the supremacy of truth and the well-being of the state.[43] The ban, however, is issued reluctantly and with assurances to Poetry that she will be welcomed back if it can be shown that she 'is useful to States and to human life'.[44]

The force of Plato's argument still lurks behind every act of censorship, and, indeed, has a debilitating effect even on opponents of censorship by diverting them down the path of defending literature by arguing, as did Quinn, that allegedly obscene literature actually teaches a moral lesson. Anderson's response to Quinn's Plato-infused approach finds its underpinnings in Wilde's classic essay 'The Decay of Lying', published in 1891, which turned Plato upside down. Mimicking the two-voice style of Plato's dialogues, Vivian, the thinly veiled voice of Wilde, asserts that the 'object of art is not simple truth, but complex beauty', and beautiful complexity involves what is essentially dissimulation, because art 'is really a form of exaggeration; and selection, which is the very spirit of art, is nothing more than an intensified mode of over-emphasis'.[45] With typical panache, Wilde manages to enlist Plato in support of his argument, observing that the advantages of lying for the sake of improving the young are 'so admirably set forth in the early books of Plato's *Republic* that it is unnecessary to dwell upon them here'.[46] Wilde blithely asserts that, although this and various other forms of lying have limitations, 'the only form of lying that is absolutely beyond reproach is lying for its own sake, and the highest development of this is … Lying in Art'.[47] Accordingly, he argues, 'those who do not love Beauty more than Truth never know the inmost shrine of art'.[48] In sum, Wilde submits,

'Lying, the telling of beautiful untrue things, is the proper aim of Art.'[49] In full stride, he easily dispatches those who would rely on Shakespeare to oppose him. He points out that the great dramatist's 'unfortunate aphorism about Art holding the mirror up to Nature, is deliberately said by Hamlet in order to convince the bystanders of his absolute insanity in all art-matters'.[50]

The essence of Wilde's argument was encapsulated in Anderson's insistence that Beauty was the only criterion for measuring what constitutes art. Quinn never engaged directly with the substance of Anderson's views. Instead, having forged ahead with his own Plato-driven argument that Lewis's story taught a good moral lesson, he wrote to Pound complaining – not of Anderson's views – but of the fact that she had chosen to quarrel publicly with Hand's decision, a choice that he could not help describing in sexual terms. Anderson, he wrote, 'is an attractive girl' but has no 'business sense', a quality he reserved to his own domineering masculinity.[51]

Quinn's reticence and Anderson's courage over the aesthetic and legal issues presented by the Cantleman case were prologues to their respective roles in the struggle to publish *Ulysses*. Indeed, at the outset of Quinn's representation of Anderson in the *Little Review* case, he wrote to Pound championing the 'moral lesson' approach, which he had used successfully in *Kennerley*, over the 'Book work of art' position.[52] He was, in essence, opting for Plato over Wilde.

The epic enterprise of defending *Ulysses* began in December 1917 when Joyce began sending episodes of the novel to Pound, who forwarded them to Anderson. Pound recognized that publishing *Ulysses* in the United States would run afoul of the Comstock Act's prohibition against transmitting obscene material through the mails. 'I suppose we'll be damn well suppressed if we print the text as it stands,' he wrote to Joyce. 'BUT it is damnwell worth it. I see no reason why the nations should sit in darkness merely because Anthony Comstock was horrified at the sight of his grandparents in copulation, and thereafter ran wode in a loin cloth.'[53] When

Anderson read the initial episode, she was not deterred by a similar warning of likely censorship perils.[54] Rather, it was in response to Pound's warning that she told Heap, 'This is the most beautiful thing we'll ever have ... We'll print it if it's the last effort of our lives.'[55] She promptly committed publicly to serial publication of the novel, announcing to her readers in January 1918 that we 'are about to publish a prose masterpiece'.

Ulysses' debut overlapped with a revealing sequel to the Cantleman case. Although Quinn had complained to Pound about Anderson's public comment on Hand's decision, Pound himself submitted an article to Anderson criticizing Hand. Pound appreciated the quality of Hand's mind – one could see, he conceded to Quinn, why he is a judge – but identified the weakness at the core of his opinion. Hand forthrightly recognized that the *Hicklin* standard would ban many indisputably great works of literature, but tried to circumvent this fundamental problem by referring to a judge-made exception for 'classics'.[56] Hand had put it this way:

> [N]umerous really great writings would come under the ban, if tests that are frequently current were applied, and these approved publications doubtless at times escape only because they come within the term 'classics,' which means, for the purpose of application of the statute, that they are ordinarily immune from interference, because they have the sanction of age and fame, and usually appeal to a comparatively limited number of readers.

Pound saw that this loose end could unravel *Hicklin's* failure to consider the literary merit of a work alleged to be obscene. Writing to Quinn, he observed that 'the judges [*sic*] excuse for permitting the classics to pass through the mails, because they are read only by a few people is TOO RICH AND FRUITY not to be made use of'.[57] In the tradition of Anderson's desire to spark a conversation with her readers, Pound's sharp pen drafted an article asking the 'gentle reader' to 'picture to himself the state of America IF the classics were widely read; IF these books which in the beginning lifted mankind from savagery, and which from a.d.1400 onward have gradually redeemed us from the darkness of medievalism, should be read by the millions who now consume Mr. Hearst and the *Ladies Home Journal* ! ! ! ! !' Having struck this blow with the hammer of Augustus Hand's partial attempt to circumvent a Plato-like ban on poets, Pound added tellingly that the exception was of no use to living writers because contemporary works could not have the requisite sanction of age.[58]

Pound's proposed article also vented his outrage at the fact that the list of non-mailable material in the federal statute involved in the Cantleman case lumped literature with contraceptive devices, which he referred to as 'the inventions of the late Dr. Condom'. Quinn wrote Pound on 2 March 1918 urging him not to publish his criticism of the Cantleman decision because it would result in Pound's being publicly identified as a champion of 'sex litera-ture'. The publication of that article 'would permanently injure you here', Quinn wrote. 'It is just the kind of thing that people would remember. You have got too much genius to be catalogued in the newspaper biographies of this country as a man chiefly interested in sex literature.' Quinn's squeamishness about sex leaps off the page when he qualifies his agreement with Pound that America 'needs waking up' by adding, 'But God damn the idea of waking this country up by rehashing nauseating sex questions.' Quinn's dire warning was one he took to heart in his own career: 'You don't want to be known as a free smut, free sex advocate.'

Quinn's letter unfairly blames Anderson for Pound's article, saying she should have seen at a glance that 'the thing was impos-sible'. With an almost willful blindness, Quinn portrays Anderson to Pound as a sexual innocent. Apparently unaware that she had written an editorial supporting Margaret Sanger that called birth control 'one of the milestones by which civilization will measure its progress',[59] he wrote to Pound that he was hampered in writing to Anderson about Pound's article because he was unable to explain

Pound's allusion to 'the works of the late Dr. Condom', and doubted she understood it.[60]

Anderson and Heap published Pound's article in the March 1918 issue, although they made some concessions to Quinn's comments, 'leaving out' as he told Pound, 'most of the objectionable parts, except the allusion in the first paragraph to Dr. Condom'. Quinn was 'sore as hell' when he saw Pound's article, although what he most objected to in the issue was 'the Joyce thing', the first episode of *Ulysses*.[61] Whereas Anderson had been captivated by the lyrical beauty of Joyce's prose, Quinn regarded much of it as 'toilet-room literature, pissoir art' that would be 'subject ... to damnation in thirty seconds by any court or jury'. He was particularly offended by what would become the famous mock-Homeric epithets: 'scrotum-tightening' and 'snotgreen' in Joyce's descriptions of the sea, and by Buck Mulligan's Ballad of the Joking Jesus.

On reflection, he conceded 'the Joyce thing standing alone might go', but it could not pass muster combined with pieces by Lewis, Ford, and Pound because all four reflected 'the obsession of women', all 'bordering on sex or women'. Quinn blamed the editors, rather than the authors, for this predilection because, in his view, the issue 'is damnable as a whole more than in any of its parts'. Although Quinn claimed that the issue manifested an obsession with sex, his harangue is an exercise in amateur psychology that might better have been directed at himself. Anybody reading the whole issue, he insisted, would say the editors 'suffered from sex mania or the obsession of sex, or that they were over-sexed' and 'unsatisfied'. He warns Pound that 'your friends won't like to have you branded in the same star class'.

Quinn himself clearly did not want his friends to brand him that way. His professional livelihood depended on the respect of a network of Irish-American, Catholic businessmen, judges and lawyers, who were likely to be put off by public perception of Quinn as a champion of 'sex literature'.

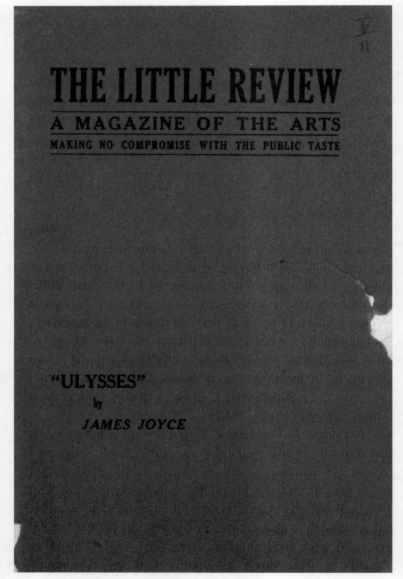

The Little Review, *March, 1918. (Special Collections,*
University of Wisconsin-Milwaukee Libraries)

THE LITTLE REVIEW

THE MAGAZINE THAT IS READ BY THOSE WHO WRITE THE OTHERS

MARCH, 1918

Ulysses, 1.	*James Joyce*
Imaginary Letters, VIII.	*Wyndham Lewis*
Matinee	*Jessie Dismorr*
The Classics "Escape"	*Ezra Pound*
Cantico del Sole	
Women and Men, II.	*Ford Madox Hueffer*
Bertha	*Arthur Symons*
A List of Books	*Ezra Pound*
Wyndham Lewis's "Tarr"	
Raymonde Collignon	
The Reader Critic	

Copyright, 1918, by Margaret Anderson

MARGARET ANDERSON, Editor
EZRA POUND, Foreign Editor

24 *West Sixteenth Street, New York*
Foreign office:
5 *Holland Place Chambers, London W. 8.*

25 cents a copy $2.50 a year

Entered as second-class matter at P. O., New York, N. Y.
Published monthly by Margaret Anderson

The Little Review, *March, 1918, showing the extraordinary conjunction of the first installment of* Ulysses *and Ezra Pound's criticism of Judge Augustus Hand's decision in the 'Cantleman's Spring-Mate' case. (Special Collections, University of Wisconsin-Milwaukee Libraries)*

One of his most lucrative clients, for example, was Thomas Fortune Ryan, controlling stockholder of the Equitable Life Assurance Society of the United States, the tenth-richest man in the country, and a major financial supporter of Catholic institutions, to which he and his wife contributed approximately $20 million.[62] Other members of this circle included Sligo native Bourke Cockran, a six-term Tammany-backed Democratic Congressman, and Democratic members of the judiciary such as Judges Martin Keough and Daniel Colahan, and Magistrate (later Judge) Joseph E. Corrigan, nephew of the Archbishop of New York.[63] Quinn, Ryan and Keough would become fellow members of the American Committee for Relief in Ireland, which was formed in 1920 to aid Irish civilians whose lives were disrupted by the Anglo-Irish War.[64] The subsidiary New York Committee was chaired by Martin Conboy, who went on to become Chairman of the Clean Books Committee, an organization founded in 1923 to press for a stricter obscenity statute – one that was 'horse-high, pig-tight, and bull-strong' – after D.H. Lawrence's *Women in Love* was found not to be obscene under the existing state statute.[65]

The hostility of Quinn's Irish-American circle to books like *Ulysses* is dramatically illustrated by Conboy's eventual role as the United States Attorney who argued passionately to the Federal Court of Appeals in 1934 that *Ulysses* was obscene, a view that, as reported in *The New Yorker*, was 'personal as well as official' for a man who was 'perhaps one of the foremost Catholic laymen in the country, and was made a Knight-Commander of the Order of St. Gregory while President of the Catholic Club'.[66] Moreover, Conboy was an officer of the New York Society for the Suppression of Vice, the entity that prosecuted Anderson and Heap for publishing Joyce.[67] The antipathy to Joyce's novel among Quinn's Irish-American colleagues is further illustrated by the fact that the only member of the three-judge panel of the Court of Appeals who agreed with Conboy's argument was Judge Martin Manton, who had also been a fellow member of the Committee for Relief in Ireland with Conboy and Quinn, and began his legal career as a partner of Bourke Cockran.[68]

Quinn's reluctance to be branded a champion of sex literature led him to re-evaluate his financial support of *The Little Review* even as he warned Pound of its potential for inflicting reputational harm. In a letter of 10 June 1918 he informed Pound that he would not support *The Little Review* beyond his original contribution, although he would make good on the commitment he had made to Pound in March to a second year of contributing $750 to Pound for himself and writers designated by Pound without regard to where their work was published.[69] He put a sharp edge on his decision in a 30 October letter to Pound, stating that he was 'glad you and I have come to a definite understanding about the *Little Review*, namely, that there will be no more subsidies from me when this year's is exhausted … They can go to hell as far as I am concerned'.[70] He informed Anderson and Heap of his decision by letter of 3 December 1918, adding that he would pay Pound the $450 remaining on his second $750 annual commitment.[71] Later in December Pound advised Joyce that '*The Little Review* will have to paddle mostly on its own after April' because 'I can't raise any more cash (after the second year's lot runs out) and can't give my time to it without that meager allowance for self and contributors.'[72] Pound resigned as foreign editor the following spring.

Events surrounding termination of the subsidy illustrated both Anderson and Heap's independence as editors and Quinn's tendency to view their conduct in sexual terms. As prelude to his exit, Pound, who was also serving as foreign editor of Harriet Monroe's *Poetry* magazine, published in *The Little Review* a condensed version of some poetry criticism by Edgar Jepson that Monroe had declined to publish in *Poetry*. Pound added a postscript stating that Monroe had turned down Jepson's work because of his 'lack of flattery' of such Chicago-based poets as Vachel Lindsay, Edgar Lee Masters and Carl Sandburg.[73] Monroe responded with an article maintaining that she had turned down Jepson's review, not because it denigrated Chicago poets, but because of 'its cheap incompetence', and went on to take Pound to task for criticizing *Poetry* in *The Little Review*, while employed by both. *The Little Review,* she suggested, was 'now under the dictatorship of Ezra Pound'.[74] Heap responded in *The Little Review,* defending Pound as editor, but skewering him as a person:

> Miss Monroe is not the first to tell us that the *Little Review* is under dictatorship of Pound. Our idea of having a foreign editor is not to sit in our New York office and mess up, censor, or throw out work sent to us by an editor in London. We have let Ezra Pound be our foreign editor in the only way we see it. We have let him be as foreign as he likes: foreign to taste, foreign to courtesy, foreign to our standards of Art. All because we believe in the fundamental idea back of our connection with Mr. Pound: the interest and value of an intellectual communication between Europe and America.[75]

Quinn could enjoy Heap's withering pen when it was directed at Pound. On 11 December 1918, after reading Heap's criticism of Pound in the November issue, Quinn wrote to Pound that it 'is a most amusing number. In it Miss [sic] J.H. takes a fall out of you.' Still, he can't help but see Heap's writing in sexual terms, suggesting that her attitude towards Pound is like that of a spurned lover.[76] Anderson and Heap had the last word. In a brief note on the inside of the cover of the June 1919 issue they informed readers with tongue in cheek that the allegedly tyrannical 'Ezra Pound has abdicated and gone to Persia' and that John Rodker was now their London editor.

Spurned or not, Anderson and Heap continued to publish episodes of *Ulysses*, but the January 1919 issue containing the so-called Lestrygonians episode was suppressed by the Post Office after it had been partially distributed. Until this point no charge of obscenity had been made against *Ulysses*, although many readers were discomfited by features of Joyce's style that are captured by a recent description of modernism as 'an assault on a more traditional understanding of narrative' in favour of an 'insistence that language is not a transparent medium of representation'.[77] Early readers encountered two aspects of Joyce's modernist style that must have appealed to Anderson's desire to inspire a more intensely lived life: an attempt 'to carve deep and even profound meaning from even the seemingly most innocuous experiences of day-to-day life' and an effort 'to regenerate language itself, to inject meaning into words and forms that have become dulled by use and age'.[78]

Even the famous opening sentence of the novel in which 'stately, plump Buck Mulligan' emerges on the roof of the Martello tower *bearing* a bowl on which a mirror and razor are *crossed* echoes the central narrative of Christianity, thus infusing old words with new meaning. Seamus Heaney captured the excitement of Joyce's opening chapter in his observation – made in the course of a visit to the Martello tower – that 'the English language opens like a pack of cards in the hands of a magician'.[79] The chapter in its entirety can be read as a parody of the Mass, with words carrying multiple meanings at every turn. Joyce's regeneration of language is also apparent in one of the mock Homeric epithets that exercised Quinn – a 'snotgreen sea' observed by Stephen in place of the Homeric 'wine-dark sea'.

Another novel aspect of Joyce's style intrudes early in the opening episode when, in the midst of a direct depiction of Stephen Dedalus's mental reaction to the events being described, the word 'Chrysostomos' (Greek for 'golden-mouthed') interrupts the narrative's description of Mulligan's gold-pointed teeth. From this point forward, much of the first three episodes of the novel reveal the 'density and complexity' of Stephen's quotidian life by recounting his experience as perceived not by an observer but by his highly philosophical and literary consciousness. For example, the phrase that first captivated Margaret Anderson occurs as Stephen tests Aristotle's theories of vision by closing his eyes and wondering, 'Am I walking into eternity along Sandymount strand?' while 'the ineluctible modality of the visible' floats through his consciousness.

W.B. Yeats immediately perceived what was new and important about *Ulysses* when he read the initial episodes in *The Little Review*. Writing to John Quinn on 23 July 1918, he commented that Joyce's 'new story in "The Little Review" looks like becoming the best work he has done. It is an entirely new thing – neither what the eye sees nor the ear hears but what the rambling mind thinks & imagines from moment to moment. He has certainly surpassed in intensity any novelist of our time.'[80]

At the outset of the fourth episode, Stephen's highly abstract consciousness gives way at the advent of Mr Leopold Bloom, who famously 'ate with relish the inner organs of beasts and fowls'. The reader begins to experience the day's events through Bloom's interior monologue, which is much more concrete and sensual than Stephen's, and reflects a highly inquisitive mind that jumps from thought to thought and memory to memory, often leaving the reader to fill in the gaps. Terence Killeen's useful companion to *Ulysses* comments that the reader's 'almost unprecedented immediacy of access to this mind … is one of the great achievements of the book'.[81] As Bloom experiences the same hours of the day already described in terms of Stephen's perception, the reader learns that Bloom's wife Molly, a singer, is planning to commence an affair with her manager Blazes Boylan at 4:30 that afternoon. In the next episode, the reader follows Bloom to Paddy Dignam's funeral and shares Bloom's meditation on death.

The sixth episode is centred in a newspaper office and is written in an exaggeratedly rhetorical style that drew no complaint from the postal authorities. The seventh episode, Lestrygonians, was the first to be suppressed. There is no record of what caused the Postmaster to intervene, but it seems fair to assume that his eye focused on the scene in which Bloom, his memory stimulated by a glass of wine over lunch in Davy Byrne's pub, reminisces about one of the central events in the novel, the occasion on which Molly, as she herself will remember in her concluding monologue, said 'yes' to Bloom in a field on Howth Head. The stimulus to Bloom's memory, although not as famous as Proust's madeleine, is gently evocative, beginning with 'Glowing wine on his palate lingered swallowed,' then continuing 'Crushing in the winepress grapes of Burgundy. Sun's heat it is. Seems to a secret touch telling me memory. Touched his sense moistened remembered.'[82] The memory silently unfolding in Bloom's mind sets the scene: 'Hidden under wild ferns on Howth below us bay sleeping; sky. No sound. The sky.' After further setting the scene, Bloom's memory focuses on the heart of the matter:

> Ravished over her I lay full lips full open kissed her mouth. Yum. Softly she gave me in my mouth the seedcake warm and chewed ... Screened under ferns she laughed warm folded. Wildly I lay on her, kissed her: eyes, her lips, her stretched neck beating, woman's breasts full in her blouse of nun's veiling, fat nipples upright. Hot I tongued her. She kissed me. I was kissed. All yielding she tossed my hair. Kissed, she kissed me.

Abruptly, Bloom returns to the present in which his wife is awaiting a liaison with her soon-to-be-lover Blazes Boylan: 'Me. And me now.'

Lionel Trilling might have had this passage in mind when he observed that 'we can perhaps consider the whole of *Ulysses* as an epiphany, the continuous showing forth of the spirit of Leopold Bloom out of the intractable commonplaces of his existence'.[83] 'The assumption of the [Joycean] epiphany', Trilling explained, in terms redolent of Anderson, 'is that human existence is in largest part compounded of the dullness and triviality of its routine, devitalized or paralyzed by habit and the weight of necessity', but that from time to time a flash of spirit suddenly 'transfigures the ordinary, suffusing it with significance'.[84] The transfiguration of Bloom's otherwise ordinary lunch is triggered by a powerful erotic memory, whose voltage is plainly of a different order of magnitude from anything in 'Cantleman's Spring-Mate' or *Hagar Revelly*. Looking back to 1919 we can reasonably postulate that this is the passage the Postmaster found objectionable, even as we disagree with his finding.

It is less clear what caused the pre-mailing suppression of the next issue, which was scheduled for publication in May 1919 and included the second half of the Scylla and Charybdis episode. Anderson had tried to avoid suppression by herself excising four passages from Joyce's text, including Buck Mulligan's assertion that Stephen Dedalus had 'pissed' on John Synge's doorstep, two lines in a ballad referring to masturbation, the subtitle 'A Honeymoon in the Hand' to Mulligan's ballad 'Everyman His Own Wife', and a list of illicit sexual relations: 'sons with mothers, sires with daughters, nephews with grandmothers, queens with prize bulls'. Anderson advised her readers of what had happened to the January issue, and added, 'To avoid a similar interference this month I have ruined Mr. Joyce's story by cutting certain passages in which he mentions natural facts known to everyone.'[85] What she published was a not-very-lust-inducing account of Stephen's disquisition on his theory of Shakespeare and Hamlet to a symposium-like group in the National Library. Nonetheless, the issue was suppressed.

Despite his antipathy for Anderson and Heap, Quinn's conception of himself as the protector of an eventual private publication of Joyce's manuscript led him to seek to mediate between *The Little Review* and the postal authorities. He wrote to Pound suggesting eighteen passages that might have been the basis for the Postmaster's suppression.[86] The letter shows how low a threshold Quinn set for what constituted non-mailable matter. None of his examples seems calculated to excite lust, and most seem unlikely candidates for exclusion from the mails even in 1919. Quinn's first example was a very mild parody of the Apostle's Creed ('He who Himself begot, middler the Holy Ghost') and his second ('Jove, a cool ruttine send them') was a near verbatim imitation of a line from Shakespeare's *The Merry Wives of Windsor*. Quinn's self-consciousness about his inoffensive litany is reflected in his comment that, 'I think you will agree that a different standard is applicable to a magazine than to a book' – a belief he based on the facts that magazines were subsidized by low postal rates and reached readers who hadn't necessarily invited all of the contents. He seemed more exercised by the Joycean language Anderson had deleted than by what she proposed to publish. Taking issue with Anderson's advice to her readers that she had omitted 'natural facts known to everyone', he observed, 'I suppose that pederasty, masturbation, defecation and urination are "known to everybody." But perhaps not … I cannot agree that the whole test of whether "natural facts" should be mentioned in stories is "that they are known to everyone."' His quarrel is more about taste or propriety than eroticism – and he blames Anderson for Joyce's writing. Anderson had deleted references to urination and masturbation from the episode as published, and, although the overall text of *Ulysses* reflects a fascination with excrement, there is no reference to defecation in the passages Quinn postulated as possible grounds for exclusion. The sole reference to one of Quinn's list of 'natural facts' in his catalogue of excludable passages is a reference to 'the charge of pederasty brought against the bard' and a response attributed to Professor Dowden that 'life ran very high in those days'.

Pound was not convinced that Quinn's tepid litany justified excluding what he called 'the Shakespeare chapter' from the mails. 'It is *typical*', he fumed, 'that they shd. have hit on Joyce's best & most intellectual chapter, typical of the way America spews when given any real food for the intellect …'[87] Although Pound felt that Joyce had 'gone rather far in one or two other places', he was convinced that 'if he gets suppressed on the Shakespeare chapter, it merely nullifies all my advice, and shows officials merely incalculable, or rather cranky in just the proportion that the work shows intellectual energy'. So convinced was Pound that he allowed he 'might listen to my wife who has assured me that the *energy* in Joyce, W[yndham] L[ewis], & myself is what upsets people. That indecency has nothing to do with it.'

Here, then, was an opportunity to tip the censorship battle in Joyce's favour by seeking a judicial determination that his 'Shakespeare chapter' was not obscene and thus the bar order was unjustified. Yet Quinn adhered to his view that 'it would be perfectly hopeless to take the matter into Court'.[88] No doubt harking back to his Cantleman experience, he maintained that the court would defer to the Postmaster's determination. But deference cannot create obscenity where there is none. Rather than seeking a public victory for Joyce in court, Quinn submitted a memorandum to the Solicitor of the Post Office in June 1919 arguing against suppression of the May issue. In a tacit admission that Joyce's Scylla and Charybdis episode was not, in fact, obscene, the Solicitor replied to Quinn that the suppression was 'not based solely upon the passage from Mr. Joyce's article, to which your brief is devoted, but is based upon the magazine as a whole, and [referring to four nude drawings by James Light] upon the cuts contained therein as well as the printed matter'.[89] The Post Office clearly would have been on the defensive in court had Quinn seized this game-changing opportunity to give Joyce the upper hand in the obscenity wars.

Readers of Quinn's memorandum were impressed. Anderson thought it a 'valiant defense'[90]; Ezra Pound called it 'the best apologia for [Joyce] that has been written'[91]; and Eliot found it 'admirable'[92] and was prepared to publish it in the *Egoist*. Apparently relying on his patron Harriet Shaw Weaver's report, Joyce himself called it 'magnificent'.[93] Despite such praise from these giants of modernism, Quinn declined to permit publication of his memorandum. He claimed that it was written too hastily and he lacked time to revise it,[94] but he was clearly following the advice he had given to Pound not to be publicly identified as a 'free smut, free sex advocate'.

It would be fascinating to know what Quinn wrote that was praised so highly but that he refused to publish. Unfortunately, the pertinent Post Office archives were destroyed, and no copy can be found.[95] Thus we know neither what 'passage' Quinn discussed nor what he said in its defence. However, a letter Quinn wrote to the Irish writer and diplomat Shane Leslie two years later suggests that his memorandum tracked a line of thinking offered to him by John Butler Yeats's letter arguing that Wyndham Lewis, like Swift in his day, was a writer 'without pity, but … of enormous value in breaking up the strength of hypocrisy and sentimental decency' by presenting life with a 'truth and honesty' that left humanity 'stripped naked'. Quinn probably had these words in mind when he wrote to Leslie that there was 'no humbug in Ulysses, no pretense about morality' but rather 'the facts and the dialogues, simple, unadorned, unashamed, without sentiment and without sentimentality'.[96] This was likely the thrust of the memorandum Quinn submitted privately to the Post Office but would not be identified with in public, where he preferred pretense about morality.

Undeterred by the Post Office's repeated interference, Anderson and Heap published further episodes of *Ulysses* throughout the remainder of 1919 and the first half of 1920 with one additional suppression, in January 1920, when the entire issue was seized and burned on the basis of the third part of the Cyclops episode. From Quinn's standpoint, the suppression and burning of issues of *The Little Review* simply proved his point. Joyce himself, always relishing the role of martyr, seemed to make light of the burning. With a subtle reference to the fact that his confirmation namesake, the sixteenth-century St Aloysius Gonzaga, was believed to have burned with love of God with such ardour during his life that he passed through purgatory quickly, Joyce observed in a letter to Weaver that the burning of the Cyclops episode was 'the second time I have had the pleasure of being burned while on earth so that I hope I shall pass through the fires of purgatory as quickly as my patron S. Aloysius'.[97] For Anderson, however, the destruction of her magazine was 'like a burning at the stake'. Her account of her reaction to the burning still crackles:

The care we had taken to preserve Joyce's text intact; the worry over the bills that accumulated when we had no advance funds; the technique I used on printer, bookbinder, paper houses – tears, prayers, hysterics or rages – to make them push ahead without a guarantee of money; the addressing, wrapping, stamping, mailing; the excitement of anticipating the world's response to the literary masterpiece of our generation ... and then a notice from the post office: BURNED.[98]

More serious than the burning, however, was the inauspicious augury for Quinn's impending role as defender of *Ulysses* that was suggested by Anderson's belief that her aesthetic ideas were faithfully presented in Quinn's private memorandum to the Post Office, but not in his public argument before Judge Hand.

NOTES

1 Lionel Trilling, *Sincerity and Authenticity* (Cambridge: Harvard University Press, 1972) ('Trilling') 6.

2 John Quinn, review, *Vanity Fair* (May 1917), reprinted in Robert H. Deming, *James Joyce: The Critical Heritage* (London: Routledge & Kegan Paul, 1970) ('Deming') I, 103–6 at 104.

3 Vincent Brome, *H.G. Wells: A Biography* (London: Longmans, Green, & Co., 1951) 112.

4 Ezra Pound, 'James Joyce: At Last the Novel Appears', *The Egoist*, 4, No. 2 (February 1917) 21–2.

5 Edward de Grazia, *Girls Lean Back Everywhere* (New York: Random House, 1992) 4.

6 16 Blatch. 338, Fed Cas. No. 14, 571.

7 L.R. 3 Q.B. 360 (1868).

8 *People v. Seltzer*, 122 Misc. 329, 334, 203 N.Y.S. 809, 813 (Sup. Ct. 1924).

9 Plato, *The Republic*, trans. Benjamin Jowett (New York: Modern Library, 1982) ('Republic') III, 387.

10 Daniel Carson Goodman, *Hagar Revelly* (New York: Macauley, 1913) 168–9.

11 'Hagar Revelly Not Immoral Says Jury', *Pub. Weekly*, LXXXV (14 February 1914) 515–16.

12 Rachel Potter's recent study *Obscene Modernism* erroneously states that Judge Hand's determination was appealed to '[t]he circuit court in

New York ... [which] chose to ignore the wider philosophical matter that had been raised by Hand, and simply overturned Kennerley's conviction by judging it not obscene by the Hicklin standard.' Rachel Potter, *Obscene Modernism: Literary Censorship & Experiment 1900–1940* (Oxford: Oxford University Press, 2013) ('Obscene Modernism') 37.

13   Letter of 5 November 1917, University of Wisconsin-Milwaukee, Archives Department ('UWM').

14   LR (October 1917) 13.

15   *Id.*

16   *Id.* at 13–14.

17   *Anderson v. Patten*, 247 Fed. 382 (S.D.N.Y. 1917).

18   Samuel Eliot Morison, *Three Centuries of Harvard, 1636–1936* (Cambridge: Harvard University Press, 1936) 330.

19   Gerald Gunther, *Learned Hand: the Man and the Judge* (New York: Alfred A. Knopf, 1994) ('Gunther') 33.

20   *United States v. Kennerley*, 209 Fed. 119, 120–21 (S.D.N.Y. 1913).

21   Letter of 6 November 1917 (QC).

22   *Id.*

23   QC.

24   Anderson Affidavit, Equity 14–379, S.D.N.Y. 1918.

25   1 December 1917 (QC); see also Quinn to JBY, 28 November 1917 (QC).

26   Letter of 14 June 1919 (UWM).

27   247 Fed. at 383.

28   Letter of 5 December 1917 from Quinn to Anderson (UWM).

29   Vanderham 17–18.

30   Quinn letter to Anderson of 5 December 1917, n. 28 above; and Quinn letter of 1 December 1917 to JBY (QC).

31   LR (December 1917) 46–9.

32   Théophile Gautier, *Mademoiselle de Maupin*, 1835, trans. Burton Rascoe (New York: Knopf, 1920) 22.

33   LR (December 1917) 46–9.

34   *Id.*

35   Letter of 2 March 1918 (QC).

36   Letter of 2 December 1917 to Pound (QC).

37   Republic II, 377.

38   *Id.* at 378.

39   *Id.*

40   Republic III, 387.

41   See Martha C. Nussbaum, *The Fragility of Goodness* (Cambridge: Cambridge University Press, 1986) 382 (citing *Republic* 392 A–B). See also Nussbaum, *Love's Knowledge: Essays on Philosophy and Literature* (New York: Oxford University Press, 1990) 387–8.

42   Republic III, 392.

43   Republic, X, 595; 600–5.

44   *Id.* at 607–8.

45   Oscar Wilde, 'The Decay of Lying', 1891, in *The Prose of Oscar Wilde* (New York: Bonibooks, 1935) ('DL') 25.

46   *Id.* at 49.

47   *Id.* at 50.

48   *Id.*

49   *Id.* at 53.

50   *Id.* at 31.

51   Letter of 2 December 1917 (QC).

52   Letter of 16 October 1920 to Pound, University of Southern Illinois Carbondale Special Collections Research Center ('SIUC').

53   Letter of 19 December 1917 to Joyce, Pound/Joyce 128–9.

54   Letter of 17 January 1918 to Margaret Anderson, EP/LR 173–4.

55   See Ch. 1, n. 1.

56   Letter of 30 December 1917 to John Quinn in Pound/Quinn Letters 132.

57   *Id.* at 135.

58   Ezra Pound, 'The Classics "Escape"', LR (March 1918) 32–4.

59   Margaret Anderson, 'Mr. Comstock and the Resourceful Police', LR (April 1915) 3.

60   Letter of 6 March 1918 (QC).

61   Letter of 14 March 1918 (QC).

62   MNY 34–5, 84, 617; Edwin Slipek, Jr., 'The Tycoon', *Style Weekly* (19 January 2005).

63   MNY 17, 85, 91, 110, 448, 617.

64   Report of the American Committee for Relief in Ireland (New York: 1922 (?) Internet Archive) ('Irish Relief Committee Report'); See F.M. Carroll, 'The American Committee For Relief in Ireland 1920–22', *Irish Historical Studies*, Vol. 23, No. 89 (May 1982) 30–49.

65   Paul S. Boyer, *Purity in Print* (2nd edn, Madison: University of Wisconsin Press, 2002) ('Boyer') 102–4.

66   *The New Yorker* (29 September 1934) 12.

67   See the Society's 1929 Annual Report, cited in Vanderham 130.

68   Irish Relief Committee Report and Joseph Borkin, *The Corrupt Judge* (New York: Clarkson Potter, 1962) ('Borkin') 29.

69   See Quinn letters to Pound of 14 March and 10 June 1918 (QC).

70   QC.

71   UWM.

72   Letter to James Joyce, 12 December 1918, Pound/Joyce 147–9.

73   Edgar Jepson, 'The Western School', LR (September 1918) 4–5.

74   Harriett Monroe, 'An International Episode', *Poetry* (November 1918) 94–5.

75   Jane Heap, 'The Episode Continued', LR (November 1918) 35–37.

76   QC.

77   Sean Latham, *Joyce's Modernism* (Dublin: National Library of Ireland, 2005) 39.

78   *Id.* at 3.

79   Seamus Heaney, quoted in J.C., N.B., *Times Literary Supplement* (6 September 2013) 32.

80   John Kelly, ed., *The Collected Letters of W.B. Yeats*, Oxford University Press (Intelex Electronic Edition) ('*CL InteLex*') 3465. Yeats later observed that the opening episodes have 'our Irish cruelty & also our kind of strength & the Martello Tower pages are full of beauty ...' Letter of 8 March 1922 to Olivia Shakespear, *CL InteLex* 4085.

81   Terence Killeen, *Ulysses Unbound* (Dublin: Worldwell, 2005) 42.

82   LR (January 1919) 47.

83   Trilling at 90.

84   *Id.* at 89.

85   LR (May 1919) 21.

86   Letter of 18 June 1919 (QC).

87   Pound letter to Quinn, 6 July 1919, Pound/Quinn Letters 176–7.

88   Letter to Pound, 17 June 1919 (QC).

89   Letter from Solicitor W.H. Lamar to Quinn, 18 June 1919 (UWM).

90   Quinn letter to Anderson (quoting Anderson), printed in TYW 225.

91   Pound to Quinn, 6 July 1919, in Pound/Quinn Letters 176.

92   Eliot to Quinn, 9 July 1919, in Valerie Eliot and Hugh Haughton, eds, *The Letters of T.S. Eliot, Vol. 1* (New Haven: Yale University Press, 2011) 373.

93   Letter of 3 August 1919 from Joyce to Quinn in Richard Ellmann, ed., *The Letters of James Joyce, Vol. II* (New York: Viking, 1966) ('JLII') 447–8.

94   Quinn letter of 22 November 1919 (QC).
95   Research at, and telephone conversation by the author with, National Archives (William Creech).
96   Letter of 21 June 1922 (QC).
97   Letter of 25 February 1920, in Stuart Gilbert, ed., *Letters of James Joyce, Vol. I* (New York: Viking, 1957) ('JLI') 137.
98   TYW 175.

The Importance of Pairing Truth with Beauty in Defending *Ulysses*

Although Anderson and Heap survived the burning and managed to publish additional episodes of *Ulysses*, danger loomed as the pioneering editors sought to bring Joyce's beautiful prose to the public. In a pre-storm lull, there was no interference with the issues of April and May–June 1920, which contained the first two parts of the episode called Nausicaa, the name of the princess who helps Odysseus when he is washed up on the shore of Phaeacia as he struggles to return to Ithaca. In a letter to Quinn of 3 September 1920, Joyce situated Nausicaa as the thirteenth of eighteen contemplated episodes that would mirror Homer's *Odyssey* according to a plan described in greater detail later that month to critic Carlo Linati.[1] The letter to Linati outlined the rarefied structure in which Joyce's sometimes earthy prose would be housed. It explained that *Ulysses* is

> an epic of two races (Israelite–Irish) and at the same time the cycle of the human body as well as a little story of a day (life) ... [and] also a

71

sort of encyclopedia. My intention is to transpose the myth *sub specie temporis nostri*. Each adventure (that is, every hour, every organ, every art being interconnected and interrelated in the structural scheme of the whole) ... [so that each] should not only condition but even create its own technique. Each adventure is so to say one person although it is composed of persons – as Aquinas relates of the angelic hosts.[2]

The Nausicaa episode unfolds on Dublin Bay's Sandymount Strand, where Gerty MacDowell is sitting on a rock while a Benediction ceremony is being conducted in the adjacent Star of the Sea church. The writing exemplifies what would eventually be seen as central features of modernism. It begins with what seems to be Gerty's interior monologue, but the texture of the voice is unremittingly the trite language of consumer-oriented magazines – what Vladimir Nabokov has described as 'a sustained parody of feminine magazine or novelette prose with all the clichés and false elegancies of that kind'.[3] The language seems to overwhelm the notion of a real Gerty separate from the language. In the final part of the episode – printed in the July–August 1920 issue – Gerty's monologue becomes startlingly alive when she notices that Bloom, sitting on a nearby rock, is staring at her. As the reader hears Gerty's perception of the Benediction, she leans back to allow the increasingly interested and excited Bloom to see her 'nainsook knickers, four and eleven on account of being white', while swinging her foot in time with the Tantum Ergo hymn in a crescendo that peaks when a rocket from the fireworks at a nearby bazaar

> sprang and bang shot blind blank and O! then the Roman candle burst and it was like a sigh of O! and everyone cried O! O! and it gushed out of it a stream of rain gold hair threads and they shed and ah! they were all greeny dewy stars falling with golden, O so lovely! O so soft, sweet soft!

As Nabokov points out, the newness of this passage emphasizes the difference between cliché – words that were once original and vivid but have become hackneyed – and live lyrical language: 'What Joyce does here,' he writes, 'is to cause some of that dead and rotten stuff to reveal here and there its live source, its primary freshness ...' He instances the 'description of the church service as it passes transparently through Gerty's consciousness', noting that it 'has real beauty and a luminous pathetic charm', as does 'the tenderness of the twilight ...' 'Of course,' he concludes, 'the description of the fireworks ... is really tender and beautiful: it is the freshness of poetry still with us before it becomes a cliché.'[4]

The fact that Bloom experienced an orgasm as the rocket burst into beautiful display becomes apparent from several musings in the Bloomian interior monologue that now takes control of the narrative:

> Near her monthlies, I expect, makes them feel ticklish ... but then why don't all women menstruate at the same time with the same moon? Wonder if it is bad to go with them then.
> Mr. Bloom with careful hand recomposed his shirt.
> Did she know that I? Course.
> Lord, I am wet.
> For this relief much thanks.
> Short snooze now if I had. And she can do the other.[5]

As Bloom pauses on the Strand after a taxing day, the reader has immediate access to his typically wide-ranging reverie, which, among other things, ponders the vagaries of sexual attraction ('Pretty girls and ugly men marrying'); philosophizes that a woman's 'First thoughts' about men 'are the best', instancing an occasion about which Molly will later elaborate ('Molly, lieutenant Mulvey that kissed her under the Moorish wall beside the gardens' when she was fifteen); sees his encounter with Gerty in a humanizing context ('Still it was a kind of language between us'); meditates on the central role of women in birth and death ('Nature. Washing child, washing corpse. Dignam.'); and postulates an erotic current connecting people and their environment ('Like to be that rock she sat on. Also the library today those girl graduates. Happy chairs under them.').

As the reverie continues, Bloom frames his encounter with Gerty in terms of his initial sexual experience with Molly on Howth, and her betrayal with Boylan, which coincides with what Nabokov calls his 'love at a distance' with Gerty. Bloom begins by noting that his watch stopped at half-past four, and then wonders, 'Very strange about my watch. Wonder is there any magnetic influence between the person because that was about the time he …' Bloom pulls all the strands together while gazing toward Howth: 'All quiet on Howth now. The distant hills seem. Where we. The rhododendrons. I am a fool perhaps. He gets the plums and I the leavings.' These musings lead Bloom to reflect on the circular pattern of life: 'Curious [Molly] an only child, I an only child. So it returns. Think you're escaping and run into yourself. Longest way round is the shortest way home. And just when he and she. Circus horse walking in a ring.'

The poignancy of Bloom's reverie fades into a traditional narrative that puts his plight in the context of Howth's age-old beauty: 'Far out over the sands the coming surf crept, grey. Howth settled for slumber tired of long days, of yumyum rhododendrons (he was old) and felt gladly the night breeze lift, ruffle his many ferns.' The episode ends in what might suggest an astonishing magnetic force linking Molly, Boylan, Bloom, Gerty and even the clock with 'a bird that came out of its little house to tell the time' that Gerty had seen in the rectory at Star of the Sea. Bloom's and Gerty's narratives coalesce as the cuckoo emerges from the clock: As Bloom writes 'I AM A' on the sand with a stick, Gerty 'noticed at once that the foreign gentleman that was sitting on the rocks looking was

Cuckoo.

Cuckoo.

Cuckoo.'

Bloom's monologue is an example of the way in which the truth of creative writers is necessary to achieving self-knowledge.

John Sumner saw it differently. He was the successor to Anthony Comstock as secretary of the New York Society for the Suppression of Vice, an unusual organization that, beginning as a committee of the YMCA, was invested by the New York legislature in 1873 with authority to enforce the state's obscenity laws. Like similar organizations in other cities, it was an outgrowth of 'deep-seated fears about the drift of urban life in the post-Civil War years'.[6] Sumner's Savonarola-like drive to obliterate offending books is apparent in the photograph showing him supervising the burning of books. The assertedly purifying flames of Sumner's book burnings are a chilling reminder of their affinity with the May 1933 book burnings in Nazi Germany, which were a direct attack on the art for art's sake rationale espoused by Margaret Anderson, Jane Heap and John Butler Yeats.

John Sumner (wearing hat in centre) *burning books.*
(Copyright Bettmann/Corbis)

The Society's seal emphasizes the seizure and burning
of books. (Granger–NYC, all rights reserved)

Propaganda Minister Joseph Goebbels' statement of the Nazi regime's aesthetic principles, which led to the burnings, stressed that, 'There must be no art in the absolute sense, such as liberal democracy acknowledges … [which] would end in the people's losing all internal contact therewith and the artist's becoming isolated in a vacuum of art for art's sake.'[7] When the concluding section of the Nausicaa episode was brought to Sumner's attention, he responded to the threat of art for art's sake by issuing a warrant complaining of the magazine's distribution. As Pound put it to Joyce, '"Nausikaa" has been pinched by the PO-lice.'[8] Anderson and Heap were charged with violating a New York statute that criminalized the distribution of 'any obscene, lewd, lascivious, filthy, indecent, or disgusting' material.

The stage was thus set for a test of whether innovative literature by a master stylist could be kept from the public on the ground that it was obscene. The task of the advocate for Anderson and Heap was to find the ideas, verbal formulae and persuasive force to convince the court to modify the judge-made law of obscenity as articulated in the *Hicklin* case so that Joyce's literary achievement would weigh more heavily than the shock effect of Bloom's wet shirt or Gerty's monthlies. Anderson and Heap almost automatically turned to their patron Quinn for representation. He was the wrong choice for a variety of reasons. His reluctance to be identified publicly as a champion of what he termed 'sex literature', coupled with a prudish notion of the degree of sexual candour that would be acceptable to the judiciary and the broader public, were fundamentally antagonistic to the goal shared by Joyce, Anderson and Heap. They wanted to break down the wall of secrecy surrounding sexual matters; Quinn took refuge behind it. His deeply felt attitudes about the narrow range of permissible sexual frankness in literature had already led him to advise Joyce that *Ulysses* could not be published other than in an expensive private edition.[9] The same views would inhibit him from accepting Judge Hand's open invitation to argue that beauty and truth in literature, however erotic, are not obscene. Quinn was more comfortable arguing that allegedly obscene writing would actually deter immoral conduct, even though, as he told Pound in connection with 'Cantleman's Spring-Mate', he did not believe in the argument.[10] Early in their relationship, John Butler Yeats had branded Quinn a 'New World Puritan'.[11] Although Quinn denied that he was a member of what he called that 'self-righteous and bitter lot', his biographer concluded that 'he was wrong about himself and Yeats was right: an unrecognized Puritanism was a deep and durable part of his composition'.[12] Perhaps that Puritan streak explains the contradiction between Quinn's ready public embrace of groundbreaking modern art and his reluctance to be a public champion of Joyce's frankness in sexual matters.

The effect of Quinn's prudery and caution on his suitability as an advocate for Anderson and Heap is illustrated by the fact that, shortly before he undertook to represent them in the *Ulysses* case, he had withdrawn from representing the publisher of James Branch Cabell's *Jurgen* because he wrongly thought the case unwinnable, even to the point that he wrote to Arthur Symons that 'it is a book that ought to have been prosecuted and ought to be condemned'.[13] He was so convinced of the correctness of this view that in a meeting with Cabell and his publisher he scoffingly dismissed their arguments as to the book's literary merit.[14]

Despite Quinn's insistence on *Jurgen's* obscenity, the novel, a mythical tale of a medieval pawnbroker's travels through earth, heaven and hell, seemed routinely inoffensive. However, *Jurgen* attracted the attention of John Sumner and the New York Society for the Suppression of Vice when New York journalists, including the widely read Heywood Broun, publicized the contention of a theatrical press agent that the book masked 'an undercurrent of extreme sensuality ... and once the trick of transposing the key is mastered one can dip into this tepid stream on every page'. Broun claimed that the novel was no more than 'a ... nasty ... barroom story refurbished for the boudoir' and that it was a best-seller among New York chorus girls who were competing to decipher its *double-entendres*.[15] Granted the double meanings, it was far from clear that hidden meanings could make a literarily significant novel obscene. Cabell himself conceded in a letter to his friend Burton Rascoe that his novel was 'a jungle of phallic hints and references', but maintained they 'will shock nobody because nobody will understand them'.[16]

The public clamour stirred by Broun triggered Quinn's reluctance to be identified publicly as a champion of 'sex literature'. He advised the publisher, Robert McBride, that 'no letters or opinions from literary experts are admissible' as to the book's literary merit, and 'we would be convicted ... in ten minutes'.[17] This dire advice convinced McBride to approve Quinn's strategy of getting the case initiated by indictment so that the resulting delay would give Quinn time to negotiate a deal in which the prosecution would be terminated in return for withdrawal of the book.[18] When Quinn's negotiations failed, Holt wrote to Cabell that 'Q is practically certain to drop the affair, considering that he has earned his thousand, and we are now assured of losing, but have no choice save to fight.'[19] Quinn did, in fact, withdraw, explaining to Pound that he did so because he didn't want to present the case to a jury with McBride taking the position 'Book work of art …'[20] 'Book work of art' would, of course, be exactly the position desired by Joyce, Anderson, and Heap.

Quinn's lack of confidence in that defence, and his certainty that the case was unwinnable, were proved wrong when his successor won a directed verdict of acquittal, with the trial judge praising *Jurgen* as a 'brilliant' work of 'unusual literary merit'.[21] The judge dismissed the argument that the book contained veiled sexual suggestions, saying that such suggestions were delicately conveyed. The judge also accepted an argument that the advocate's mind cannot resist, that it was in any event 'doubtful if the book could be read or understood at all by more than a very limited number of readers'.

Quinn's poor judgment as to what courts would find acceptable was exacerbated by a paternalistic and elitist belief that unwitting readers of magazines delivered by the postal system should be protected from works like *Ulysses*, an attitude antagonistic to his clients' desire to foster a wide-ranging conversation about new kinds of writing. Anderson and Heap would hardly have agreed with his comment in his 16 October 1920 letter to Pound that 'There are things in "Ulysses" published in number after number of "The Little Review" that never should have appeared in a magazine asking privileges of the mails. In a book, yes, in a magazine, emphatically no.'[22] Quinn believed that 'there ought to be', and that reasonable judges would likely find, 'a distinction between matter published in a magazine which is openly sold and offered and distributed for almost nominal cost through the mail, and matter published in expensively printed private editions … which are bought only by a few, presumably experts of literature, who are interested in such books'.[23] Thinking that serialization would lead to a criminal conviction that would interfere with his efforts on Joyce's behalf to negotiate a contract for private publication of the completed novel as a book, Quinn urged Joyce, via Pound, to withdraw serialization rights from *The Little Review*.[24] Joyce was unconvinced. He declined to accept Quinn's view that conviction of *The Little Review* would frighten book publishers. Rather, he told Quinn that he thought withdrawal of the book would be 'a sign of weakness'.[25] He explained to his patron Harriet Shaw Weaver that withdrawal would suggest that he was passing sentence on his own writing and blaming the editors of *The Little Review* for publishing it, thereby prejudicing their position in court.[26]

More concerned about Joyce than his other clients, Anderson and Heap, Quinn plunged ahead, purporting to represent the *Little Review* editors, but actually advancing his own erroneous conception of what was best for Joyce. Even as he began to defend the editors against criminal charges that would stop publication of Joyce's novel in *The Little Review*, Quinn was writing to Pound in his 16 October letter that, 'If further publication of "Ulysses" in "The Little Review" is stopped, the result will be that all of those who have been interested in it will have to buy the book, that it will be the best advertisement for the book.' On the other hand, Quinn remarked, 'If the further episodes are published to the end, many will be content with having it in "The Little Review" and not buy the book.' Quinn's belief that conviction of his clients Anderson and Heap would benefit his client Joyce posed a serious ethical issue. Undertaking to defend Anderson and Heap ran counter to the duty of undivided loyalty imposed on Quinn by then applicable Canon 6 of the ethical rules governing New York lawyers. The rule permitted clients to waive its applicability 'by express consent of all concerned given after full disclosure of the facts',[27] and Quinn made no bones about his belief that serialization of *Ulysses* was not in Joyce's interest. However, there is no evidence that Quinn advised Anderson and Heap of the full extent to which their interests diverged from Joyce's, and suggested that they consult independent counsel. To the contrary, when Anderson suggested she would obtain different counsel, Quinn insisted that he continue and it was clear to her that 'no power on earth could have wrested that privilege from him'.[28]

Quinn's unsuitability was aggravated by misogyny compounded by prejudice against Anderson and Heap's lesbianism. This prejudice, which had hitherto hovered at the edges of his consciousness, crystallized as the trial approached. Quinn's vicious 16 October 1920 letter to Pound rants against the 'female urinal' from which *The Little Review* was published and accuses his clients of having the 'perverted courage of the bugger and the Lesbian'. Projecting his distorted emotions onto Anderson and Heap, he saw issues of their periodical not as the product of their extraordinary artistic sensibility but as 'monthly mensurations' that 'menstrually' violated the law. His follow-up letter of 21 October continues the same terrible trope. Borrowing a word from one of the Bloomian musings attacked by Sumner, Quinn refers to issues of *The Little Review* as 'monthlies'.[29] Quinn was a man of great abilities and a ready patron, but he suffered from painful limitations as an advocate for Molly Bloom, Gerty MacDowell, Margaret Anderson, Jane Heap and James Joyce. Quinn's characterization of the periodic publication threatened by the prosecution of Anderson and Heap as an expression of their femininity was so hostile a view of his clients and their business enterprise as to constitute an additional factor vitiating the notion that they could give effective consent to the conflicted representation. The gulf between lawyer and clients is illustrated by the fact that, as Quinn was undertaking to represent editors who believed they were publishing prose of extraordinary beauty, he confided to Pound that their magazine was 'a sewer that covers [its contents] with the common stench and filth'.[30]

Quinn's limitations had serious consequences. Despite the generally forbidding legal terrain created by the Victorian judicial precedents, Joyce's masterful prose was well suited as a vehicle with which to pursue Judge Learned Hand's suggestion that lawyers advance the argument that the law should not prevent an adequate portrayal of the serious and beautiful way in which reality reveals itself in the sexually tinged imagination. Moreover, that very case was articulated for Quinn in a long letter from John Butler Yeats that emphasized the value of Joyce's 'terrible veracity'.[31] JBY added a lifetime's meditation on the importance of truth to Anderson and Heap's focus on the overriding importance of beauty. His emphasis on the value of truthfulness in literature as an end in itself supplied for use in the twentieth century the argument that Plato had hoped for as a justification for inviting poets back to his ideal city.

The overriding value of truth for its own sake, ignored by Plato as he wrote *The Republic,* had great persuasive force as applied to Joyce's prose, but such an argument ran the risk of being lost beneath Anderson's emphasis on, as Tietjens put it, 'Beauty with a still bigger B' than the 'A' in Art. Anderson's commitment to Beauty was derived from Wilde, whose enthusiastic emphasis on the writer's imaginative – and thus arguably deceptive – shaping of nature needed a counterbalance if an argument based on the societal value of literature were to prevail in court. This need was illustrated by Sir Edward Carson's fascinating cross-examination of Wilde about his aesthetic theory in the libel prosecution Wilde instigated against the Marquess of Queensberry for leaving his card at Wilde's club describing him as 'posing as somdomite [*sic*]'. Part of Queensberry's defence of justification rested on Wilde's writings, including *The Picture of Dorian Gray.* In response to Carson's question whether he thought his writings were likely to tend toward immorality, Wilde asserted that 'My work never aims at producing any effect but that of literature.'[32] Attacking Wilde for the famous assertion in *Dorian Gray* that literature was neither moral nor immoral, Carson asked if a well-written book would be a good book no matter how immoral. Wilde tellingly dodged the word 'good', and answered that it would be beautiful. An expansion of the critical vocabulary to make room for the value of truthful depiction of life was necessary to an effective legal argument. JBY's emphasis on the value of truth in all cultural pursuits was exactly what was needed.

The elder Yeats's longstanding commitment to artistic truth-telling was galvanized by his personal recognition of Joyce's veracity when he read the Nausicaa episode of *Ulysses* in the July–August 1920 issue of *The Little Review*. His reaction to a profound truthfulness in Joyce reminiscent of the works of Irish playwright John Synge bursts into his 14 August 1920 letter to Lady Gregory. An off-handed reference in the letter to a friend's visit to France leads to a comment on French veracity, which immediately brings to mind the episode of *Ulysses* then appearing in *The Little Review*. 'Surely *veracity* is *the* French quality – from France have come all the great movements toward fact and reality,' he observes, adding, 'It is England and not France who cultivate falseness & humbug. That awful fiction written by Joyce have [*sic*] this quality. I dislike it yet have for him and it a profound respect – his portrait published in this month's "Little Review" reminds me of Synge.'[33]

The reference to Synge evokes the famous controversy that greeted the opening of his *The Playboy of the Western World* at Dublin's Abbey Theatre in 1907, an event that captured the imaginations of both JBY and Joyce, and was a precursor to the furor provoked by *Ulysses*. The opening-night audience disrupted the performance to protest what it claimed was Synge's maligning of Irish women with his verbal picture of 'a drift of chosen females standing in their shifts'. In the midst of the outcry, JBY mounted the stage to defend Synge's truthfulness and its importance. 'Ireland', he said, 'was a land of saints,' then adding over the cheers, 'a land of plaster saints.'[34] His core point – one that would later shape his reaction to *Ulysses* – was that 'Ireland is also an island of sinners – only unfortunately in this Country [*sic*] people cannot live or die except behind a curtain of deceit.'[35] Thirty years later, W.B. Yeats celebrated his father's performance as one of the 'Beautiful Lofty Things': 'My father upon the Abbey stage, before him a raging crowd: / "This

Land of Saints," and then as the applause died out, / "Of plaster Saints," his beautiful mischievous head thrown back.'[36]

JBY restated his views in his 1909 obituary of Synge, writing that Synge's plays were reviled because they revealed the 'manifold existence' of 'an island of sinners as well as of saints'. Critics admitted privately, he said, that 'Synge's picture was a true rendering, that the facts were true but should not be revealed to the world.'[37] The condition, in JBY's view, was societally debilitating. The cure for Ireland's woes, he wrote elsewhere, was 'freedom of thought and the intoxication of truth ...'[38]

Even though he was living in Italy at the time of the *Playboy* disturbance, Joyce was as captivated as JBY by its significance. He wrote to his brother lamenting that he had missed this iconic dispute over truthful writing about sexually tinged issues: 'I feel like a man in a house who hears a row in the street and voices he knows shouting but can't get out to see what the hell is going on.'[39] Not yet started on the novel that would later come under fire for its references to Gerty MacDowell's and Molly Bloom's knickers, Joyce devoured the account in *The Freeman's Journal* of the protests that greeted Synge's use of the word 'shift'. He was captivated by the comments of his friend Daniel T. Sheehan, who observed that 'when the artist appears in Ireland who was not afraid of life and his nature, the women of Ireland would receive him'. The newspaper reported that, in response to Sheehan's comment, 'many ladies, whose countenances plainly indicated intense feelings of astonishment and pain, rose and left the place'. Joyce was intrigued: 'I would like', he wrote to his brother, 'to hear the phrases which drove out the ladies with expressions of pain on their faces.'

The reactions of Joyce and JBY to the *Playboy* controversy were rooted in values they had championed since their student days. Both had made truth the centrepiece of speeches they delivered to student debating societies. The importance of truth dominated the young JBY's thoughts on the night of 21 November 1865 when, seemingly on the verge of a promising legal career, he took the stage to deliver the prestigious annual address of the auditor to the Law Students' Debating Society of Dublin. Instead of committing himself to the ancient traditions of the profession, however, he challenged the received understanding of the very purpose of legal education and debate: he would attempt, he announced, 'to show that our present purpose – the cultivation of oratory – is one which defeats itself …'[40] Rather, he insisted, the purpose of the Society must be pursuit of 'truth for its own sake'. A 'restless craving for truth', the young auditor maintained, would lead the members of the society 'to desert their mimic debates and devote their faculties and energies, in real debate, to the attainment and promotion of truth'. He supported his argument with an aphorism from John Stuart Mill that would animate his approach to the struggle between law and literature: 'Eloquence, as well as poetry, is impassioned truth.'

JBY's challenge to the traditional notion of the barrister as the single-minded advocate for a particular position must have astonished the audience, which included the Lord Chancellor, the Lord Chief Baron, numerous judges and Oscar Wilde's father, Sir William Wilde. The ideas that burst forth in this groundbreaking address had been nurtured in JBY's early upbringing by his clergyman father, a lifetime habit of wide-ranging reading, and his self-guided study before and during his studies at Trinity College Dublin.[41] He was thoroughly grounded in works he would later read to his son, the future poet who was five months old at the time of the Debating Society lecture: Macaulay's *Lays of Ancient Rome* and Scott's *Ivanhoe* and *The Lay of the Last Minstrel* and, as the children grew older, Shakespeare, Chaucer, the Brontës, Dickens, Shelley and Keats.[42] JBY had read deeply in Mill and August Comte the summer before entering Trinity.[43] He wrote in a draft memoir that he read Mill's two volumes of Political Economy 'and then all his books', thus beginning 'the long climb of accurate and careful logical thinking never to be abandoned'. So thoroughly did JBY imbibe Mill that, looking back in 1918, he could insist that 'His methods are still my methods, though it is many years since I took interest in anything except Art and Literature.'[44]

JBY found much food for thought in Mill's insistence on the writer's freedom from government control. Mill's fundamental point was that 'the only purpose for which power can be rightfully exercised over any member of a civilized community, against his will, is to prevent harm to others. His own good, either physical or moral, is not a sufficient warrant.' Rounding out his argument, Mill asserted that a person cannot rightfully be compelled to do or refrain from doing something 'because it will be better for him to do so, because it will make him happier, because, in the opinion of others, to do so would be wise or even right'.[45] With particular reference to freedom of expression, Mill emphasized that silencing opinion robbed the human race because, 'If the opinion is right, they are deprived of the opportunity of exchanging error for truth; if wrong, they lose, what is almost as great a benefit, the clearer perception and livelier impression of truth produced by its collision with error.'[46]

The ideas that JBY developed from his self-study departed so sharply from the traditional notion of the lawyer as an advocate for a client, rather than a searcher for the truth, that he abandoned the law within a year of his admission, and began the career as a painter and writer that eventually brought him to New York and to his relationship with John Quinn.

JBY was energized when he learned in the autumn of 1920 that Quinn would be defending Joyce's novel. 'I think really that in fighting for Joyce', he wrote on 14 October, 'you have a most important cause for which to fight. Freedom of the press is good, but far better is freedom of literature.'[47] His first reaction was to draw Quinn's attention to a passage in Joyce's *A Portrait of the Artist as a Young Man* in which Stephen Dedalus advances the idea, based on his study of the thirteenth-century philosopher St Thomas Aquinas, a Joyce favourite, that 'the feelings excited by improper arts' – defined as pornographic and didactic – are 'kinetic desire or loathing'. By contrast, the 'esthetic emotion is static. The mind is arrested and raised above desire and loathing.'[48] Joyce, JBY argued, sought esthetic emotion, which was inconsistent with obscenity. Given Quinn's emotional investment in the argument that works like 'Cantleman's Spring-Mate' and *Hagar Revelly* were not obscene because they induced loathing, it is no surprise that he showed no interest in this argument.

JBY had another. No sooner had he posted this first letter than he sent Quinn a long defence of Joyce as a truth-telling artist.[49] Although Mill is not named, his thinking suffuses JBY's opening assertion that Joyce's gospel as artist and poet is 'the freedom of the individual, or … *each man's right to be himself. That such a man should write filthiness is incredible.*' JBY then makes a point that will ultimately figure in Augustus Hand's 1934 opinion lifting the ban on *Ulysses*: 'There is no great book or great literature that would not be dangerous reading to some people … For them we can do nothing.' As an afterthought, he adds, 'Joyce brings with him what will protect him from the silly … for Joyce is very difficult reading.'

In a long postscript that dwarfed the main body of the letter, JBY drew on his extensive knowledge of literature to construct the schema of a potentially winning legal argument that positioned Joyce's adherence to truth-telling – his 'intense feeling for what is actual and true' – midway between Wilde's exaltation of beauty (on which Anderson and Heap relied so heavily) and an obsession with 'the ugly', as exemplified by another great Irish writer, Jonathan Swift. Without addressing in so many words Wilde's argument that artistic selectivity is a form of lying, JBY comments, with avuncular familiarity, that 'Wilde said to my son that the intellect could refine anything; that is to say, he prided himself on superabundance of the kind of intellect that seeks artistic refinement. Beauty was the god of his heaven, and ugliness its devil.' The inability of an argument based exclusively on beauty to carry the day for *Ulysses* is apparent in JBY's comment that 'We can easily guess how [Wilde] would have regarded Joyce's books and how he would have flung them into the fire.' In fact, no guess is needed because Wilde had already made clear his preference for beauty over truth by lamenting, in 'The Decay of Lying', how a young man with 'a natural gift for exaggeration' might fall into 'careless habits of accuracy' that would be 'fatal to his imagination'. Developing 'a morbid and unhealthy faculty of truth-telling', he might end 'by writing novels which are so lifelike that no one can possibly believe in their probability'.[50]

Turning to the opposing idea of the ugly, JBY pointed out that 'Dante, the greatest of the medieval poets ... never shrank from the hideous and the obscene.' Joyce, he adds, is 'and has always been, a great student of Dante' and it 'is from Dante he gets that terrible hardness, that hardness of which Wilde had so little and Swift too much'. It is this hardness of Joyce's veracity, situated midway between the beautiful and the ugly, that 'inspires Joyce when he writes those so-called filthy passages to which people object'. Defining Joyce's 'hardness' in terms of his veracity supplied the context that was missing from Quinn's *Vanity Fair* praise of the hardness of Joyce's prose in *Dubliners* and *Portrait*.

Against this background, JBY tells Quinn that the objection to Joyce is not based on moral indignation. Rather, in language that parallels Anderson's idea of literature as a stimulus to a more deeply experienced life, JBY insists that 'the whole movement against Joyce and his terrible veracity, naked and unashamed, has its origin in the desire of people to live comfortably, and, that they may live comfortably, to live superficially'. Joyce, he says, 'has exquisite gifts of writing by which he could make a great deal of money if only he would praise what his readers like to see praised'. But, 'his genius, which loves the truth because it is genius, will not have it so'. JBY's insistence on the importance of self-knowledge to a life fully lived is an overwhelmingly powerful argument for the value to society of truthful writers like Joyce.

John Quinn and the Governor *by Jack B. Yeats. Sketch of the artist's father, John Butler Yeats, who suggested a potentially winning argument, and New York lawyer John Quinn, who failed to use it. (NGA Yeats Archive Y1/JY1/1/48/18. Copyright Estate of Jack B. Yeats. All rights reserved. DACS London/IVARO Dublin 2016. Photo copyright National Gallery of Ireland)*

As part of an argument that Quinn would misuse as though it were the whole, JBY observes that writers and artists 'who insist on the hideous and the repulsive and the obscene ... make the man who studies them much stronger to resist evil'. In a counterpoint that Quinn would ignore, JBY goes on to make clear that such champions of the repulsive are not the greatest artists. Rather, the 'great poets are men of great character who know too well the value of both the ugly and the beautiful to side with either' in the recurring conflict 'between the people who love beauty and those who love the ugly ...'

Melding the values of both beauty and truth embodied in the Nausicaa episode, JBY says that

while I enjoy beyond words many passages of Joyce because of their beauty and delicacy and poetry, I shrink a good deal when sometimes he strips off the covering of sentiment that long convention and easy good nature have woven around women and sexual love; I shrink, yes, but I do not ... take refuge in hating Joyce. On the contrary, I admire him for his courage and wonder at his unselfishness.

Joyce's 'sin, in the eyes of his enemies' is that his 'unflinching veracity' shatters the dream that 'the world is a smiling garden'.

JBY's emphasis on Joyce's veracity focuses on precisely the quality that Joyce himself urged as the essence of art in an address he gave to a college debating society as a student in Dublin almost thirty-five years after JBY gave his career-changing talk on the importance of truth to another debating society in the same city. Joyce's talk on 'Drama and Life' before the University College Dublin Literary and Historical Society on 20 January 1900 carved out a position in opposition to Wilde's aesthetic as embodied in W.B. Yeats's Abbey Theatre. Pulling no punches, he denigrated the claim of beauty to be the aim of drama as 'insidious'. Employing the name of one of Hinduism's heavenly worlds, Joyce declared that 'Beauty is the swerga of the aesthete', but 'truth has a more ascertainable and more real dominion. Our art is true to itself when it deals with truth' and literature must deal with 'life – real life.' Sounding the note that would guide his writing – and lead him into conflict with the law – the young student proclaimed, 'Life, we must accept as we see it before our eyes, men and women as we meet them in the real world, and not as we apprehend them in the world of faery.'[51]

Like the lead character in his draft novel *Stephen Hero*, Joyce read his speech 'quietly and distinctly, involving every hardihood of thought or expression in an envelope of low innocuous melody'.[52] The effect on the packed audience was electric. One after another, Joyce's listeners attacked his artistic credo, but Joyce, apparently imbibing the energy of his audience, spoke without notes for thirty minutes answering each critic in turn.[53] Impassioned defence of truth was a potent elixir for both JBY and Joyce.

Truth was no enemy of artistic beauty. Joyce, whose familiarity with Aristotelian aesthetics is abundantly clear in *A Portrait of the Artist as a Young Man,* no doubt saw the relevance to his own artistic enterprise of Aristotle's observation that it was possible to create beauty through a masterful imitation of the repulsive.[54] Truth about life, including its repulsive aspects, could be beautiful. Across the generational divide, Joyce and JBY spoke as with one voice on the beauty and necessity of artistic truth. JBY's schema was perfectly tailored to Joyce's work.

NOTES

1   JLI, 145.
2   Letter to Linati, *id.* 146–7 (original in Italian).
3   Vladimir Nabokov, *Lectures on Literature* (New York: Harcourt Brace Jovanovitch, 1980) ('Nabokov') 345–6.
4   *Id.*
5   John Quinn appended the offending passages to his 16 October 1920 letter to Ezra Pound: Ch. 2, n. 52.
6   Boyer at 3.
7   Quoted in 'Putting Art in Its Place', *Nation,* CXXXVI (10 May 1933) 519 (quoted in Boyer at 263).
8   Letter *circa* October 1920, Pound/Joyce 184.
9   Letter of 15 August 1920 (QC).
10 Letter of 2 December 1917 to Ezra Pound (QC), discussed in Chapter 2.
11 Letter of 25 November 1902 to JBY (QC).
12 MNY 11–12.
13 Letter of 11 April 1920 (QC).
14 MNY 443–4; Letter of 11 March 1920 to Mitchell Kennerley (QC).
15 *New York Tribune* (17 November 1919, 3 January 1920), quoted in 'Emergency Committee Organized to Protest against the Suppression of James Branch Cabell's "Jurgen"' in *Jurgen and the Censor* (New York, privately printed, 1920) 15–16.
16 Letter of 21 June 1919 in Padraic Colum and Margaret Freeman Cabell, *Between Friends: Letters of James Branch Cabell and Others* (New York: Harcourt, Brace & World, 1962) ('Between Friends') 121.

17 Letter of 1 March 1920 from Robert McBride to Cabell, *Between Friends* 166–7.

18 *Id.*

19 Letter of 8 May 1920 from Guy Holt to Cabell, *Between Friends* 173–4.

20 Letter of 16 October 1920 to Pound, Ch. 2, n. 52.

21 *People v. Holt, McBride & Co.*, printed in Guy Holt, *Jurgen and the Law* (New York: Robert McBride & Co., 1923) 73–4.

22 See n. 5 above.

23 Letter of 5 February 1921 to Anderson (SIUC).

24 *E.g.*, 16 October 1920 letter to Pound (Ch. 2, n. 52) which Pound forwarded to Joyce via the letter cited in n. 8 above.

25 Letter of 17 November 1920 from Joyce to Quinn (QC).

26 Letter of 10 November 1920, British Library ('BL').

27 The American Bar Association Canons ('Canons') had been adopted in New York. (http://www.americanbar.org/content/dam/aba/migrated /cpr/mrpc/Canons_Ethics.authcheckdam.pdf)

28 TYW 215.

29 Letter of 21 October 1920 to Pound (SIUC).

30 Letter of 28 October 1920 (QC).

31 Letter of John Butler Yeats to John Quinn, 14 October 1920 (QC), printed in Donald J. Torchiana and Glenn O'Malley, eds, 'A Letter: J.B. Yeats on James Joyce', *Tri-Quarterly* (Fall 1964) 70–76.

32 Merlin Holland, ed., *Irish Peacock and Scarlet Marquess* (London: Fourth Estate, 2003) 73–80.

33 Berg.

34 *Freeman's Journal* (5 February 1907); James Kilroy, *The Playboy Riots* (Dublin: Dolmen, 1971) 85.

35 Letter of 29 December 1915 to Joseph Hone (JBY Letters 214).

36 W.B. Yeats, 'Beautiful Lofty Things' in Peter Allt and Russell K. Alspach, eds., *The Variorum Edition of the Poems of W.B. Yeats* (New York: Macmillan, 1957) 577.

37 *New York Evening Sun* (2 April 1909), quoted from PF 346, which uses the typescript prepared for JBY by Quinn's assistant, Thomas Curtin.

38 J.B. Yeats, 'Ireland to be saved by Intellect', *The Independent*, NYC (n.d.), National Library of Ireland, John Butler Yeats Miscellaneous Papers. Murphy dates the article 1912. (PF 391–2).

39 Letter of 11 February 1907 to Stanislaus Joyce, JLII, 211–13. The material

from *The Freeman's Journal* quoted in the text is taken from Ellmann's annotations.

40 John Butler Yeats, *An Address Delivered Before the Law Students' Debating Society of Dublin at the Opening Meeting of the Fourteenth Session, in the Lecture Hall, King's Inns, on Tuesday Evening, 21 November 1865, By the Auditor John Butler Yeats A.B., Student of the King's Inns, Dublin, and of the Middle Temple, London.* (Dublin: Joseph Dollard, 1865) 9–33.

41 PF 33–4.

42 PF 95.

43 PF 29–31.

44 John Butler Yeats, Notebook quoted in PF 558, n. 92.

45 J.S. Mill, *On Liberty* (1859; London: Penguin, 1985) ('On Liberty') 68.

46 *Id.* at 76.

47 QC.

48 See James Joyce, *A Portrait of the Artist as a Young Man* (New York: Viking, 1962) ('Portrait') 205.

49 John Butler Yeats's letter of 14 October 1920 to John Quinn, n. 31 above.

50 DL 13.

51 James Joyce, 'Drama and Life' in Ellsworth Mason and Richard Ellmann, eds, *The Critical Writings of James* Joyce (New York: Viking 1959) 38–46.

52 James Joyce, *Stephen Hero* (New York: New Directions, 1963) 100–01.

53 Richard Ellmann, *James Joyce* (rev. edn, New York: Oxford University Press, 1982) ('Ellmann') 73.

54 Aristotle, *Poetics* 1448b in W. Rhys Roberts and Ingram Bywater, trans., *The Rhetoric and the Poetics of Aristotle* (New York: Modern Library, 1954) ('Roberts').

John Quinn: The Advocate as Cynic

Unfortunately, JBY's compelling argument based on Joyce's terrible veracity never made it to the courtroom. Although Quinn praised JBY's ideas as 'very brilliant, very true, very searching, very illuminating', and generously sent him a check 'for $85 as a fee to you as my associate counsel in the matter of "Ulysses"', he misused the ideas he praised so lavishly.[1] The New York statute under which Anderson and Heap were charged was susceptible to JBY's argument. Since the statute did not define obscenity in terms of a 'tendency to corrupt', it was open to Quinn to urge the court to ignore arguably inapplicable language in *Hicklin* about a tendency to corrupt, and hold that *Ulysses* was not obscene because of its truth and beauty as literature. Such an argument would insist, as JBY's initial letter of 14 October did, on the importance of freedom of literature. But Quinn, just two days after JBY's letter, proclaimed in his 16 October letter to Pound that there was no issue of freedom of literature involved in defending *Ulysses*.[2] Instead, he insisted on presenting the case in terms of whether or not *Ulysses* tended to corrupt, an approach better suited to the social-hygiene theories of *Hagar Revelly* than the terrible veracity of Joyce.

Quinn perverted JBY's letter terribly in his argument at a preliminary hearing on 21 October 1920 before New York City Magistrate Joseph E. Corrigan, whom he described to Pound as an 'old friend'.[3] In other words, the magistrate was one of the circle of Irish Americans before whom Quinn did not want to present himself as a champion of sex literature. Converting JBY's aesthetic argument into a moral one, and reviving the idiosyncratic vocabulary he had employed in his *Vanity Fair* commentary on Joyce's *Portrait*, Quinn argued that it is beauty that corrupts, but filth that deters, and contrasted 'the strong hard filth of a man like Joyce with the devotion to art of a soft flabby man like Wilde'.[4] This is bad criticism and worse advocacy. Joyce, Anderson and Heap deserved better than the concession that Joyce's prose was filthy and thus escaped the corruption of beauty. Quinn managed to avoid championing 'sex literature' by arguing that *Ulysses* could not corrupt, thus ignoring JBY's realistic argument that, while 'there is no great literature that would not be dangerous reading to some people', Joyce's terrible veracity was too valuable to society to be barred as obscene. Although Quinn was willing to depart from one of *Hicklin*'s subsidiary points by arguing that filthiness should be tested by a work's 'effect on the average man or woman',[5] he declined to challenge *Hicklin*'s core.

Quinn's further argument as to why the Nausicaa episode would not corrupt the reader did Joyce the double disservice of branding as disgusting language that bore no resemblance to the text for which Anderson and Heap were being prosecuted. As he recounted to Pound, Quinn urged the court:

> If a young man is in love with a woman and his mother should write to him saying: 'My boy, the woman you are infatuated with is not a beautiful woman ... She sweats, she stinks, she is flatulent. Her flesh is discolored, her breath is bad. She makes ugly noises when she eats and discharges other natural functions ...' Those remarks might be

considered by some refined person as filthy, but they are not filthy within the meaning of the law. They would not send the aforesaid son to the arms of that fairy, but would be more likely to turn him from her in disgust.[6]

Of course, this imaginary text is not Joyce's, and Quinn neglected to point out the beauty of what Joyce did write.

Quinn's next argument reduced JBY's subtle observation that Joyce's difficult prose would 'protect him from the silly' to the absurdist 'syllogism' that the reader would either understand the Nausicaa episode, or not, and, 'If he understood what it meant, then it couldn't corrupt him, for it would either amuse or bore him. If he didn't understand what it meant, then it could [not] corrupt him.' Magistrate Corrigan, who was the nephew of Michael Corrigan, Archbishop of New York from 1885 to 1902, and held undergraduate and graduate degrees from Seton Hall College and a law degree from Columbia, had no trouble penetrating and dismissing Quinn's syllogism.[7] The passage 'where the man went off in his pants', Corrigan ruled, was unmistakable in meaning and 'smutty, filthy within the meaning of the statute'.[8] So much for the syllogism. Corrigan ordered a trial on the merits before three city court judges in the Court of Special Sessions.

Quinn sought to delay the ultimate outcome – which he was convinced would be adverse – by filing a motion in the Court of General Sessions, a court at a higher tier of the judicial system, asking that the case be transferred there.[9] Following the strategy he had employed in the *Jurgen* case, his thinking, as explained in a letter to Shane Leslie, was that the case would move at a slower pace, being commenced by a grand jury indictment and tried to a jury, and thus *Ulysses* could be privately published and sold during the delay.[10] Quinn's moving papers cited Judge Learned Hand's opinion in *Kennerley* in support of the proposition that the question whether a work was obscene was normally a question to be determined by a jury. Quinn's letter to Leslie recounts that his tactic boomeranged.

His argument that significant property interests were at stake convinced the court that the case should be tried promptly, and thus a quicker trial in the Court of Special Sessions was preferable. The motion was denied.

The defence Quinn presented at the February 1921 trial before three Court of Special Sessions judges was even more tawdry and cynical than his presentation at the preliminary hearing. Whereas Anderson and Heap wanted a defence based on Anderson's belief that *Ulysses* was 'the prose masterpiece of my generation',[11] the essence of Quinn's case, as reported in the 22 February 1921 *New York Tribune*, was that average readers would not be harmed by Joyce's prose 'because if they read the magazine, which was improbable, they would be either unable to comprehend Joyce's style, or would be bored and disgusted'.[12] Quinn's account of the trial in a 21 April 1921 letter to Joyce omitted reference to his argument based on the disgusting nature of Joyce's prose, but emphasized its incomprehensibility. He told Joyce that he impressed upon the judges that the Nausicaa episode could not corrupt because 'no one could understand what the thing was about'. He sought to justify this insulting argument – which he claimed many in court called 'brilliant' – by asserting that the judges were 'stupid' and thus this was 'the only tack that could be taken with the three stupid judges'[13] – an approach he characterized to Leslie as 'a frank appeal to the three Judges' ignorance'.[14] But it was Quinn's duty to educate the judges about *Ulysses*, whatever their intellectual attainments. Moreover, it is the trial lawyer's job to lay the basis for an appeal in the event of an adverse ruling.

To Quinn's credit, he did begin his presentation by referring to Joyce's reputation as a man of letters, but he dropped the point as soon as the judges questioned its relevance.[15] Quinn likely welcomed the judges' reaction because it confirmed his own view that the quality of Joyce's work was irrelevant.[16] But he was an advocate, and his job was to press the case on behalf of his client. Judicial skepticism is the advocate's invitation to engage and persuade, not to retreat.

Instead, rather than establishing the quality and importance of Joyce's writing, Quinn followed his 'incomprehensibility' argument with what he told Joyce was the 'good point' that the anger manifested in the prosecutor's argument was 'my best exhibit'. Recalling his argument with relish, Quinn boasted to Joyce that, 'pointing to the prosecutor, I said':

> There is my best exhibit. There is proof that 'Ulysses' does not corrupt or fill people full of lascivious thoughts. Look at him! He is mad all over. He wants to hit somebody. He doesn't want to love anybody. He wants somebody to be punished. He's mad. He's angry. His face is distorted with anger, not with love. That's what Joyce does. That's what 'Ulysses' does. It makes people angry. They want to break something. They want somebody to be convicted. They feel like prosecuting everybody connected with it, even if they don't know how to pronounce the name 'Ulysses'. But it doesn't tend to drive them to the arms of some siren. And after all it isn't a crime to make people angry.

Confusing the effect of being the prosecutor in an obscenity trial of *Ulysses* with the effect of reading the book, Quinn deprived the occasion of the seriousness it demanded. 'The judges were rocking with laughter,' Quinn wrote to Joyce, 'and again I thought I had them'. Quinn did not report to Joyce that, as Anderson informed her readers, he had told the court that 'I think Joyce has carried his method too far in this experiment.'[17] Whereas the core of a potentially winning argument – and certainly what Joyce, JBY, Anderson and Heap believed – was that *Ulysses* was great literature that the public was entitled to read, Quinn presented it as a failed and unintelligible experiment. According to the *New York Times*, Quinn told the court that the unintelligibility of Joyce's prose 'was principally a matter of punctuation marks', which Joyce didn't use, 'probably on account of his eyesight'.[18] Quinn suggested to the judges that *Ulysses* was 'cubism in literature',[19] but stopped short of explaining the importance of experimentation in art, settling instead for the limp concession that the experiment was a failure.

Given Quinn's distaste for championing 'sex literature' and in view of his arguments of unintelligibility and failure, it is no surprise that he did not make a record of expert testimony as to the beauty and truthfulness of Joyce's prose as literature. At the time of the trial, the law of New York on the admissibility of such evidence was in a state of flux that presented an opportunity for a vigorous advocate to obtain an appellate ruling that a writer or publisher accused of obscenity should have a right to present expert opinion as to the quality of the allegedly obscene work as literature. New York's highest court, the Court of Appeals, had held in 1884 that expert opinion was not admissible on the question of obscenity because 'to permit such evidence would put the witness in the place of the jury, and the latter would have no function to discharge'.[20] The Court reasoned that 'testimony of experts is not admissible upon matters of judgment within the knowledge and experience of ordinary jurymen'.[21] Nonetheless, within a decade of this decision, lower courts in New York, consistent with the general trend of admitting expert testimony when it might be helpful to the jury, were allowing expert testimony on the question of obscenity.[22] Quinn himself had successfully read a letter from the 'muckraker' author Ida Tarbell to the jury on the question whether *Hagar Revelly* was obscene. Nonetheless, Quinn failed to present expert critical opinion on the merit and significance of *Ulysses* as literature.

Welcoming the ban on further serialization, and convinced that an appeal would fail, Quinn had decided in advance of trial that there would be no appeal from the assumed conviction. Thus he informed Anderson on 5 February 1921 that 'the Appellate Court will with absolute certainty affirm the decision of the lower court' and thus he would not make a record of 'witnesses, experts and critics, and passages of comparative literature' for an appeal as he would have done had he 'thought there was a fighting chance in the matter'.[23] Quinn further advised in his 5 February letter that Anderson and Heap needed to 'think about what your personal defenses will be in mitigation of the penalty or sentence'. This dire warning must have provoked a sufficiently alarmed reaction from Anderson that Quinn altered his view at the last minute and decided to present expert testimony for the limited purpose of mitigating punishment. He wrote Anderson on 8 February – six days before trial – that she should suggest at least two witnesses whom he could offer to prove 'the serious nature of Joyce's work ...' Such testimony, he said, 'is not admissible but sometimes the court may receive it in mitigation of sentence'.[24] At trial, Quinn offered limited expert testimony, but its thrust was not that *Ulysses* was great literature, but only that it would not corrupt readers. John Cowper Powys, the accomplished novelist whose lecture on Ruskin and Pater had inspired Anderson to start *The Little Review*, was pressed into service to give testimony that fit Quinn's theory of the case by saying, as recounted by Anderson, that '*Ulysses* was too obscure and philosophical a work to be in any sense corrupting.'[25] Quinn called Phillip Moeller of the Theatre Guild to the stand to say that 'the objectionable chapter is an unveiling of the subconscious mind, in the Freudian manner, and that he saw no possibility of these revelations being aphrodisiac in their influence'.[26] Both witnesses were competent to testify to the value of Joyce's work as literature, but neither was offered for that purpose or gave testimony to that effect.[27]

Instead, Quinn presented *Ulysses* as a failed experiment, and treated the prospect of a criminal conviction for publishing innovative literature as an occasion for provoking the judges to laughter by personal ridicule of the prosecutor. The joke was on Joyce, Anderson, and Heap. Anderson and Heap were convicted, with one of the judges (Justice McInerney) concluding that 'this novel is unintelligent, and it seems to me like the work of a disordered mind'.[28] Anderson and Heap were fined fifty dollars each, and it was stipulated that no further installments of *Ulysses* would be published in *The Little Review*.[29]

Anderson and Heap were deeply disappointed. They had devoted enormous energy at great personal sacrifice and risk to publishing about 60 per cent of the eventual novel over the period from the spring of 1918 through the end of 1920, and had strong convictions about how their efforts should be defended. Nonetheless, they had reluctantly agreed to what Anderson later described as 'John Quinn's idea' that she and Heap 'remain inconspicuous, meek and silent ...'[30] Quinn's patronizing treatment of his clients illustrates the sage observation of Shaw's Sir Patrick Cullen that 'all professions are a conspiracy against the laity'.[31] Anderson had maintained that 'the question that *should* be up for discussion in court ... is the relation of the artist – the great writer – to the public.' '*I state clearly*', she insisted, '*that the (quite unnecessary) defense of beauty is the only issue involved.*'[32] The tragedy of Quinn's silencing of his clients was epitomized in the moment when one of the judges paternally suggested that Anderson be excused before the prosecutor read the allegedly obscene passages. Quinn pointed out that she was the publisher, but the judge insisted that she couldn't have known the significance of what she was publishing.[33] Unlike the male judges and lawyers, she did. She and Heap had powerful ideas about the relation between law and literature, and risked liberty and livelihood in support of their artistic convictions.

Heap's closely argued essay in *The Little Review* on the eve of trial artfully blended the claims of both beauty and truth in support of *Ulysses*. She insisted on literature's right to portray life honestly, noting that Gerty MacDowell's leaning back on Sandymount Strand was perfectly ordinary and natural. As she put it with quiet force: 'Girls lean back everywhere.' Imaginative treatment of natural acts, she argued, does not corrupt: 'It was the poet, the artist, who discovered love, created the lover, made sex everything that it is beyond function. It is the Mr. Sumners who have made it an obscenity.' Echoing – and performing – the creed of Pater and Wilde, Heap insisted that 'the only question relevant at all to "Ulysses" is – "Is it a work of Art?"'[34]

Anderson made a similar point after the trial in her report of the proceedings in *The Little Review*. Identifying the crucial failure to present expert opinion on the quality of Joyce's prose as literature, she complained that literary experts were denigrated 'because they know only about literature but not about law: "Ulysses" has suddenly become a matter of law rather than of literature ...'[35] This was the central flaw at the heart of the defence presented by Quinn.

Not having presented evidence as to the literary importance of Joyce's work, but having conceded that it was a failed experiment, Quinn adhered to the decision he had made even before the trial commenced that no appeal would be taken from the conviction he regarded as inevitable. If an appeal had been taken, and reached the Court of Appeals on an appeal as of right from the intermediate appellate court,[36] the appeal would have arrived at about the time that the Court of Appeals accepted, in another case, arguments of the kind that JBY, Anderson and Heap wanted to advance in defence of Joyce. The case, *Halsey v. New York Society for the Suppression of Vice*, 234 N.Y. 1 (1922), on which the Second Circuit Court of Appeals would later rely in holding that *Ulysses* was not obscene, arose out of a much more aggressive approach to Sumner than employed by Quinn. Sumner had arrested and prosecuted Halsey for selling an English translation of *Mademoiselle de Maupin*, the nineteenth-century novel by Théophile Gautier in the preface to which Gautier insisted that literature follows morals and not vice versa, and articulated the notion of art for art's sake. Halsey was acquitted. Thereafter, he commenced an action for malicious prosecution against the New York Society for Suppression of Vice, and won a jury verdict against Sumner's Society.

In the course of upholding the jury's verdict that Sumner lacked probable cause to prosecute Halsey for selling Gautier's novel, the court, in an opinion by Judge William Andrews, departed from the *Hicklin* rule that *any* obscenity doomed the entire book. Rather, the court held that, although the book contained many paragraphs 'which taken by themselves are undoubtedly vulgar and indecent', a work may not 'be judged by a selection of such paragraphs alone', but rather the book 'must be considered broadly as a whole'. Moreover, Andrews took account of critical opinion, noting, for example, that Saint-Beuve – described as 'that distinguished critic' – was 'astonished by the variety and richness of [Gautier's] expression', that 'Henry James refers to him as a man of genius,' and that a number of other named critics 'all speak of him with admiration' and 'tell of his command of style, his poetical imagery, his artistic conceptions, his indescribable charm, his high and probably permanent place in French literature'. Analogous evidence and argument might have been advanced by Quinn but for his view – shown to be erroneous by the decision in *Halsey* – that they could not possibly succeed.[37]

Quinn could have made and presented an appellate record of expert opinion of the merit of the entire Nausicaa episode in the context of the book's overall parallel of Homer's *Odyssey*, which Joyce had described to him in his 3 September 1920 letter.[38] Application of the principles of *Halsey* would have required that Anderson and Heap's convictions be reversed because the court had erroneously considered passages in isolation and failed to consider expert opinion as to the work's literary merit. Instead, Joyce's prose was found obscene without Quinn having sought an appellate ruling on these important issues or otherwise forced the judicial system to focus on the fundamental issue of the quality of Joyce's writing as literature.

Having peremptorily informed Anderson prior to trial that there would be no appeal, Quinn did not discuss appellate possibilities after the trial, or suggest that Anderson and Heap seek a different lawyer. As Anderson later observed, Quinn liked having control, and was not about to cede it.[39] Nor did Quinn bother to consult Joyce about the decision not to appeal. It was Quinn's nature to be certain he knew what was best. Joyce, focused on writing, took only sporadic interest in the legal proceedings. In fact, Joyce generally stood in relation to the many people struggling to help him much as his character Stephen Dedalus situates the artist in relation to his work: 'The artist,' Stephen declares, 'like the God of the creation, remains within or behind or beyond or above his handiwork, invisible, refined out of existence, indifferent, paring his fingernails.'[40] Joyce's remoteness and Quinn's arrogance combined to create a situation that allowed Quinn to eschew an appeal that could have reversed Anderson and Heap's convictions and hastened Joyce's ability to bring *Ulysses* to the public.

This communication gap bedeviled the case from the outset. The 21 October preliminary hearing before Judge Corrigan had already taken place before Joyce was even aware that proceedings had been commenced against Anderson and Heap. He wrote to Pound on 5 November 1920 that 'I knew nothing of the affair till yesterday' when he received a letter from Scofield Thayer saying 'he was sorry about the *Little Review*'.[41] By 10 November Joyce had received the letters of 16 October and 21 October that Quinn had asked Pound to forward, and wrote to Harriet Shaw Weaver that he had received from Pound 'two very long letters from Mr. Quinn of New York concerning *Ulysses* and *The Little Review* but before I reply I should like to know whether you have had any communication from anybody in New York on the subject'.[42]

Despite the great length and detail of Quinn's 21 October account of the hearing before Corrigan, Joyce's response was terse, focusing only on an aspect of Quinn's report that had played to the Joycean fondness for scatology that Quinn found so offensive in writings intended for publication, but was happy to stoke in private. Setting the scene for Joyce, who had playfully entitled a book of poems *Chamber Music*, Quinn reported that 'the judge was in his legal chambers', and expressed uncertainty whether the 'judicial urinal or judicial water closet abutted his chambers'. Apparently not realizing that Joyce would not share his view of *The Little Review* as a sewer, he added that, 'at any rate, chambers struck me as the right place for him to read the July–August number'. Joyce's 17 November response was silent with respect to the substance of Quinn's argument, and limited itself to thanking Quinn for his defence of *Ulysses* and noting his amusement at the letter in the context of his hope 'that the magistrate enjoyed himself in his judicial chambers as much as he appears to have done in court'.[43]

The failure of attorney-client communication was fuelled by the way in which Quinn's overconfidence meshed with Joyce's remoteness, and aggravated by the personal circumstances of both Joyce and Quinn. As the trial approached, Joyce was frantically writing the Circe and Eumaeus episodes of his novel, while trying to find suitable living accommodations in Paris and suffering from debilitating eye problems.[44] Quinn, exhausted and angry that Joyce had disregarded his advice to withdraw *Ulysses* from *The Little Review*, felt that in diverting time from a busy practice to defend Anderson and Heap, he was 'pay[ing] the price of other people's stupidity'.[45] On the eve of trial, when communication should have been at its maximum, Quinn imposed a moratorium on communication with Joyce, instructing him by cable of 24 January 1921, 'Do not cable me again on any subject. Have endeavored to make you and Pound understand am working limit of my endurance.'[46] The silence between Joyce and Quinn leading up to the trial continued through the time when an appeal might have been taken. Quinn had good reason to be annoyed that he was taking time away from pressing business without compensation, but he had volunteered to take charge of the case and had a duty to do so competently and conscientiously, a duty that precludes abandoning the case, and requires seeking informed client consent on significant decisions.[47]

As a result of Quinn's failure to apprise Joyce of developments in the case, the author of *Ulysses* learned that one of its episodes had been found obscene only by reading the *New York Tribune*'s 23 February 1921 editorial comment on the trial,[48] which had found

its way by chance to Sylvia Beach, proprietor of the now legendary
Paris bookstore, Shakespeare and Company.[49] The expatriate book-
seller had been captivated by *Ulysses* when she read the episodes
published in *The Little Review*, and thus was thrilled to meet Joyce at
a social event in Paris to which Pound brought him after convincing
him to move to the French capital.[50]

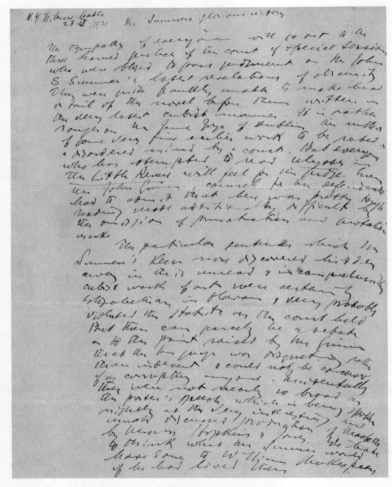

Joyce's transcription of the New York Tribune *article from which he learned that
Anderson and Heap had been convicted of obscenity for publishing an episode of*
Ulysses. *(Beinecke Rare Book and Manuscript Library, Yale University)*

Sylvia Beach and James Joyce in front of Shakespeare and Company, 1921.
(James Joyce Collection, The Poetry Collection of the University Libraries,
University at Buffalo, The State University of New York. Item 3.4)

On a subsequent visit to Beach's bookstore, Joyce learned from the newspaper clipping that Quinn's defence of his masterpiece was essentially that it was disgusting and incomprehensible. The effect on Joyce was so dramatic that he took the trouble to transcribe the article in his own hand.[51] Contemplating reports of the trial, Joyce wrote to Harriet Shaw Weaver that the offence was less grotesque than the defence.[52]

At this perilous point on *Ulysses'* voyage, Anderson and Heap's publication of instalments of Joyce's novel led to the book's rescue: after hearing Joyce lament that the New York conviction meant his novel would never be published, Beach, primed by reading *The Little Review* installments, made an astonishing offer to publish the novel in France under the imprint of her bookstore.[53]

When Quinn finally provided Joyce with an account of the trial in his letter of 13 April 1921 Joyce's response was brusque, noting tersely that 'The publication of *Ulysses* (complete) was arranged here [in Paris] in a couple of days,' and adding only perfunctory 'best thanks for your advocacy'.[54] According to Joyce's biographer Richard Ellmann, Joyce 'never wholly accepted' Quinn's approach to *The Little Review* case, 'feeling that a chance for a brilliant defense of the book had been muffed'.[55]

Joyce was right. Quinn lacked the personal conviction to force the courts to confront the right of *Ulysses* to be heard. By relying on an argument in which he didn't believe – that Joyce's prose deterred immoral conduct because of its filth – he undermined his *ethos,* the quality of personal credibility that Aristotle lists as the first tool of persuasion, giving it priority over both *pathos* and *logos.*[56] Moreover, his unpardonable bias against Anderson and Heap and his antipathy to their enterprise disqualified him for the fundamentally important task of protecting their right to publish. Joyce's biographers, Richard Ellmann and Gordon Bowker, and John Butler Yeats's biographer, William Murphy, have tended to defer to Quinn's judgment that the case against Anderson and Heap was unwinnable.[57] But, as already mentioned, Quinn had thought the same thing about the case against *Jurgen,* and he turned out to be wrong when his successor as counsel proved victorious. Without hindsight or speculation, it is clear that the arguments that Quinn did advance were poor ones, and unworthy of *Ulysses* and Joyce. Quinn's biographer B.L. Reid adopts what he characterizes as Quinn's view – that he 'behaved ... as a practical hodman of the law trying to save what he could of another man's bad cause'. Even Reid, however, laments the cynical, near-farcical tone of Quinn's arguments, and finds it 'distressing that Quinn did not rise to mount a crusade for *Ulysses* on general principles as well as upon tricky manipulations of law and of prejudice'.[58] Reid's appraisal evokes JBY's assessment:

> Quinn is the brainiest man I know *but he has no intellect* ... As a rule lawyers have no intellect, only brains, clever in argument and in getting the better of all their opponents. But intellect is something different. It is *insight*, a power of vision, by which men paint pictures and write poetry and evolve philosophical theories, and it never never argues and never gets excited and feverish, though very eager to explain itself.[59]

Paul Vanderham's *James Joyce and Censorship* suggests, 'Given the limitations imposed upon him by his own view of literature and the unwillingness of the judges to place much value on literary merit, Quinn made the best argument he could.'[60] But Quinn's view of literature should have been of no significance. His duty was to advance the position of his clients that *Ulysses* was a 'prose masterpiece' of compelling beauty and truth. Moreover, the judges' unwillingness to place much value on literary merit was exactly what needed to be changed, either by convincing the judges to think otherwise or reversing them on appeal.

The most recent assessment of Quinn's handling of the case, Kevin Birmingham's *The Most Dangerous Book*, startlingly lauds 'sophisticated legal creativity' by a 'savvy defense attorney'.[61] Birmingham's view is heavily influenced by his assertion that Quinn introduced a completely out-of-context-discussion of Learned Hand's *Kennerley* opinion in the midst of an argument avowedly addressed to the 'ignorance' of judges he perceived as 'stupid'.[62] Neither Quinn himself, nor Anderson and Heap, who longed for an argument based on truth and beauty, recount any such *Kennerley*-based argument. Birmingham cites no account of the trial that states that Quinn made an argument based on truth and beauty, rather than pursuing what Quinn himself called the 'only tack' he could take with the 'stupid' Special Sessions judges, which consisted of his insistence on Joyce's unintelligibility, his concession that Joyce's writing was a failed experiment, and his buffoonish ridiculing of the prosecutor. Birmingham supports his claim that Quinn discussed *Kennerley* by referring to Quinn's 'memorandum'. But Quinn filed no memorandum in connection with his oral presentation to the Court of Special Sessions judges. In response to a query by the author of the present book, Birmingham has clarified that his reference to a memorandum was meant to describe written papers Quinn had previously filed in a different court, the Court of General Sessions, in support of his unsuccessful motion to have the case transferred to that court.[63] Quinn cited *Kennerley* in those papers for the proposition that obscenity charges should be resolved by a jury. But papers filed at a different time in a different court do not support an account of what was said about the alleged obscenity of *Ulysses* at the trial before the three judges who decided the case. Birmingham's praise of Quinn's performance at trial thus rests on what is essentially a fictional account of the trial. Birmingham concedes in a footnote that 'The order of events, exchanges and particular arguments during the trial isn't always clear, and it varies from account to account. I've arranged it for narrative purposes.'[64]

Birmingham also suggests that Quinn's citation to *Kennerley* resulted in an unusual ruling by the Court of Special Sessions to allow expert literary opinion on the question of obscenity.[65] In fact, as discussed above, New York trial courts had been allowing expert testimony on the question of obscenity. Moreover, Quinn offered his experts only to mitigate punishment, not to defeat the charge of obscenity. Birmingham's creative approach to narrative obscures the sad fact that Quinn consciously chose not to rely on Learned Hand's analysis at trial, but preferred a cynical argument that precluded an appellate ruling on the issues raised in Judge Hand's *Kennerley* opinion.

More interested in his novel than the legal proceedings, Joyce wrote on. In a fascinating example of the relation between law and literature, he used the material Quinn sent him about the trial as part of the life he fashioned into literature. For example, Anderson and Heap's statement to Sumner that they were the publishers of *The Little Review* 'and that they gloried in it', which was contained in the Sumner Affidavit that Quinn sent Joyce in April 1921, found its way into the Circe episode of *Ulysses*, where The Veiled Sibyl's enthusiastic support of Bloom prompts her to declare, 'I'm a Bloomite and I glory in it.'[66] Joyce also found good use for a news clipping forwarded by Quinn about Phillip Moeller's testimony that Joyce's technique involved 'an unveiling of the subconscious mind in the Freudian manner'. The report of Moeller's testimony seems to have sparked the appearance of Dr Malachi Mulligan as a sex specialist at Bloom's fantastical trial in Circe where he analyses Bloom in pseudo-Freudian terminology.[67] Ever the victim, Joyce saw to it that Dr Mulligan concludes that Bloom is 'more sinned against than sinning'.[68]

Although Quinn's timidity denied Anderson, Heap and Joyce an appellate ruling on the right of *Ulysses* to be heard, the valiant editors were not entirely silenced. The Autumn 1921 issue of *The Little Review* kept the cause alive. Initiating a tactic that would later prove useful to Joyce, the editors announced in bold letters inside the front cover:

> As protest against the suppression of the Little Review containing various installments of the "Ulysses" of James Joyce, the following

artists and writers of international reputation are collaborating in the autumn number of Little Review: Brâncuși, Jean Cocteau, Jean Hugo, Guy Charles Cros, Paul Morand, Francis Picabia, Ezra Pound.

The editors made clear that the battle would continue, but with different players now that Beach had offered to publish an edition of Joyce's novel in Paris. A note on the last page signed 'jh' reported that *Ulysses* had been announced for publication in book form, and lamented, 'We limp from the field.' Anderson and Heap had, indeed, been wounded, but their perceptivity and courage had succeeded in bringing Joyce's prose to the attention of a wide audience and a publisher who would bring out the novel in book form. Moreover, their forceful insistence that the beauty and truth of literature ought not be barred by obscenity laws kept that important principle at the forefront of the marketplace of ideas.

Constantin Brâncuși (far left) *greets Margaret Anderson and Jane Heap* (far right and second from right) *in his studio with Berenice Abbott and Mina Loy. (Library of Congress)*

NOTES

1   Letter of 22 October 1920 (QC).
2   See Ch. 2, n. 52.
3   Letter of 21 October 1920. See Ch. 3, n. 29.
4   *Id.*
5   *Id.*
6   *Id.*
7   *New York Times*, 2 August 1917 and 12 June 1930.
8   Quinn letter of 21 October 1920 to Pound, n. 3 above.
9   Court of General Sessions, Affidavit and Notice of Motion For the Transfer of Cause From Court of Special Sessions to Court of General Sessions, Jan. 12, 1921 (USIC). The different New York criminal courts are discussed in James Randall Creel, 'The Statutory Disorganization of the Inferior Courts of New York City', 24 Fordham L. Rev. 635 (1955).
10 Quinn letter of 21 June 1922 to Shane Leslie (QC).
11 Ulysses in Court 24.
12 'Ulysses Adjudged Indecent; Review Editors Are Fined', *New York Tribune* (22 February 1921).
13 Letter from Quinn to Joyce, 13 April 1921 (QC). A similar account is contained in Joyce's 21 June 1922 letter to Shane Leslie, n. 10 above.
14 Letter of 21 June 1922, n. 10 above.
15 TYW 220.
16 E.g. Quinn letter of 5 February 1921, Ch. 3, n. 23.
17 Ulysses in Court 24.
18 'Improper Novel Costs Women $100', *The New York Times* (22 February 1921).
19 '"Ulysses" Finds Court Hostile As Neptune', *The World* (22 February 1921).
20 *People v. Muller*, 96 N.Y. 408, 412 (1884).
21 *Id.*
22 See, e.g., Stephen Gillers, 'A Tendency to Deprave and Corrupt: The Transformation of American Obscenity Law from Hicklin to Ulysses II', *85 Washington University Law Review 215* (2007) ('Gillers') at n. 122 (collecting cases).
23 See n. 16 above.
24 Letter of 8 February 1921 (SIUC).
25 Ulysses in Court 23.

26 *Id.* at 23–4.

27 Although Anderson later wrote that Scofield Thayer of the *Dial* also testified (TYW 220), her contemporaneous *Little Review* account reports that Thayer's testimony was waived as repetitive. (Ulysses in Court)

28 'Greenwich Village's Editoresses Fined', *New York Herald* (22 February 1921) 8.

29 MNY 455.

30 TWY 219–20.

31 George Bernard Shaw, *The Doctor's Dilemma*, in George Bernard Shaw, *Complete Plays with Prefaces* (New York: Dodd, Mead & Co., 1963) I, 110.

32 Margaret Anderson, 'An Obvious Statement (for the millionth time)', LR (September–December 1920) 8–9.

33 TYW 221.

34 Art and the Law 5–7.

35 Ulysses in Court 23.

36 See Gillers 265, n. 231.

37 Gillers's careful study suggests, at 270, that an appeal might well have succeeded.

38 Ch. 3, n. 1.

39 TYW 215.

40 Portrait 215.

41 Richard Ellmann, ed., *The Letters of James Joyce, Vol. III* (New York: Viking, 1966) ('JLIII') 27.

42 JLI 149.

43 QC.

44 Ellmann 498; Gordon Bowker, *James Joyce* (London: Weidenfeld & Nicholson, 2011) ('Bowker') 283–4.

45 Letter of 21 January 1921 (QC).

46 MNY 481.

47 See Canon 44.

48 'Mr. Sumner's Glorious Victory', *New York Tribune* (23 February 1921). Joyce's transcription of the editorial, which he sent to Weaver, is in the Beinecke Rare Book and Manuscript Library, Yale University, James Joyce Collection, Box 17, Folder 325. Lawrence Rainey identified the location of Joyce's transcription in *Institutions of Modernism* (New Haven: Yale University Press, 1998) 49 and 189 n. 23.

49 Letter of 3 April 1921 from Joyce to Harriet Shaw Weaver, JLI, 160;

Noel Riley Fitch, *Sylvia Beach and the Lost Generation* (New York: W.W. Norton, 1983) ('Fitch') 77.

50 Fitch 62–4; Pound/Joyce 181.

51 See n. 48 above.

52 Letter postmarked 30 March 1921 (BL).

53 Sylvia Beach, *Shakespeare and Company* (New York: Harcourt, Brace & Company, 1956) ('Beach') 47; Ellmann 504.

54 Joyce letter of 21 April 1921 to Quinn, JLIII, 40–41.

55 Ellmann 558.

56 Aristotle, *Rhetoric*, Book I, Chapter 2 in Roberts.

57 Ellmann 503–4; Bowker 286; PF 521.

58 MNY 455–7.

59 Letter of 13 September 1921 from JBY to Jack Yeats in Declan J. Foley, ed., *The Only Art of Jack B. Yeats* (Dublin: Lilliput Press, 2009) 172–3.

60 Vanderham 55.

61 Birmingham 168, 194.

62 Birmingham 193–4.

63 31 March 2015 email from Kevin Birmingham to the author. Quinn's motion in the Court of General Sessions is described at n. 9 above and the related text.

64 Birmingham 377.

65 *Id.* at 193–4.

66 James Joyce, *Ulysses* (New York: Modern Library, 1934) ('*Ulysses*') 481. Joyce's use of incidents from *The Little Review* trial is discussed in David Weir, 'What Did He Know, and When Did He Know It: *The Little Review*, Joyce, and *Ulysses*', *James Joyce Quarterly*, Vol. 37, No. 3/4 (Spring/Summer 2000) 389–412.

67 *Ulysses* at 483.

68 *Id.*

5
Between the Trials: *Ulysses* Wanders

If nothing else, the conclusion of *The Little Review* trial accomplished Quinn's goal of terminating serial publication of *Ulysses*, thus ridding him from what he regarded as the nettlesome interference of Anderson and Heap in his effort to find a publisher for the book as a whole. Although he had been in discussions with B.W. Huebsch of Viking, the American publisher of *Dubliners*, *A Portrait of the Artist as a Young Man*, and *Exiles,* Quinn seems to have been less intent on moving toward publication of *Ulysses* than on demonstrating that he had been right all along to maintain that serialization in *The Little Review* would jeopardize his ability to do so.

Huebsch's reaction to the conviction of Anderson and Heap was not to drop Joyce like a hot potato, but to suggest 'such alterations in the condemned chapter as will make it conform to the law'.[1] This was a reasonable enough reaction, as was Joyce's long-standing position that he would not alter his text to suit the dictates of judicial arbiters of obscenity. What Joyce needed was a negotiator who could convince Huebsch and other publishers that the city court ruling against Anderson and Heap occurred at the bottom of the judicial totem pole, and that energetic advocacy at higher levels of the state court system or in the federal courts could pave the way to general publication of the book as a whole. This approach apparently never occurred to Quinn. He had just declined to pursue appellate review of the trial court decision in *The Little Review* case, and was personally convinced that *Ulysses* was not fit reading material for most people. Quinn did not hesitate to share this attitude with Joyce. He made it starkly clear in his 5 June 1921 response to Joyce's request that he return a portion of the manuscript of *Ulysses*. Quinn wrote that the husband of one of Joyce's typists 'found the typewritten copies of some of your MS on his wife's table, read it, tore it up and burned it'. Quinn volunteered that he 'rather admire[d] that husband' and felt that the wife 'should have been much pleased at what he did ... shielding her, protecting her, guarding her, and learning what she was doing and disapproving where disapproval was due'.[2] It is no surprise that Quinn answered Huebsch's overture about excisions with a curt response calculated to break off communication, rather than open a dialogue about the possibility of publishing the book without changes in the text. He peremptorily informed Huebsch that, in view of Joyce's position that no changes would be made, he assumed 'you do not care to consider further the publication of "Ulysses"'.[3]

Quinn's reports to Joyce about the negotiations reflect an unnecessary belligerence toward someone who had been Joyce's American publisher and continued to be interested in publishing *Ulysses*. When Huebsch wrote Quinn referring to 'a change of some kind' in the manuscript, Quinn dismissed the suggestion as overly vague, and reported to Joyce that he addressed the vagueness by '[putting] my heel down on the head and body of the wriggler and [giving] him no chance to wriggle further'.[4] When Huebsch wanted to keep open the possibility of publication, Quinn 'squelched' it.[5] After discussions with Huebsch predictably broke down, Quinn wrote the publisher suggesting that Huebsch 'rejoice yourself and be glad that you escape the long arm of the criminal law and that you won't ever have to stand up in the stinking atmosphere of a New York criminal court' to defend against publication of *Ulysses*. It was better, he suggested, 'to lose twenty Ulysses than spend thirty days in Blackwell's Island for one'.[6]

Horace Liveright of Boni & Liveright, another leading publishing house, also contacted Quinn about publishing *Ulysses*. Quinn was quick to remind Joyce that publication was unlikely because his failure to follow Quinn's advice to cease serialization in *The Little Review* resulted in a situation in which Liveright faced serious risk of criminal prosecution and financial loss by publishing *Ulysses*. These risks could have been avoided, Quinn insisted, had Joyce followed his recommendation rather than 'side-stepp[ing] and evad[ing] it repeatedly ...'.[7] Liveright nonetheless offered to publish the book, but Quinn, having read the recently received text of the Circe and Eumaeus episodes, telephoned him to say 'that I would waste no more time on it for the concluding parts were such that I would not advise him that it could be published here without the certainty of prosecution and conviction'.[8] This dire warning terminated discussion with Liveright. Quinn's gratuitous legal advice to both Huebsch and Liveright was diametrically opposed to the interest of his own client.

With the door seemingly closed on publication in the United States, Joyce had proceeded with Sylvia Beach's offer to publish *Ulysses* privately in Paris under the imprint of her bookstore, Shakespeare and Company. This course of action posed a serious problem under the very restrictive provisions of the United States Copyright Act of 1909, which provided that an English-language book published outside the United States could obtain US copyright only if a copy of the book was deposited in the US Copyright Office not later than sixty days after its publication abroad, and the book was manufactured and published in the United States no later than four months after the initial deposit. Full protection was contingent upon compliance with the general provisions of the statute, which required registering, depositing two copies of the book, filing an affidavit, and printing a copyright notice on the work.

Rushing to publish *Ulysses* to coincide with his fortieth birthday, 2 February 1922, Joyce asked Quinn about US copyright protection when they met in Paris in the summer of 1921. Quinn told him that Margaret Anderson's copyright of episodes of the book in *The Little Review* 'would protect the copyright of the book as a whole' – advice that 'relieved Joyce very much'.[9] When, in January 1922, Beach relayed to Quinn Joyce's query whether it was 'necessary to place two sets of the proofs' of her forthcoming edition with the Library of Congress in order to 'insure' American copyright, Quinn replied testily that Joyce must have forgotten his advice of the previous summer that such action was unnecessary because of *The Little Review* copyrights.[10] Quinn also implied that, in any event, it would be impossible to deposit copies of the book in the Copyright Office because, following the conviction of Anderson and Heap, John Sumner 'was sure to have instructed the customs authorities to confiscate all copies of "Ulysses" that come by mail or any other way'.

Quinn's copyright advice was incomplete or erroneous in multiple respects. Preliminarily, as Robert Spoo's informative *Without Copyrights* points out, it was far from clear that Anderson's having copyrighted issues of *The Little Review* would operate for the benefit of Joyce because copyright was not claimed for him as the author.[11] In addition, *The Little Review* had published only about 60 per cent of the novel. Moreover, although Quinn had assumed that all issues of the magazine were filed with the Copyright Office, only four of the twenty-three issues containing parts of *Ulysses* were in fact filed, and thus protection would be incomplete even if Joyce were treated as beneficial owner of Anderson's copyright.[12] Finally, Quinn was wrong to the extent he implied that the customs authorities could block all copies of *Ulysses* from entering the United States. Indeed, Quinn himself wrote to Beach in March 1922, within the statutory sixty-day deadline for depositing Beach's edition, that copies of *Ulysses* were circulating in New York.[13] Although it is possible that the Copyright Office might have refused to accept copies of a book containing episodes that had been found obscene, Spoo points out that the Office had registered many works of questionable morality under its 'rule of doubt'.[14]

Perhaps Quinn was cavalier about protecting Joyce's opportunity for American copyright because, as reflected in his approach to *The Little Review* case and his dealings with publishers, he believed that widespread dissemination of *Ulysses* was impossible. He simply didn't believe in Joyce's right to reach the general public with his groundbreaking novel.

Nonetheless, the publication of *Ulysses* in Paris on 2 February 1922 was an epochal event. Pound, whose labours had contributed to the extraordinary birth of both *The Waste Land* and *Ulysses* in 1922, wrote to Scofield Thayer with deep satisfaction that Eliot's poem 'is as good in its way as Ulysses in its way – and there is so DAMN little genius, so DAMN little work that one can take hold of and say "this at any rate stands, and makes a definite part of literature"'.[15]

The reception of Beach's edition revived interest in the possibility of publication in America. Horace Liveright, free at least temporarily from Quinn's pessimism, made an offer in Paris to bring out the book in the United States and, as Pound colourfully reported, 'hand over 1,000 bones to J.J.'[16] Liveright's willingness to pay for the right to publish *Ulysses* in the United States suggests that he may have been assuming that US copyright was still available. Alternatively, he may have been following the 'trade courtesy' custom described by Spoo pursuant to which American publishers paid royalties to European authors whose works were in the American public domain in the belief that they would be protected from competition by the informal practice of established publishing houses not to compete with the first authorized publisher of uncopy-righted works from abroad.

Quinn promptly put the damper on Liveright's interest. Writing to Joyce on 4 April 1922, he said he had received a letter from Liveright about an American edition, but reminded Joyce that Liveright had withdrawn his previous offer.[17] Quinn neglected to mention that he was the one who had convinced Liveright to do so. On 27 July Quinn concluded the matter by definitively advising Joyce's patron and confidante Harriet Shaw Weaver that *Ulysses*, 'unexpurgated, unchanged, cannot be published in the United States without the certainty of prosecution and conviction ...'[18] In the same letter, Quinn sounded the death knell for a proposal by Samuel Roth to pay Joyce $250 thirty days after the publication of *Ulysses* in its entirety in a quarterly entitled *Two Worlds*. Quinn advised not only that unexpurgated publication would lead to conviction, but that publication of the entire novel in a single magazine was impossible, and that Roth had a reputation as 'a nut poet' who was 'full of crazy ideas'. On the strength of Quinn's report, Weaver responded to Roth's proposal by 'definitely declining on Mr. Joyce's behalf'.[19]

Quinn never permitted his invincible certainty that *Ulysses* was unpublishable to be put to the test. That was the clear – and arguably intended – effect of his failure to seek appellate review of the convictions of Anderson and Heap. Nor did he pursue other possible avenues of testing whether *Ulysses* was, in fact, unpublish-able. For example, beginning in 1921, the New York Civil Practice Act authorized suits for declaring the rights of parties to a dispute, thus opening the door to a suit seeking a determination that the book as a whole was not obscene.[20] Alternatively, since copies of the Shakespeare and Company edition of *Ulysses* were being seized by US customs authorities, Quinn could have advised Joyce to have a friendly recipient contest the seizure, or contest the legality of a postal bar order, much as Margaret Anderson had done with respect to 'Cantleman's Spring-Mate'. Clearly, Quinn did not want to test his view that *Ulysses* was unpublishable, unimportable and unmailable.

Both before and after Quinn's untimely death in 1924, Joyce took no action to address the continuing seizures of *Ulysses* by customs authorities. The *ad hoc* seizures were accorded some degree of formality in 1928 when the Customs Court upheld the seizure of a lot of forty-three items, representing eleven different titles, one of which was *Ulysses*, and all of which were generally held to be obscene.[21] The combination of the customs ban and the absence of any authorized American edition of *Ulysses* left a vacuum that might be filled by an unauthorized version. Beginning in July 1926 Samuel Roth, without authority from Joyce, filled the vacuum by publishing an expurgated text of installments of *Ulysses* in each of the eleven published issues of his *Two Worlds Monthly*.[22]

Although Roth was perfectly within his legal rights because *Ulysses* was not protected by US copyright, Joyce sensed an opportunity to glory in portraying himself as a victim. With his intuitive and prescient sense of the power of publicity, Joyce took a cue from *The Little Review*'s international writers' protest of the suppression of *Ulysses*. Under Sylvia Beach's energetic direction, Joyce launched a massive publicity campaign that stigmatized Roth as a 'pirate' who had 'mutilated' Joyce's text and misappropriated his property. What began as a letter-writing campaign evolved into an international protest signed by more than 160 authors and intellectuals that was released in time for yet another Joyce birthday on 2 February 1927. Signers included W.B. Yeats, T.S. Eliot, Virginia Woolf, Albert Einstein and Bertrand Russell.[23]

On the heels of the international protest, Joyce, always fascinated with the law, added litigation to his campaign to brand Roth as a pirate while presenting himself to the world as a martyr. Using a New York law firm with a Paris office, Joyce took the extraordinary step of initiating a lawsuit in his own name against Roth in state court in New York. The case, styled 'James Joyce against Samuel

Roth and Two Worlds Publishing Company', was filed in March 1927. Joyce alleged that Roth had used his name for advertising and trade purposes in violation of a New York statute creating a right of publicity. The urgency of Joyce's desire to preserve the American market for *Ulysses* is apparent from the fact that, in contrast to his remoteness from *The Little Review* case, he was willing to take on the burdens of a plaintiff, who can be required to produce documents and give testimony.[24] Had Joyce taken an active role in defending his novel in the *The Little Review* case, he clearly would not have acquiesced in Quinn's approach, and would have been able to insist on a defence that relied on the beauty and truth of his prose, and pressed for an appellate ruling on the important issues presented by the suppression of his masterpiece.

The complaint against Roth was all but defective on its face because of an exception in the statute for the use of the name of an author who has used it in connection with sale of his work. Nonetheless, Roth's personal circumstances left him with little choice but to consent to an injunction against further publication of *Ulysses*. His publishing company was insolvent and, ironically, he was imprisoned on the basis of unrelated obscenity charges brought by John Sumner and the New York Society for the Suppression of Vice, the same forces that had succeeded in convicting Margaret Anderson and Jane Heap for publishing an installment of *Ulysses* in *The Little Review*.[25] Although Anderson and Heap's un-appealed convictions remained an obstacle to publication of *Ulysses* in the United States, Joyce, with a new legal team, was at last taking the offensive.

NOTES

1   Letter of 24 March 1921 to Quinn, quoted in Gorman at 279.
2   QC.
3   Letter of 25 March 1921, quoted in Gorman at 279–80.
4   Letter of 5 June 1921 (QC).
5   *Id.*

6   Letter of 13 April 1921 from Quinn to Huebsch quoted in NNY 486.

7   Letter of 5 June 1921 from Quinn to Joyce (QC).

8   *Id.*

9   Letter of 4 February 1922 from Quinn to Beach (recounting conversation with Joyce) (Poetry Collection, State University of New York at Buffalo ('SUNYB').

10   *Id.*

11   Robert Spoo, *Without Copyrights: Piracy, Publishing, and the Public Domain* (New York: Oxford University Press, 2013) ('Spoo') 156–8.

12   *Id.*

13   MNY 532.

14   Spoo 86.

15   Letter of 9–10 March 1922, Walter Sutton, ed., *Pound, Thayer, Watson and The Dial: A Story in Letters* (Gainesville: University Press of Florida, 1994) 236.

16   Letter of Ezra Pound to Quinn, 21 February 1922 (Pound/Quinn Letters 206).

17   SUNYB.

18   QC.

19   Weaver letter of 15 September 1922 to Quinn (QC).

20   Harold R. Medina, 'Some Phases of the New York Civil Practice Act and Rules', XXI *Columbia Law Review*, No. 2 (February 1921) 113–25.

21   *A. Heymoolen v. United States* (Treasury Decision 42907, Cust. Ct. Aug. 1, 1928).

22   In the interim between Weaver's declining Roth's offer to publish *Ulysses* and his unauthorized publication, Roth had published without authorization episodes of Joyce's *Work in Progress*, which had been published in England before eventually morphing into *Finnegans Wake*. Following correspondence with Sylvia Beach, Roth, who had exchanged friendly letters with Joyce in 1921, made *ex-gratia* payments to Joyce. Spoo 165–72.

23   The protest appears in JLIII, 151–3.

24   Birmingham (at 279) erroneously identifies Beach as the plaintiff.

25   Spoo (193–232) provides a detailed account of the matter based on his careful review of the files of the lawyers who represented Joyce in the litigation.

Ernst, Woolsey and the Hands: *Ulysses* Unbound

In the summer of 1931 two impulses converged that would ultimately end *Ulysses'* exile. One was Joyce's concern that unauthorized editions of *Ulysses* would deprive him of the American market, which led him to direct his agent James Pinker to explore the possibility of an authorized American edition.[1] The second was the interest of the New York lawyer Morris Ernst in waging a legal battle to permit American publication of *Ulysses*. Ernst, whose father had immigrated to the United States from Eastern Europe, grew up in New York City, attended Horace Mann School, and received his BA from Williams College. He was particularly influenced by the broadly humane ideas of English professor Ted Lewis, a former major league baseball player known as 'the Pitching Professor', who discussed poetry with Robert Frost as the two played catch.[2]

Ernst's writing suggests that he drank from the same spring as John Butler Yeats, whose argument for Joyce's 'terrible veracity' had been mutilated by Quinn. For example, Ernst prominently cited

JBY's master J.S. Mill in articulating 'The Case Against Censorship' in one of his memoirs and, as we shall see, relied on another JBY favourite, Macaulay, in urging the courts to recognize the value of *Ulysses*' truthfulness.[3] Not surprisingly, Ernst was bored with his post-college job of selling furniture. Intrigued by a friend's experience of attending New York Law School at night, Ernst did the same while selling shirts and furniture by day. After law school, his earnest interest in free expression fuelled a busy practice and led him to serve as general counsel to the American Civil Liberties Union from 1929 to 1954.[4] He had a number of high-profile successes challenging obscenity charges, including those against Radclyffe Hall's *The Well of Loneliness*.

In the summer of 1931 Ernst and his partner Alexander Lindey discussed their desire to wage a battle to legalize *Ulysses* in the United States. Lindey referred to their discussions in his very interesting 6 August 1931 memorandum to Ernst about his lengthy interview with Sylvia Beach's sister, Holly Dennis, who was visiting New York from California.[5] Dennis told Lindey that Beach 'has the sole and exclusive world rights with respect to *Ulysses* ... and is tremendously interested in the legalization of *Ulysses* and would be glad to cooperate in every respect if a responsible American publisher could be found.'[6] Holly Dennis's statement about her sister's rights was legally correct because Joyce, in a cynical effort to convince his lawyers in the Roth litigation that he was not obliged to pay them, had entered a contract with Beach in 1930 ceding her sole worldwide rights to *Ulysses* to support his dubious position that she was the party to whom his lawyers should look for payment.[7] Lindey further recounted that Beach's sister had said that, although B.W. Huebsch's firm, Viking, would have the American rights to Joyce's *Work in Progress,* the working title of what became *Finnegans Wake,* Viking did not have the rights to *Ulysses*. Lindey's excitement at the prospect of fighting to legalize *Ulysses* is palpable: 'I still feel very keenly that this would be the grandest obscenity case in the history of law and literature, and I am ready to do anything in the world to get it started.' Not wanting to miss this opportunity, he observed that, in view of another law firm's relationship with Viking, 'I realize that you would not be very anxious to see *Ulysses* sponsored by them.' The sage Ernst responded with a note expressing a desire to pursue the matter, but, knowing there are multiple ways of skinning a cat, cautioned his colleague, 'Be sure not to knock Viking to her. It will get back.' Significantly, Ernst saw himself as the moving force in the matter and expressed confidence that 'I am sure I can get a good publisher.'

By 21 October Ernst was writing to Huebsch following up their meeting the previous day that had concluded with Ernst's promise to the publisher that he would 'drop you a line in regard to possible services that we might render in connection with the legalization of Joyce's *Ulysses*'.[8] Ernst laid out the realistic situation respecting *Ulysses,* coupled with a very positive statement as to the course he might pursue 'in order to win a court decision in favor of *Ulysses*'.[9] He explained that *Ulysses* might be in the public domain, that the injunction entered against Roth was 'not very impressive', and that the real problem lay in the fact that 'any attempt to legalize the volume will be faced at the outset with the condemnation previously enunciated by various courts against the volume'.[10] Although he didn't mention *The Little Review* case by name, Ernst likely had that case and the *Heymoolen* Customs Court case in mind. Ernst's files contain a copy of the *Heymoolen* decision.[11] There was no official report of the trial court's ruling in *The Little Review* case. Neither the Customs Court nor the New York State court decision would be binding on a federal district court, but both decisions applied the traditional obscenity test to *Ulysses*. The real task for Ernst would be to supplant the traditional *Hicklin* test upon which the earlier decisions were based. He concluded his letter on a positive note, saying that to win the case would involve 'substantial reversals of opinions laid down by our courts about a decade ago ... but we were confronted with the same situation in the reversals which we have had to obtain in other cases such as the works of [birth control advocate] Dr. Marie C. Stopes ...'[12]

Huebsch had never lost interest in *Ulysses*, but his dealings with Pinker and Beach hit an unanticipated snag. Irked at being treated by Joyce and others as his 'representative' rather than his publisher, Beach sought to ensure fair treatment in the event of an English or American edition by asserting the value of the rights that Joyce had too cleverly assigned to her. Thus, on 4 July 1931, she issued her own declaration of independence in the form of a letter to Pinker saying, 'Will you kindly take note of the fact that I have a contract' with Joyce granting publication rights. Observing that she had brought out the first edition in 1922, had published the book ever since, and that 'if an American edition appeared I should probably have to cease publication here', she instructed Pinker that 'any offers must therefore include the sum of twenty five thousand dollars to be paid to me on signing the contract'.[13]

As 1931 drew to a close, Huebsch despaired of success, and so advised Bennett Cerf of Random House, who also wanted to publish *Ulysses*, but had deferred to Huebsch as a matter of trade courtesy. On 17 December a frustrated Huebsch wrote to Cerf that 'Pinker writes from London that he thinks it's hopeless to try to wrench *Ulysses* away from Miss Beach.' Although noting that he would try again next time he saw Beach, Huebsch told Cerf, 'You graciously stood aside for us, and naturally we cannot object if you should now determine to try to get the book ...'[14] Huebsch also let Ernst know of his temporary retreat, and Ernst, who had obviously been discussing the subject with Cerf, wrote to Cerf on 21 December suggesting they 'hop a boat and spend a weekend with Miss Beach in Paris'.[15] Cerf responded the next day suggesting they talk 'soon after the turn of the new year'.[16]

Cerf promptly went to Paris on his own where he met with Beach and Joyce, and returned with the right to publish *Ulysses* in the United States. The breakthrough occurred, according to Beach, when Joyce's old friend Padraic Colum, speaking on Joyce's behalf, told her there was 'no contract'. When she disagreed, Colum told her she was standing in the way of Joyce's interests.[17] 'Floored', she immediately telephoned Joyce to tell him she relinquished any claim to *Ulysses*, and he was free to proceed as he wished.[18] An epic legal battle over obscenity was assured when Cerf, who had sought the assistance of Ernst's firm in drafting the contract with Joyce, retained the firm in March 1932 to 'handle the legal end of this matter'.[19] Although the ideas championed by Margaret Anderson, Jane Heap and John Butler Yeats went unheard in *The Little Review* case, they foreshadowed the arguments that Ernst would advance on behalf of Random House.

Ernst's fight to legalize *Ulysses* took advantage of a provision of the Tariff Act of 1930 that accorded a right of judicial review to the putative importer of a book seized as obscene. Specifically, the Act required the government to commence a legal proceeding against the book and authorized the would-be importer to intervene in the proceeding to contest the legality of the seizure.[20] Energetically taking the battle to the enemy, Ernst and Cerf had Joyce mail a copy of *Ulysses*, into which favourable reviews had been pasted, to Random House and made sure that it was seized.[21]

Ernst and Cerf had a piece of extraordinary good fortune in the prosecution's concurrence in their effort to steer assignment of the ensuing case to Judge John Munro Woolsey. A graduate of Phillips Academy, Yale University and Columbia Law School, Woolsey had a variety of non-legal interests and was a serious reader with wide-ranging tastes. Especially attuned to the late eighteenth century, he admired and collected the works of Dr Johnson, and was also a student and collector of 'Colonial and republican architecture, furniture, woodwork [and] glassware'.[22] He was a devoted member of the Century Association, a club of 'amateurs of letters and the fine arts', and regularly attended Saturday lunch at the club.[23] The opinion he would write in the *Ulysses* case was the work of a master of prose style.

The United States Attorney, George Medalie, thought *Ulysses* was a very important book and was amenable to trying to time the case's early activity with a view to having it assigned to a literate judge like Woolsey.[24] There was much to commend Woolsey to Ernst. He was the judge who, two years earlier, had ruled in favour of Ernst's client Marie Stopes that her book *Married Love* was not obscene. The government had challenged the importation of the book from England even though all references to contraception had been excised. Woolsey's opinion made no secret of his wide reading, observing that 'to one who had read Havelock Ellis, as I have, the subject-matter of Dr. Stopes' book is not wholly new, but it emphasizes the woman's side of sex questions', making a plea 'for a better understanding by husbands of the physical and emotional side of the sex life of their wives'.[25] Woolsey held that the book could not be found to be obscene, and thus ended the case without trial by dismissing it as a matter of law. Taking a characteristically sweeping approach that neither cited *Bennett* and *Hicklin*, nor discussed their requirement that obscenity be judged on the basis of the work's effect on the most susceptible reader, Woolsey pronounced that 'I cannot imagine a normal mind to which this book would seem to be obscene ...'

Fortunately, the legal analysis that supported this result had been undertaken a year earlier by Augustus Hand in his opinion for the Second Circuit reversing the conviction of Mary Dennett for using the mails to distribute her pamphlet *The Sex Side of Life*, which Hand characterized as 'a truthful exposition of the sex side of life, evidently calculated for instruction and for the explanation of relevant facts'. Vaguely adverting to the First Amendment's protection of freedom of expression, Hand wrote that 'while there can be no doubt about its constitutionality, [the statute barring the mailing of obscene books] must not be assumed to have been designed to interfere with serious instruction regarding sex matters unless the terms in which the information is conveyed are clearly indecent.'[26] Woolsey's opinion in the *Married Love* case piggybacked on this analysis by saying that 'Dr. Stopes treats quite as decently and with as much restraint of the sex relations as did Mrs. Mary Ware Dennett in "The Sex Side of Life, An Explanation for Young People," which was held not to be obscene by the Circuit Court of Appeals for this Circuit ...' In typically pithy prose, Woolsey summed the matter up by saying, 'The present book may fairly be said to do for adults what Mrs. Dennett's book does for adolescents.' Shortly after his *Married Love* decision, Woolsey also ruled in favour of Ernst's challenge to the seizure of Stopes' book *Contraception*.[27] In that same year, 1931, Ernst praised Woolsey's *Married Love* opinion in a preface to Stopes' *Enduring Passion*, which was described in a subtitle as a 'continuation of *Married Love*'.[28] It is not surprising that Ernst carefully played the case-assignment system to get the *Ulysses* case assigned to Woolsey.

Woolsey's role would be especially important because the parties waived the right to jury trial and stipulated that Woolsey would, in effect, be both judge and jury. In a jury trial, Woolsey would have ruled on legal issues and instructed the jury as to the law, but the jury would find the facts, including the ultimate fact of whether the book was obscene. The parties stipulated, however, that Woolsey 'would decide all questions of law and fact involved and render a general finding thereon'. In other words, Woolsey would both decide the law and sit as trier of fact.

Ernst's role as defender of *Ulysses* benefited from the fact that, following Sylvia Beach's publication of the complete novel in Paris in 1922, it had received some (if far from overwhelming) critical approbation. The usually above-it-all Joyce had contributed to this helpful aura of high-mindedness. Following the suppression of *The Little Review* he had revised his text to add additional parallels between *Ulysses* and the *Odyssey*,[29] thus strengthening the link between his work and Homer that he had previously identified

131

in his letter to Carlo Linati.[30] Even as he made efforts to inoculate his text against suppression, Joyce did not hesitate to spit in the censor's eye, adding, for example, additional graphic detail to the Nausicaa episode, such as that, as Gerty leaned back, Bloom's 'hands and face were working and a tremor went over her'.[31] As publication approached, Joyce doubled down on the parallels with Homer by providing a more detailed elaboration of the Homeric correspondences (and other stylistic features) to the distinguished French novelist, translator, and critic Valery Larbaud, and helping to arrange a lecture and article by Larbaud that emphasized the link between Joyce and Homer.[32] Here, once again, Joyce was the beneficiary of Anderson and Heap's courage: Larbaud had become a 'raving mad' admirer of *Ulysses* when Sylvia Beach sent him *The Little Review* issues containing episodes of the novel and was thus disposed to promote its reception.[33]

While publication of the complete novel facilitated the comparison with Homer, it also meant that Ernst was burdened by the concluding Molly Bloom monologue, a highly sexual reverie that Joyce himself called 'probably more obscene than any preceding episode'.[34] Molly's long reverie filtering the events of her day through her memory of the past begins with the word 'Yes' and concludes with her recollection of the occasion when Bloom said 'the sun shines for you … the day we were lying among the rhododendrons on Howth Head' and 'I asked him with my eyes to ask again yes and then he asked me would I say yes to say yes my mountain flower and first I put my arms around him yes and drew him down to me so he could feel my breasts all perfume yes and his heart was going like mad and yes I said yes I will Yes.'[35] The following passages from Molly's reverie particularly attracted the government's attention:

> [...] he must have come 3 or 4 times with that tremendous big red brute of a thing he has I thought the vein or whatever the dickens they call it was going to burst though his nose is not so big after I took off all my things …

I never in all my life felt anyone had one the size of that to make you feel full up he must have eaten a whole sheep after what's the idea making us like that with a big hole in the middle of us like a Stallion driving it up into you because thats all they want out of you with that determined vicious look in his eye I had to halfshut my eyes still he hasn't such a tremendous amount of spunk in him when I made him pull it out and do it on me considering how big it is …

… hes heavy too with his hairy chest for this heat always having to lie down for them better for him put it into me from behind the way Mrs Mastiansky told me her husband made her like the dogs do it and stick out her tongue as far as ever she could …

… I wished he was here or somebody to let myself go with and come again like that I feel all fire inside me or if I could dream it when he made me spend the 2nd time tickling me behind with his finger I was coming for about 5 minutes with my legs round him I had to hug him after O Lord I wanted to shout out all sorts of things fuck or shit or anything at all …

… I tried with the Banana but I was afraid it might break and get lost up in me somewhere yes because they once took something down out of a woman that was up there for years covered with limesalts theyre all mad to get in there where they come out of youd think they could never get far enough up and then theyre done with you in a way till the next time yes because there's a wonderful feeling there all the time so tender how did we finish if off yes O yes I pulled him off into my handkerchief pretending not to be excited but I opened my legs I wouldn't let him touch me inside my petticoat I had a skirt opening up the side I tortured the life out of him first tickling him I loved rousing that dog in the hotel rrrsssst awokwokawok his eyes shut and a bird flying below us he was shy all the same I liked him like that morning I made him blush a little when I got over him that way when I unbuttoned him and took his out and drew back the skin it had a kind of eye in it they're all Buttons men down the middle on the wrong side of them Molly darling he called me what was his name Jack Joe Harry Mulvey was it yes …

… yes Ill sing Winds that blow from the south that he gave after the choir stairs performance Ill change that lace on my black dress to show off my bubs and Ill yes by God Ill get that big fan mended make them burst with envy my hole is itching me always when I think of him I feel I want to ...

Ill put on my best shift and drawers let him have a good eyeful out of that to make his micky stand for him Ill let him know if thats what he wanted that his wife is fucked yes and damn well fucked too up to my neck nearly not by him 5 or 6 times handrunning theres the mark of his spunk on the clean sheet I wouldnt bother to even iron it out that ought to satisfy him if you dont believe me feel my belly unless I made him stand there and put him into me Ive a mind to tell him every scrap and make him do it in front of me serve him right its all his own fault if I am an adulteress ...

... thats what a woman is supposed to be there for or He wouldn't have made us the way He did so attractive to men then if he wants to kiss my bottom Ill drag open my drawers and bulge it right out in his face as large as life he can stick his tongue 7 miles up my hole as hes there my brown part then III tell him I want £1 or perhaps 30/ – Ill tell him I want to buy underclothes then if he gives me that well he wont be too bad I dont want to soak it all out of him like other women do I could often have written out a fine cheque for myself and write his name on it for a couple of pounds a few times he forgot to lock it up besides he won't spend it Ill let him do it off on me behind provided he doesnt smear all my good drawers O I suppose that cant be helped Ill do the indifferent 1 or 2 questions Ill know by the answers when hes like that he cant keep a thing back I know every turn in him Ill tighten my bottom well and let out a few smutty words smellrump or lick my shit or the first mad thing comes into my head then Ill suggest about yes O wait now sonny my turn is coming III be quite gay and friendly over it ...[36]

Ernst clearly had some obstacles to overcome, but he approached his task with a commitment to the value and veracity of Joyce's work. At the outset of the case, he filed with the court a thick compendium of materials designed to show the importance of *Ulysses*.[37] These included a map of the United States showing the location of libraries interested in obtaining and circulating *Ulysses*, and endorsements by distinguished literary figures, including John

Cowper Powys, whose lecture in Chicago many years earlier had inspired Margaret Anderson on her path to founding *The Little Review*. Whereas Quinn had used Powys only for the back-handed observation that *Ulysses* was too obscure and philosophical to corrupt, Ernst submitted Powys's robust pronouncement that *Ulysses* was one of the 'very few books that by sheer force of genius mount up during an author's lifetime to an unassailable and classical position'.[38]

Ernst's brief continued the theme of *Ulysses'* distinction, explaining how Joyce presented the events of a single day in the context of the structure of the *Odyssey*, and noting that a copy of the book resided in the Widener Library at Harvard and was on the reading list for a course taught there by T.S. Eliot.[39] The brief quoted encomia from J. Middleton Murry, Rebecca West, Arnold Bennett and Ernest Boyd. Moreover, Ernst delivered to Woolsey, who already had a copy of Stuart Gilbert's *James Joyce's Ulysses*, copies of Herbert Gorman's *James Joyce: The First Forty Years* and Paul Jordan Smith's *A Key to the Ulysses of James Joyce*.[40] These efforts paid off: Woolsey's decision noted that his reading of *Ulysses* was accompanied by perusal of 'a number of other books which have now become its satellite'. Ernst's summation of Joyce the man echoed John Butler Yeats, who had argued, 'That such a man as Joyce should write filth is incredible.' The voice of JBY, who had died in 1922, was finally heard in Ernst's assertion that, 'It is monstrous to suppose that a man of the stature of Joyce would or could produce a work of obscenity.'[41]

It remained necessary to come to grips with the text. Confronted with a charge that *Ulysses* is obscene, the mind of the advocate seems incapable of resisting the argument that it is too obscure to excite. Ernst put it this way: *Ulysses* 'is far too tedious and labyrinthine and bewildering for the untutored and the impressionable who might conceivably be affected by it. Such people would not get beyond the first dozen pages.'[42] Referring to the New York decision in which – after Quinn had dropped the case – the court referred to the difficulty of James Branch Cabell's *Jurgen* in finding it not to be obscene, Ernst argued that 'beside [*Ulysses*], Jurgen is a child's primer. It is not only the language that is baffling; the construction is almost unbelievably involved'.[43] As an example of the difficulty of the language, Ernst cited some words selected at random from the book, including whelks, cataletic, houyhnhnm, crubeen, parallax, cygnets, entelechy, yogibogeybox, apocrypha, tympanum, demisemiquaver, videlicet, cruiskeen, oxter, topiary, and epicene.

Moreover, Ernst argued, 'incomprehensible paragraphs' recur again and again. The primary example he offered was the one whose content first attracted Anderson. It contained both the Quinn-offending adjective 'snotgreen' and the passage that Anderson told Heap was the most beautiful thing they would ever see, and convinced her to risk prosecution to make Joyce's lyrical prose part of her conversation with her readers. The passage as it appeared in Ernst's brief illustrates the text's difficult beauty:

> Ineluctable modality of the visible: at least that if no more, thought through my eyes. Signatures of all things I am here to read, seaspawn and seawrack, the nearing tide, that rusty boot. Snotgreen, bluesilver, rust: colored signs. Limits of the diaphane. But he adds: in bodies. Then he was aware of them, sure. Go easy. Bald he was and a million-aire, maestro di color che sanno. Limit of the diaphane in. Why in? Diaphane, adiaphane. If you can put your five fingers through it, it is a gate, if not a door. Shut your eyes and see.[44]

Ernst refrained from quoting Molly's soliloquy or other passages that drew the ire of the government. One can empathize with the advocate's desire to elude the question of obscenity with the red herring of obscurity. But, sooner or later, a rigorous assessment of whether *Ulysses* was barred by the statutory ban on obscene works must come to grips with the fact that the essence of *Ulysses* – its warp and woof – is its author's conviction that sexual desire lies at the heart of things. Ernst sought to whistle his way past this core issue, arguing that 'though the element of sex is present, it is relegated to a position of relative unimportance'.[45] Fortunately, Ernst's brief provided the building blocks needed to construct the rationale within which *Ulysses* was not obscene and, to their credit, the appellate judges faced with the task of applying the statute to the book recognized that the current of erotic imagination that drives *Ulysses* could not be ignored and courageously altered judge-made legal doctrine to accommodate it.

Ernst laid the groundwork for a change in legal doctrine by emphasizing Learned Hand's suggestion in *Kennerley* that the standard for obscenity should vary with the mores of the time, and his anticipation of the time when society will 'believe that truth and beauty are too precious to society at large to be mutilated in the interests of those most likely to pervert them to base uses'.[46] Ernst also relied on the decision of the New York Court of Appeals in the *Halsey* case, which, at about the time that an appeal on behalf of Anderson and Heap would have been decided if Quinn had appealed, recognized that the claimed obscenity of a book could not be judged from a selection of paragraphs, but that the book 'must be considered broadly as a whole'.[47] The federal court was not bound to follow a decision of the New York court, but the decision by the distinguished New York judges was inherently persuasive.

Within this legal framework, Ernst's brief wove an argument that sounded the important notes of the beauty and veracity of Joyce's writing. Whereas he was more comfortable relying on quotations from critics to establish the beauty of *Ulysses*, he spoke in his own voice in support of the novel's truthfulness:

> It is a many-faceted crystallization of life and thought. It records the doubts and fears, the joys and torments, the swirling consciousness, of a handful of characters, and informs the experiences of those characters with the quality of universality. Sex is present, to be sure; but sex is part of man's existence. One can no more say that *Ulysses* is obscene than that life or thought is obscene.[48]

In the concluding section of his brief Ernst sought to fortify the judges who would have to deal with the eroticism and earthiness of

Joyce's prose by forcefully stating the importance of truth in literature as an end in itself. Adopting Shakespeare's metaphor of the mirror being held up to nature that Wilde had rejected, Ernst insisted, 'The notion of pornography is wholly inconsistent with an artist's serious effort to mirror and perpetuate truth in literature.'[49] In a turning of the tables worthy of Wilde himself, Ernst supported his argument by reference to critic Holbrook Jackson's comment, a variation of Wilde's pronouncement in the preface to *The Picture of Dorian Gray*, that *Ulysses* is 'neither moral nor immoral ... [Joyce] simply records like Homer'.[50] Whereas Wilde insisted that literature's beauty protected it from claims of immorality, Ernst emphasized that *Ulysses* transcended issues of morality because of its truth.

The most impassioned paragraph in the brief reflects the influence of JBY's mentors J.S. Mill and Macaulay. Much as Mill's influence had led JBY to praise Joyce's 'terrible veracity', Ernst's view of Joyce's importance was informed by Mill's warning of the harm caused to humanity by the stifling effect on thought and expression of a charge of immorality or irreligion – the passage he quoted in 'the case against censorship' in his memoir.[51] Ernst's brief came alive when Mill's warning intersected with Macaulay's praise of Milton's fearless carrying of 'the torch of truth'. Ernst argued that Macaulay's praise of Milton's willingness to speak out in favour of divorce and regicide 'applied with equal force to Joyce'. His quote from Macaulay's essay on Milton set a high bar for Joyce to scale:

> There is no more hazardous enterprise than that of bearing the torch of truth into those dark and infected recesses in which no light has ever shone. But it was the choice and pleasure of Milton to picture the noisome vapours and to brave the terrible explosion ...[52]

Ernst urged that Joyce was equal to the challenge:

> It may be that in *Ulysses* [he argued,] Joyce has seen fit to cast light into some of the murky chambers of the human mind. It is only by such exposure that we can hope to banish darkness and taint. Joyce's penetration and courage deserve praise, not condemnation.[53]

Judge John Munro Woolsey. (Courtesy John M. Woolsey III)

Ernst's powerful argument found a receptive audience in Judge Woolsey. Significantly for subsequent prosecutions of literature, Woolsey dealt with *Ulysses* primarily in terms of its imaginative and stylistic originality. His supple mind identified and articulated the link between beauty and truth. In essence, he found that the beauty of Joyce's style enabled the written word to convey the truth of human consciousness. His articulation of this insight broke new ground by deciding a legal question on the basis of an analysis of literary technique. Without explicitly using the term 'stream of consciousness', Woolsey observed that Joyce was experimenting in a new literary genre in which he attempted

> to show how the screen of consciousness with its ever-shifting kalei-doscopic impressions carries, as it were on a plastic palimpsest, not only what is in the focus of each man's observation of the actual things about him, but also in a penumbral zone residua of past impressions, some recent and some drawn up by association from the domain of the subconscious.[54]

This approach, Woolsey wrote, required him to focus on Joyce's veracity, what Woolsey called 'his honest effort to show exactly how the minds of his characters operate'.

The important point here is that, according to Woolsey, the characters are not consciously indulging themselves in erotic imagin-ings. Instead, the reverse is true. The primal energy of Eros is forcing itself on the characters. Accordingly, if there is a strong sexual undercurrent in *Ulysses*, it is not attributable to any fault of either Joyce or the reader: 'If Joyce did not attempt to be honest in developing the technique which he has adopted in "Ulysses" the result would be psychologically misleading and thus unfaithful to his chosen technique,' said Woolsey, adding that 'such an atti-tude would be artistically inexcusable'. Woolsey's analysis brought him to the precise point John Butler Yeats made in his 1920 letter to Quinn: the reason for the outcry against Joyce was his terrible veracity. As Woolsey framed the point: 'It is because Joyce has been loyal to his technique and has not funked its necessary implica-tions, but has honestly attempted to tell fully what his characters think about, that he has been the subject of so many attacks and that his purpose has been so often misunderstood and misrepre-sented.' Woolsey realized – and had the courage to say – that Joyce was considered obscene because 'his attempt sincerely and honestly to realize his objective has required him incidentally to use certain words which are generally considered dirty words and has led at times to what many think is a too poignant preoccupation with sex in the thoughts of his characters.' Again emphasizing Joyce's veracity, Woolsey found that 'each word of the book contributes like a bit of mosaic to the detail of the picture Joyce is seeking to construct for his readers'. There is no 'dirt for dirt's sake'.

Law and literature blend seamlessly here because it is Joyce's mastery as a writer that convinces Judge Woolsey of the grievous wrong that would be done were the law to silence him. Woolsey's opinion responds to a feature of Joyce's writing pinpointed by the great University College Dublin professor Gus Martin when he wrote that Joyce's achievement was the invention of 'a range of technical and linguistic resources' of the necessary 'power and range' to break 'the sound barrier of ... social reticence, the wall – at least the façade – between the public and private self that Victoria's reign had so consolidated, and which the Catholic Church in Ireland had so reinforced'.[55] Molly Bloom's piercing of the sound barrier between public and private showed Woolsey the way to break the hold of the Victorian *Hicklin* case on the law of obscenity. Importantly, Ernst's emphasis on the quality of *Ulysses* as literature had provided Molly a platform from which she commanded serious attention for the argument she crafted from her bed in Eccles Street. Woolsey could not help but find it a compelling case for putting off pretence and recognizing the role of the erotic imagination in daily life. Molly's question – 'what else were we given all those desires for Id like to know' – demanded an answer from a judge being asked to ban a book that draws attention to them. They 'didnt make me blush', argued Molly: 'why should it either it's only nature'.[56] Molly knew her target. When, after the litigation was over, Ernst asked Woolsey to inscribe 'some sweet phrases' on his photograph, Woolsey sent a paraphrase of a fragment of eighteenth-century writing that had long fascinated him and suggested his susceptibility to an argument like Molly's: 'I fear, Sir,' the text read, 'that you may consider these protestations unmaidenly, but by the laws of Nature we are bound to love, although the Rules of Modesty oftentimes compel us to conceal it.'[57]

Woolsey's implicit acceptance of Molly's argument is apparent in his framing of the core issue in terms of what JBY called Joyce's 'terrible veracity'. Woolsey put the question this way: 'when such a real artist in words, as Joyce undoubtedly is, seeks to draw a picture of the lower middle class in a European City, ought it be impossible for the American public legally to see that picture?' Woolsey's appreciation for the value of the truth and beauty of Joyce's novel enabled him to swallow the admittedly 'strong draught' of *Ulysses*. It remained to reconcile his conclusion with the federal law of obscenity, which still adhered to the teaching of *Hicklin* that a book was obscene if even isolated passages excited sexual desire in the most susceptible reader. Woolsey ignored *Hicklin*, and simply plunged ahead with the *ipse dixit* that the proper test was a reading of the book in its entirety in terms of how it would affect 'a person with average sex instincts – what the French would call "*l'homme moyen sensuel*" …'

Even the valiant Woolsey paled at the prospect of offering himself as the barometer of whether *Ulysses* excited lustful thoughts. Instead, he reported what was, in effect, the combined decision of himself and two friends, who retained their anonymity in Woolsey's opinion, but who are identified in Ernst's files as Henry Seidel Canby, editor of *The Saturday Review of Literature*, and Charles E. Merrill Jr, a scholar and publisher.[58] This private consultation was an extraordinary departure from the normal procedure pursuant to which the parties have an opportunity to be heard on whether the court can consider expert opinion in reaching a decision. Under today's Federal Rules of Evidence, a trial court may appoint an expert whose 'scientific, technical or other specialized knowledge will help the trier of fact to understand the evidence or to determine a fact in issue', but the parties participate in the process. The court must inform the expert of his or her duties either by a writing that is filed in the court file or orally at a conference in which the parties have an opportunity to participate. Moreover, the expert must advise the parties of any findings; may be deposed by any party; may be called to testify; and is subject to cross-examination.[59] Woolsey was operating in a more informal atmosphere, and no objection was made to his consultation. Interestingly, both Merrill and Canby were fellow members of Woolsey's in the Century Association.[60] Woolsey's carefully hedged report avoided the question whether and to what extent any of the three had been stimulated to lustful thoughts in the course of duty. Instead, the report was that 'in its entirety' the 'net effect' of *Ulysses* was not 'to excite sexual impulses or lustful thoughts'. Woolsey added that '... whilst in many places the effect of Ulysses on the reader undoubtedly is somewhat emetic, nowhere does it tend to be an aphrodisiac.'

Woolsey's favourable decision was vulnerable to the argument that, whatever the 'net effect' of *Ulysses*, it contained specific passages that were obscene, and the book thus ran afoul of the statute under the traditional *Hicklin* rule. There were other bases for challenging Woolsey's decision on appeal. He had also departed from *Hicklin* in substituting '*l'homme moyen sensuel*' for 'those most susceptible' as the barometer of obscenity, and had ignored precedent by considering the opinion of critics as to *Ulysses'* literary merit on the question of its obscenity.

Although all of the above issues were subject to appellate review, Ernst's files suggest that the prosecution was not inclined to appeal Woolsey's decision.[61] However, following Franklin Roosevelt's election as president, the Republican United States Attorney George Medalie resigned. His replacement, Martin Conboy, who, as noted above, was a former officer of the New York Society for the Suppression of Vice, seized this opportunity to preserve the fruits of Sumner's victory over Quinn. Sumner had greeted Woolsey's opinion by branding it 'a literary review trying to explain away the appearance of admitted obscenity and filth'.[62] Conboy agreed, and sought permission to appeal from the solicitor general, a presidential appointee who oversees the government's appellate litigation. The solicitor general appointed by Roosevelt in May 1933 was James Crawford Biggs, who had suffered a 'series of stumbles' as the government's advocate in the Supreme Court before resigning in March 1935.[63] His decision permitting an appeal was based on a memorandum by the Assistant Attorney General in charge of the Criminal Division, Joseph B. Keenan, a graduate of Brown and Harvard Law School, who would soon gain a national reputation prosecuting the notorious bank robber and kidnapper Machine Gun Kelly, and was later chief prosecutor in the International Military Tribunal in the Far East following World War II.

Keenan's memorandum shows how a legal judgment as to whether a book is obscene can be affected by the reader's perception of the book's literary merit. His analysis began with the observation – likely shared by many readers – that 'the book is very hard to read, [and] seems to have little if any plot ...' Turning the '*Ulysses* is too obscure to excite' argument on its head, Keenan posited that *Ulysses* 'depends for its success, if it may be deemed to be successful, upon the filthy, obscene and coarse matter contained in its pages, which appears to make it popular with certain elements of the American public'. Keenan thought the book obscene 'unless it is lifted out of such class by its artistic attainments'. On that point, he believed that *Ulysses* had not attained 'a position in the field of literature' capable of lifting it out of the class of the legally obscene.[64] Thus an appeal was authorized because Keenan was not impressed by Joyce's accomplishments as a writer.

Conboy's brief to the Second Circuit argued that Woolsey had erred by disregarding *Hicklin* in all the respects enumerated above, and asserted that a mere reading of the book established its obscenity under the *Hicklin* test.[65] Interestingly, in view of the fact that Keenan's authorization of the appeal turned on his view of the quality of Joyce's writing, Conboy's brief argued that it was revers-ible error for Woolsey to have considered the 'literary importance' of the work on the question of obscenity. Finally, recognizing the importance of Woolsey's reliance on Joyce's truthfulness, Conboy argued that a 'book that is obscene is not rendered less so by reason of the fact that the matter complained of is in fact truthful'.[66] Ernst's brief essentially repeated his written submissions to Woolsey.

At oral argument Conboy condemned the book as 'filthy, offen-sive to modesty, [and] subversive of decency',[67] spending hours reading allegedly offending passages aloud, with emphasis on the concluding forty-six pages consisting of, as the *New York Herald Tribune* put it, 'the stream-of-thought soliloquizing of Mrs. Molly Bloom'.[68] The *New York World-Telegram* depicted Conboy 'blushing, stammering, rocking nervously on his heels' as he read twenty-five offending passages, while the three judges 'looked solemn'.[69] Asked if he was going to read the whole book, Conboy promised 'a generous sampling'.[70]

Conboy had no trouble convincing one of the three judges, his old colleague on the Committee for Relief in Ireland, Martin Manton, whose dissenting opinion rhetorically inquired, 'Who can doubt the obscenity of this book after a reading of the pages referred to, which are too indecent to add as a footnote to this opinion?'[71] Manton, who was appointed to the District Court in New York in 1916 at age thirty-six, and to the Second Circuit two years later, had proceeded directly to Columbia Law School from public schools in Sayville, Long Island. He put himself through law school by working nights and weekends.[72] After a long and influential judicial career, he was convicted of bribery in 1939 for soliciting and accepting bribes of $664,000 (more than $11 million in today's dollars) from litigants in cases pending before him.[73] Manton's opinion sounded unattributed echoes of Plato's rationale for banning poets from his ideal state. For example, his pronounce-ment that 'the court cannot indulge any instinct it may have to foster letters' is reminiscent of Plato's banning of poets, as is his rationale that 'the statute is designed to protect society at large ... [and thus] notwithstanding the deprivation of benefits to a few, a work must be condemned if it has a depraving influence'.

Fortunately for Joyce and his readers, the two other members of the panel were Learned Hand, who had questioned the soundness of the *Hicklin* rule twenty years previously in *Kennerley*, and his cousin Augustus Hand, judges of robust intellect and trenchant pen. The *Ulysses* case presented Learned Hand as an appellate judge with exactly the occasion he had hoped for when, as a district judge, constrained by *Hicklin* from dismissing the indictment against Kennerley, he questioned 'whether in the end men will regard that as obscene which is honestly relevant to the adequate expression of innocent ideas, and whether they will not believe that truth and beauty are too precious to society at large to be mutilated in the interests of those most likely to pervert them to base uses'.[74]

Learned Hand's private memorandum to his fellow judges in the *Ulysses* case, now available in the Harvard Law School library, provides unvarnished insight into his thinking as he approached the oral argument. The core of his view was that, while some passages of the novel

> could excite lustful feelings ... [,] there are themes whose truthful and complete expression involves what taken alone ought to have no immunity ... [and in the case of *Ulysses*] the offending passages are clearly necessary to the epic of the soul as Joyce conceived it, and the parts which might be occasion for lubricity in the reader are to my thinking not sufficient to condemn a very notable contribution to literature.[75]

Both Hands agreed that Woolsey's decision should be affirmed, but placed on a more solid legal footing, preferably in language that, unlike Woolsey's colourful prose, which Cerf had published as a preface to the Random House *Ulysses*, could not be mined for quotable phrases. Recognizing that Learned's vigorous imagination was incapable of producing an opinion devoid of quotable phrasing, they agreed that Augustus would write the affirmance.[76] Years later, reminiscing in his late eighties, Learned Hand remarked that Woolsey was 'a bit of a show-off ... given to phrases'. In an interesting observation on the relation of law and literature, Hand noted that Woolsey thought himself 'literary', adding 'that's a very dangerous thing for a judge to be. I didn't say it was a *bad* quality; I said it was a dangerous one', fine if a judge is 'brilliant' and exhibits 'a complete aptness for the occasion'.[77]

Judge Learned Hand. (Copyright Corbis)

Augustus Hand's published opinion for the majority rationalized affirmance of the District Court in terms of existing legal precedent and framed general principles to govern future cases. In view of the heated dissent filed by Manton, Augustus Hand succumbed to the need to write convincingly and, thus, quotably. Reflecting appreciation for Woolsey's reliance on Joyce's technique, his opinion begins by identifying Joyce 'as a pioneer of the "stream of consciousness" method of presenting fiction', which 'attempts to depict the thoughts and lay bare the souls of a number of people ... with a literalism that leaves nothing unsaid'. Hand's description of the text highlights its truth and beauty: 'it seems', he wrote, 'to be sincere, truthful, relevant to the subject, and executed with real art'.

Then, in one of those touches that makes judging an art, Hand brought *Ulysses* within a line of precedents that permitted a greater range of sexual reference in scientific works by framing 'the question before us' as 'whether such a book of artistic merit *and scientific insight* should be regarded as "obscene" within section 305(a) of the Tariff Act (emphasis added)'. Molly would have been proud to see her insight lauded as scientific. Significantly, Hand's recognition of the novel's 'scientific insight' focused on Joyce's truthfulness as a counterpart to what the opinion recognized as Joyce's 'artistic merit'. These twin aspects of the book are captured in the opinion's observation that Joyce's novel 'is a sincere portrayal with skillful artistry of the "streams of consciousness" of his characters'.

Characterizing his decision in *United States v. Dennett* as holding that 'works of physiology, medicine, science and sex instruction are not within the statute, though to some extent and among some persons they may tend to promote lustful thoughts', Hand concluded that 'we think the same immunity should apply to literature as to science, where the presentation, when viewed objectively, is sincere, and the erotic matter is not introduced to promote lust and does not furnish the dominant note of the publication'.[78] In finding that *Ulysses* was entitled to such immunity,

Hand emphasized the book's 'evident truthfulness in its depiction of certain types of humanity'.

Hand's recognition that society could no more thrive without truthful works of fiction than without truthful works of science transformed the law of obscenity. His equation of literature and science in a formula with truth at its core provided an encouraging answer to Ezra Pound's lament over Joyce's earlier inability to find a publisher for *A Portrait of the Artist as a Young Man*: 'If we can't write plays, novels, poems or any other conceivable form of literature with the scientist's freedom and privilege, with at least the chance of at least the scientist's verity, then where in the world have we got to, and what is the use of anything, *anything*?'[79]

Tacitly recognizing that his approach was contrary to *Hicklin* and *Bennett*, Hand looked to the New York Court of Appeals decision in *Halsey v. New York Society for Suppression of Vice* – the case decided by the New York Court of Appeals about the time an appeal from Anderson and Heap's conviction would have been heard had Quinn appealed – as reflecting the correct standard that a work should be judged as a whole, and not on the basis of isolated passages, and that 'the proper test of whether a given book is obscene is its dominant effect'. In this context, Hand found that while it could not be doubted 'that numerous long passages in *Ulysses* contain matter that is obscene under any fair definition of the word … yet they are relevant to the purpose of depicting the thoughts of the characters and are introduced to give meaning to the whole, rather than to promote lust or portray filth for its own sake', and thus the book as a whole was not within the statutory prohibition. Reflecting his careful attention to Conboy's long quotations from Molly's monologue, Hand found that the 'net effect even of the portions most open to attack, such as the closing monologue of the wife of Leopold Bloom, is pitiful and tragic, rather than lustful'. Hand showed that he had also attended to Ernst's 'incomprehensibility' argument, but did not find it determinative. 'Page after page of the book is, or seems to be, incomprehensible', he wrote, but the important point for him was that 'many passages show the trained hand of the artist'.

Hand created an important role for literary critics in applying the 'dominant effect' test by holding that persuasive evidence of the dominant effect included, in addition to relevancy of the objectionable parts to the theme, 'the established reputation of the work in the estimation of approved critics ...' Literature and law thus coalesce to enable great works of the mind to find their audience. Opening the courtroom door to literary critics eliminated the anomaly of the rickety two-tiered structure created by the stringent general prohibition of all erotic matter with a jerry-built exception for 'classics'. Ernst's brief had tried to bring *Ulysses* within the traditional exception for classics, and supported his argument by pointing to the fact that he had obtained permission from the Secretary of the Treasury to import a copy of *Ulysses* under a provision of the Tariff Act of 1930 that, as construed by the customs authorities, permitted the Secretary to allow entry to a copy of a classic for personal use by the applicant.[80] Hand's opinion, however, wisely ignored Ernst's invitation to create a separate rule for classics. Instead, while adverting to *Ulysses* as 'a sort of contemporary classic', Hand established a standard and procedure sufficiently capacious to apply uniformly to all books. The trier of fact would assess the 'dominant effect' of the book, without regard to the particular susceptibilities of those most open to potential depravity, and, in doing so, could consider the views of critics both favourable and unfavourable. By explicitly recognizing the traditional exception for 'classics' and broadening it to include all works of literary value, Hand's opinion had the effect of encouraging the work of new authors by facilitating their access to a wide audience.

The admission of critical opinion as to an allegedly obscene work's literary merit was an important development in the law of obscenity. It came about because Woolsey and the Hands were convinced that the cases precluding such evidence were wrongly decided. Ernst and Cerf's stratagem of attaching copies of favourable reviews to the book that was imported and became the subject of the action under the Tariff Act was irrelevant to this important development in the law.[81] Contrary to Birmingham's suggestion that the presence of the opinions permitted Ernst to 'base arguments on them',[82] their mere presence did not make them relevant or admissible evidence, either for the truth of their contents, or simply for the fact that the various critics held these opinions. Ernst could have as easily brought them in his briefcase. It took the Second Circuit's changes in the law of obscenity and the rules of evidence to make the opinions admissible and probative.

Hand's opinion forthrightly conceded

> that numerous long passages in Ulysses contain matter that is obscene under any fair definition of the word cannot be gainsayed; yet they are relevant to the purpose of depicting the thoughts of the characters and are introduced to give meaning to the whole, rather than to promote lust or portray filth for its own sake.

With characteristic candour, Hand recognized that his entire approach broke new ground. 'It is argued,' he said, 'that United States v. Bennett ... stands in the way of what has been said, and it certainly does'. Observing that *Bennett* and *Hicklin* 'would exclude much of the great works of literature and involve an impracticability that cannot be attributed to Congress', the Hands exercised their power as appellate judges to overrule *Bennett*, thus consigning *Hicklin* to the museum of discarded Victorian ideas and unburdening society from the leash identified by Learned Hand two decades earlier when he wrote in *Kennerley* that 'to put thought in leash to the average conscience of the time is perhaps tolerable, but to fetter it by the necessities of the lowest and least capable seems a fatal policy'.[83]

Judge Manton's dissent portrayed the majority decision as elevating 'the benefits and pleasures derived from letters by those who pose as the more highly developed and intelligent' over the 'protection of the morals of the susceptible', among whom he counted 'the average less sophisticated member of society ...'[84] The elitism inherent in the judiciary's taking it upon itself to 'protect' certain categories of readers from the benefit of what many others regarded as great literature seems to have been lost on Manton.[85]

Augustus Hand concluded his *Ulysses* opinion on a note that, echoing Woolsey's emphasis on the experimental nature of Joyce's writing, stressed the retarding effect on cultural growth of an overly 'protective' approach to the law of obscenity. 'Art', he cautioned, 'cannot advance under compulsion to traditional forms, and nothing in such a field is more stifling to progress than limitation of the right to experiment with a new technique.' Whereas Quinn had believed – and harmfully conceded to the court – that Joyce had pushed his experiment too far, Hand declared it a fundamental precept governing the relation of law and literature that law must avoid stifling experimentation in literature.

This historic determination that literature is entitled to a qualified immunity from the law of obscenity validated at last the ideas of Margaret Anderson, Jane Heap and John Butler Yeats. The notion that literature could not be obscene was Anderson's bedrock belief, and the Hands' reliance on the value of truthfulness in literature sounded the characteristic note of JBY. Heap's essay 'Art and the Law' had blended the claims of both truth and beauty in support of her conclusion that the only question the law could properly pose to *Ulysses* was 'Is it literature?' As to truth, Heap argued simply 'girls lean back everywhere'; as for beauty, she insisted it is the artist who creates love.

The *Ulysses* opinion was not as absolute as Anderson and Heap would have wanted. It contained the qualifications that literature's immunity applied only where 'the presentation, when viewed objectively, is sincere and the erotic matter is not introduced to promote lust and does not furnish the dominant note of the publication'.

The United States Supreme Court would eventually refine to a minimum – but not totally eliminate – these qualifications. Even given the qualifications on literature's immunity, however, the Hands' focus on the truth and beauty of *Ulysses* as literature fundamentally altered the law of obscenity, and vindicated one of the ideas on which *The Little Review* was founded, Anderson's belief, as stated in her inaugural 'Announcement', 'that all beautiful things make a place for themselves sooner or later in the world'.

Hand's opinion for the Second Circuit was not necessarily the last word. Conboy vigorously urged the Department of Justice to petition the United States Supreme Court to grant a writ of *certiorari* to review the Second Circuit's decision, and expressed his confidence that if discretionary review were granted, the Court would reverse.[86] In a memorandum concurred in by Assistant Attorney General Keenan, who had authorized the appeal to the Second Circuit, career attorney Harry S. Ridgely recommended to Solicitor General Biggs that Supreme Court review not be sought.[87] His conclusion was that 'unless the Government is prepared to insist that the obscenity of a book or publication is to be determined by the obscenity of any particular passage of such a book or publication, ... we could not succeed in reversing the judgment below even though we ...' convinced the Court to review the Hands' decision. The implication that such an argument would not succeed is reinforced by Ridgely's observation that '[o]ne reading the carefully prepared and exhaustive brief of the claimant [Random House] is not surprised at the holding of the Circuit Court of Appeals'.

Logic, and perhaps the vigour of Conboy's recommendation, suggested that Ridgely also address the question whether the Supreme Court would review the case at all. Based on a highly technical and detailed analysis of *Hicklin* and *Bennett*, Ridgely concluded that, although those decisions had said that an allegedly obscene book should not be considered as a whole, the precise facts of those cases were not inconsistent with permitting the trier of fact to consider the work as a whole, and that therefore Woolsey's decision was merely a determination of fact, and the Supreme Court would not review the Second Circuit's affirmance of a finding of fact. In this highly abstract universe, it seemed to Ridgely that 'the question presented cannot be characterized as one of gravity or one of general importance'. Whether by accident or design, Ridgely's memorandum did not take into account that in the real world courts had long been acting on their understanding that *Bennett* and *Hicklin* meant what they said, and that the Second Circuit's opinion had expressly overruled *Bennett*, consigned *Hicklin* to the dustbin, changed the test for measuring obscenity, and authorized reliance on expert testimony by scholars and critics on the question whether a book was obscene. The ever-vigilant John Sumner had no doubt of the need to reverse the Second Circuit's decision. His view, as conveyed by letter to the Solicitor of the Post Office Department, was that 'certainly if the decision of the Circuit Court of Appeals stands it is difficult to know what book may be successfully prosecuted under the Federal law for obscenity'.[88] Sumner's letter did not alter the decision of Solicitor General Biggs, endorsed on Ridgely's memorandum: 'No certiorari.' Thus did *Ulysses*' turbulent voyage through the courts come to an end. Sumner lamented this reversal of the triumph he had achieved over Quinn a decade earlier, writing to Keenan that 'the good old American fighting spirit is lacking when the Department fails to follow up on a hard-won partial victory ...'[89]

Ernst's forceful use of literary criticism was a critical factor in turning the tables. This is apparent from the fact that Augustus Hand was more receptive to Ernst's vigorous arguments in support of *Ulysses* than he had been to Quinn's moralistic defence of 'Cantleman's Spring-Mate'. While it is true that 'a decade of sustained onslaught on social prudery of all kinds'[90] preceded Hand's *Ulysses* decision, that assault was well underway by the time of Cantleman in 1917. Learned Hand's opinion in *Kennerley* in 1913 shows that the judiciary was then open to a forceful argument based on a literary work's truth and beauty. That argument could have prevailed for Lewis in 1917 and for Joyce in 1921 had Quinn had the wisdom and courage to advance it.

Quinn's biographer cites approvingly Jackson Bryer's statement that Ernst's arguments in defence of *Ulysses* 'were not very different from those of John Quinn'.[91] This reflects a fundamental misunderstanding. Although JBY had handed Quinn the argument that Joyce's veracity enhanced humanity's ability to live more deeply in fuller understanding of itself, Quinn failed to advance that argument. Conversely, Ernst argued forcefully that Joyce banished darkness and taint by carrying the torch of truth into the murky chambers of the human mind. Moreover, while Ernst presented *Ulysses* as one of the most significant and beautiful works of our time,[92] Quinn ran away from the beauty of Joyce's prose, and denigrated it as a failed experiment. Bryer cautiously says that Quinn 'suggested ... the literary excellence' of *Ulysses*.[93] This is true, but Quinn abandoned the argument the moment it met judicial scepticism, and never developed a record or forced an appellate determination on the point that *Ulysses*' beauty and truth as literature were a defence to its asserted obscenity. To the contrary, an appeal would have been doomed by Quinn's concession that Joyce's 'strong, hard filth' rescued him from 'the devotion to art of a soft flabby man like Wilde'. The other ground of similarity instanced by Bryer – the work's 'probable effect on the reader'[94] – simply underscores how different Quinn's approach was from Ernst's. Although neither was able to resist the argument that the book was too obscure to excite, they differed fundamentally on its effect on those who engaged with its difficulty. Whereas Quinn argued that Joyce's 'filth' would act as a deterrent to certain kinds of sexual conduct, Ernst lauded Joyce's prose as the 'torch of truth'.

Ernst's commitment to freedom of expression contrasted sharply with Quinn's deeply ingrained and culturally reinforced reluctance to be identified as a champion of sex literature, and this difference affected the arguments they made and the results they achieved. Did differences in educational background contribute to these different approaches and results? Significantly, Quinn had only one year of undergraduate education, while Ernst studied at a liberal arts college that featured the kind of education the American Academy of Arts and Sciences credits with 'emphasizing critical perspective and imaginative response' and developing 'inquisitiveness, perceptiveness, the ability to put a received idea to a new purpose, and the ability to share and build ideas with a diverse world of others'.[95]

A liberal education's focus on the value of beauty and truth is particularly apparent in the study of literature. As suggested by Judge Richard Posner – a Yale English major and a great exemplar of the fertile impact of literature on the legal mind – literature is a fruitful component of a judge's education 'because of its effects in stretching students' imaginations, multiplying their perspectives, broadening their intellectual and emotional horizons, offering them a range of vicarious experiences, and assisting them to read difficult texts, express complex thoughts, and write and speak correctly, fluently and persuasively'.[96] No one knew or exemplified this better than Judge Learned Hand, who observed that in cases presenting issues about societal values

> it is as important that a judge ... have a bowing acquaintance with Acton and Maitland, with Thucydides, Gibbon, and Carlyle, with Homer, Dante, Shakespeare and Milton, with Machiavelli, Montaigne and Rabelais, with Plato, Bacon, Hume and Kant, as with the books which have been specifically written on the subject ... for in such matters everything turns upon the spirit in which the question is approached.[97]

Posner and Hand represent two particular ways of expressing the general idea that an education in the humanities fosters a humane approach to the development of the law.

Although Quinn was a serious reader and a connoisseur of art, he approached the law as a series of rules existing independently of the body of ideas developed in a university education. Quinn's 16 October 1920 letter to Pound reflects his belief that the law consists of a series of fixed and isolated precepts. He insists that there is a clear 'law' that governs the situation of *Ulysses*, that he knows what that law is, and that the way for the law to be changed is through legislation brought about by a change in public opinion.[98] Indeed, Quinn is so certain that nothing more is at stake than application of existing law to *The Little Review* that he hectors Pound that 'if you should get the idea into your head that there is any principle involved in this thing, or that the freedom of literature is at stake, ... then I have nothing more to say'.[99]

Quinn's way of thinking about *Ulysses* reflects the way law was taught at Georgetown when he received his initial legal education. No undergraduate education was required as a prerequisite, and classes presented the law as a series of rules to be memorized. Professors assigned passages from a textbook to students in advance of class 'which the student is expected to master as thoroughly as he can before the recitation hour', following which the 'lecturer then goes over the ground covered by the text, explaining what is obscure or difficult ...'[100] This kind of legal education, which fostered Quinn's approach to *Ulysses*, differed sharply from a competing approach that located law school within the university as a whole and employed a methodology, the case method, that was based on the idea that existing legal precedents can be 'read in light of the dominant and emergent values of the pertinent culture' to yield a governing principle that should apply at the time and place of decision.[101]

Ironically, it was the introduction of this competing approach at Columbia University that led to the creation of the law school attended by the three New York Court of General Sessions judges whom Quinn denigrated as 'stupid'. All three were graduates of New York Law School, an institution – not to be confused with New York University School of Law – founded in 1891 by the erstwhile leaders of the Columbia Law School to escape what they regarded as the 'Harvardizing' of Columbia, and to continue teaching law as a series of rules as it had been taught at Columbia and as Quinn learned it at Georgetown.[102] One of the principal aspects of 'Harvardizing' to which they objected was the integration of a practice-oriented law school into the academic setting of a university. The new president of Columbia, Seth Low, incurred their enmity by following the example of Harvard, which, under the leadership of Dean Christopher Columbus Langdell in the 1870s, had required an undergraduate degree as a prerequisite to admission to law school, expanded the programme from two years to three, and made the study of law an academic discipline rather than a programme of practical training.[103] While the longtime dean of Columbia Law School, Theodore Dwight, thought of legal education as a means of training practitioners, Low defined it in scholarly and academic terms.[104] Low's views were reflected in the observation of one of the reformers, Nicholas M. Butler, that 'the student who lives in an atmosphere of literature, art, science and philosophy can hardly pursue his professional course in an unthinking and routine way'.[105]

The founders of New York Law School also objected to Low's insistence on introducing to Columbia the case method of teaching law that had been pioneered by Langdell at Harvard. Whereas Langdell maintained that the proper method of learning law was to require students to distill governing principles from judicial opinions by the inductive method, the founders of New York Law School wanted to continue using the so-called Dwight method, employed at Columbia during Dwight's thirty-three years as dean, in which students learned a series of legal principles by reading textbooks.

Judge Benjamin Cardozo, one of the giants of the American judiciary, a member of the majority in the *Halsey* decision that reformed the New York law of obscenity, and author of the seminal 1925 article 'Law and Literature', was a student at Columbia when the case method replaced the Dwight approach.[106] Cardozo praised the new method, writing that 'no longer did the student

learn by rote out of a text book some hasty and imperfect generalization, swallowed whole as it was given him ...' Rather, 'with
the cases themselves before him, he analyzed the facts, dissected
the reasoning, criticized the conclusion'.[107] This approach was
fundamentally different from the slavish application of fixed rules
reflected in Quinn's letter to Pound about *Ulysses*.

To be sure, Quinn was exposed to the case method at Harvard
Law School, where his two years coincided with two of Learned
Hand's three years.[108] Conversely, Ernst was a graduate of New
York Law School, an institution founded to resist the case method.
Nonetheless, Quinn's first experience of legal education at Georgetown, which emphasized rote learning of so-called 'black letter law',
is consistent with his approach to the question of *Ulysses*' alleged
obscenity. Ernst's creativity and ability to put a received idea to a
new purpose survived the 'law as a received text' approach of his
legal education. Ernst readily accepted Learned Hand's suggestion
in *Kennerley* that lawyers should lead what Ernst's brief in *Ulysses*
called 'the salutary forward march of our courts' to 'liberalize the
law of obscenity and to thrust back the narrow frontiers fixed by
prudery'.[109] These admittedly limited facts suggest that perceiving
law as part of what Columbia reformer Nicholas M. Butler called
an 'atmosphere of literature, art, science and philosophy' inculcates
qualities of mind conducive to effective advocacy, but it matters little
whether that education occurs in law school or elsewhere. Certainly
the atmosphere described by Butler permeates Ernst's briefs and
Woolsey's and Hand's opinions, but is sorely missing from Quinn's
approach to the case. The federal decisions in the *Ulysses* cases are a
testament to the ability of lawyers and judges to apply pre-existing
precedent to new situations on the basis of core principles like the
societal importance of beauty and truth.

NOTES

1   Beach 201.

2   Alden Whitman, 'Morris Ernst, "Ulysses" Case Lawyer, Dies', *New York Times* (23 May 1976) 40 ('Whitman'); Morris Ernst, *A Love Affair with the Law* (New York: Macmillan, 1968) 28–30; Mark C.N. Sullivan, 'Never on Sunday', *University of New Hampshire Magazine* (Spring 1912).

3   Morris Ernst and Alexander Lindey, *The Censor Marches On* (New York: Da Capo Press, 1971) ("Censor") 235.

4   Whitman.

5   Lindey's memo is reprinted in a useful compendium of Ernst's files and related documents in Michael Moscato and Leslie LeBlanc, eds, *The United States of America v. One Book Entitled Ulysses By James Joyce, Documents and Commentary – a 50-Year Retrospective* (Frederick: University Publications of America, 1984) ('Documents') 77. The original Ernst firm files are located at the Harry Ransom Center for the Humanities at the University of Texas ('HRC').

6   *Id.*

7   Beach printed the contract in Beach 203.

8   Documents 98–100.

9   *Id.*

10 *Id.*

11 Documents 142–4.

12 Documents 98–100.

13 Keri Walsh, ed., *The Letters of Sylvia Beach* (New York: Columbia University Press, 2010) 136.

14 Documents 100.

15 HRC.

16 Documents 101.

17 Beach 204–5; Fitch 322–3. See also Joyce letter of 17 December 1931 to Harriet Shaw Weaver, in Richard Ellmann, ed., *Selected Letters of James Joyce* (New York: Viking, 1975) ('Selected Letters') 358–9. Spoo provides the context in detail at 193–232. Colum, a prolific Irish novelist, poet and dramatist, who had known Joyce since their days using the National Library in Dublin, was one of his closest friends in Paris.

18 *Id.*

19 Documents 108.

20 19 U.S.C. §1305. Reference in the *Ulysses* decisions to the terms 'libel' and 'libellant' arises from the fact that, by analogy to the name of the initial pleading in a proceeding in admiralty to seize a vessel, the proceeding to confiscate an obscene book seized by the customs authorities was called a 'libel'. Potter erroneously refers to the *Ulysses* case as 'a libel trial'. Obscene Modernism at 133.

21 Bennett Cerf, *At Random* (New York: Random House, 1977) ('Cerf') 92–3.

22 Forrest Davis, 'Judge Woolsey etc.', *New York World Telegram* (13 December 1933); Obituary, 'John M. Woolsey, Retired Jurist, 68', *New York Times* (5 May 1945) 15.

23 John M. Woolsey, Jr, 'Judge John M. Woolsey', *James Joyce Quarterly*, Vol. 37, No. 3/4 (Spring/Summer 2000) 363–70.

24 Ernst to Alexander Lindey office memorandum, 12 August 1932 (Documents 158).

25 *United States v. One Obscene Book Entitled 'Married Love'*, 48 F.2d 821 (S.D.N.Y. 1931).

26 *United States v. Dennett*, 39 F.2d 564 (2d Cir. 1930).

27 *United States v. One Book Entitled 'Contraception,' by Marie C. Stopes*, 51 F.2d 525 (S.D.N.Y. 1931).

28 Morris Ernst, Preface in Marie Stopes, *Enduring Passion* (Garden City: Blue Ribbon Books, 1931) xix–xx. Spoo draws attention to Ernst's preface in an unpublished paper generously provided to the author.

29 See, e.g., Michael Groden, *Ulysses in Progress* (Princeton: Princeton University Press, 1977) 77.

30 See Ch. 3, n. 2.

31 *Ulysses* 359.

32 Ellmann 519–30.

33 Fitch 94; Beach 57–8.

34 Letter of 16 August 1921 from Joyce to Frank Bugden (Selected Letters 285).

35 *Ulysses* 723–68.

36 The United States Attorney cited these passages in seeking permission from the Department of Justice to appeal the trial court's determination that *Ulysses* was not obscene. Martin Conboy, Letter to the Attorney General, 5 March 1934, File 97–51–7, Record Group 60, Department of Justice Files, National Archives, Washington, DC (quoted by Vanderham).

37   The compendium appears in Documents 227ss.

38   *Id.* at 433.

39   *Id.* at 235 *et seq.*

40   Letter of 14 September 1933 from Alexander Lindey to Bennett Cerf. Documents 230.

41   Documents 241.

42   *Id.* at 257.

43   *Id.* at 258.

44   *Id.* at 260.

45   *Id.* at 266.

46   See Ch. 2, n. 20.

47   *Halsey v. New York Society for the Suppression of Vice,* 234 N.Y. 1 (1922). See Ch. 4.

48   Documents 255.

49   *Id.* at 266.

50   *Id.* at 267.

51   Censor 235.

52   Documents 267, quoting Thomas Babington Macaulay, *Essay On Milton,* 1825, reprinted in Herbert Augustine Smith, ed., *Macaulay's Essays on Addison and Milton* (Boston: Athenaeum Press, 1902) 60.

53   Documents 267.

54   *United States v. One Book Called "Ulysses",* 5 F. Supp.182, 183–4 (S.D.N.Y. 1933).

55   Augustine Martin, 'Sin and Secrecy in Joyce's Fiction' in S. Bushrui and B. Benstock, eds, *James Joyce: An International Perspective* (Gerrard's Cross: Colin Smythe, 1982) 143, 155.

56   *Ulysses* 762.

57   Letter of 3 April 1935 from Ernst to Woolsey, and Woolsey's 4 April response, HRC, Ernst Papers, Box 36.3; and Jack Alexander, draft profile entitled 'Federal Judge' 15 (courtesy John M. Woolsey III). Birmingham, at 328, connects Judge Woolsey's letter to the draft profile.

58   Documents 317. Birmingham's diligent research has clarified Merrill's identity based on unpublished notes of John Woolsey, Jr. (Birmingham 327, 399.)

59   Federal Rules of Evidence 702 and 706.

60   The Century Association, *List of Members for the Year 1922* (New York: Knickerbocker Press, 1922); Yale University Library, *Guide to Henry Seidel Canby Papers.*

61 Documents 358.

62 John S. Sumner, quoted in *Censor* at 22.

63 Jeff Shesol, *Supreme Power* (New York: W.W. Norton, 2010) 94.

64 Joseph B. Keenan, 'Memorandum for the Solicitor General', 6 March 1934, File 07–51–7, Record Group 60, Department of Justice Files, National Archives, Washington, DC.

65 Documents 374 *et. seq.*

66 *Id.* at 375.

67 *New York Daily News* (17 May 1934).

68 *New York Herald Tribune* (17 May 1934).

69 *New York World Telegram* (16 May 1934).

70 *Id.*

71 *United States v. One Book Entitled Ulysses By James Joyce*, 72 F.2d 705 (2d. Cir.1934).

72 *New York Times* (16 August 1916); Borkin 28–9.

73 'Judge Manton is Convicted of Selling Justice', *New York Times* (4 June 1939) 1; Borkin at 80.

74 *United States v. Kennerley*, 209 Fed. 119, 120–1 (S.D.N.Y. 1913).

75 Learned Hand Papers, Harvard Law School Library, box 194, file 2. The memo is quoted in Gunther 337–8.

76 Gunther 338–9.

77 Gunther interview of Learned Hand, 1957–9, quoted in Gunther 338.

78 Rachel Potter's *Obscene Modernism* misidentifies the author of the Second Circuit's opinion in *Dennett* as Learned, rather than Augustus Hand, and overstates its import by saying that it effectively overruled *Hicklin* and *Bennett* by holding that '[r]ather than deciding on whether a portion of a work could be considered obscene, ... the work be evaluated as a whole'. (Obscene Modernism 38) That landmark event did not occur until four years later in the *Ulysses* case.

79 Ezra Pound, 'Meditatio', *Egoist*, No. 3 (1 March 1916) 37–8.

80 The ruling was quoted in Ernst's brief to the Second Circuit, Documents 401–2. The Collector of Customs' position is stated in Letter of Assistant Collector to Alexander Lindey, 31 January 1933, Ernst Collection Box 95, HRC.

81 Cerf 92.

82 Birmingham 304.

83 209 Fed. at 121.

84 72 F.2d at 711.

85 Learned Hand likely had Manton's critique in mind two years later when, writing for the majority in *United States v. Levine*, 83 F.2d 156, 157 (2d Cir. 1936), he noted that the *Hicklin* doctrine 'presupposed that the evil against which the statute is directed so much outweighs all interests of art, letters or science, that they must yield to the mere possibility that some prurient person may get a sensual gratification from reading or seeing what to most people is innocent and may be delightful and enlightening. No civilized community not fanatically puritanical would tolerate such an imposition, and we do not believe that the courts that have declared it, would ever have applied it consistently.'

86 Martin Conboy, Letter to Attorney General Homer S. Cummings, 31 August 1934, File 97–51–7, Record Group 60, Department of Justice Files, National Archives, Washington, DC. Vanderham's diligent research identified the pertinent documents in the National Archives.

87 Harry S. Ridgely, Memorandum for the Solicitor General, 10 September 1934, File 95–51–7, Record Group 60, Department of Justice Files, National Archives, Washington, DC.

88 John S. Sumner, Letter to Karl A. Crowley, 13 October 1934, File 95–51–7, Record Group 60, Department of Justice Files, National Archives, Washington, DC.

89 John S. Sumner, Letter to Joseph B. Keenan, 24 October 1934, File 95–51–7, Record Group 60, Department of Justice Files, National Archives, Washington, DC.

90 Eric Larrabee, 'The Cultural Context of Sex Censorship', 20 *Law and Contemporary Problems* (Autumn 1955) 672, 675.

91 MNY 455–6, citing Jackson Bryer, 'Joyce, *Ulysses*, and the *Little Review*', *The South Atlantic Quarterly*, 66 (Spring 1967) ('Bryer') 148.

92 Documents 240–2.

93 Bryer at 163.

94 *Id.*

95 American Academy of Arts and Sciences, *The Heart of the Matter* (Cambridge: American Academy of Arts and Sciences, 2013) 9, 32.

96 Posner 502.

97 Learned Hand, 'Sources of Tolerance' in Hand, *The Spirit of Liberty: Papers and Addresses* of *Learned Hand* (New York: Knopf, 1952) 81.

98 16 October 1920 Letter (see Ch. 2, n. 52) at 4, 6.

99 *Id.* at 6.

100 Georgetown University Law Center, *The First 125 Years: An Illustrated History of the Georgetown University Law Center* (Washington: Georgetown University Law Center, 1995) 19–20.

101 Paul Carrington, *Stewards of Democracy* (Boulder: Westview Press, 1999) 206.

102 James A. Wooten, 'Law School Rights: The Establishment of New York Law School, 1891–1897', N.Y.L. SCH. L. REV. 36 (1991) 337 ('Wooten'); 'Must the Law School Go,' *New York Times* (4 March 1891) 8.

103 LaPiana 88–9; 92–9.

104 Wooten 347.

105 Nicholas M. Butler, 'On Permitting Students to Take Studies in Professional School While Pursuing a Regular Undergraduate Course', 3 Educ. Rev. 54, 56 (1892).

106 Andrew L. Kaufman, *Cardozo* (Cambridge: Harvard University Press, 1998) ('Kaufman') 29–50; and Benjamin Cardozo, 'Law and Literature', *Yale Review* (July 1925), reprinted in Cardozo, *Law and Literature* (New York: Harcourt Brace, 1931).

107 Benjamin Cardozo, 'Modern Trends in Law', Andrew L. Kaufman Papers, Harvard Law School, quoted in Kaufman 49–50.

108 Quinqennial Catalogue 61, 111.

109 Document 239.

7 The Impact of the *Ulysses* Decisions

The broad implications of the *Ulysses* decisions are apparent from Judge Woolsey's joint appearance with Morris Ernst on 24 April 1935 at an exhibition of books that had been burned by the Nazis in May 1933.[1] Paul Boyer suggests that this conjunction of Woolsey and Ernst around Nazi-burned books reflected the fact that the '*Ulysses* decision, coming as the full magnitude of the Nazi attack on books unfolded, was widely seen as America's answer to Hitler's repressions.'[2] But the impulse to burn threatening books dies hard, and the photograph (p. 75) of John Sumner overseeing a conflagration of books was taken in November 1935. The full import of the ideas that drove the *Ulysses* decisions unfolded slowly.

In the legal realm, those ideas found fuller expression in the Supreme Court's 1957 ruling in *Roth v. United States,* 354 U.S. 476 (1957), a case that, ironically, reviewed the obscenity conviction of Samuel Roth, who had been pilloried by Joyce in 1927 as a 'pirate' for publishing an unauthorized *Ulysses.* The Supreme Court effectively held that the test of obscenity articulated in the Second Circuit's decision in *Ulysses* was required as a matter of constitutional law. Justice Brennan's opinion for the Court seemed to uphold the traditional view that the First Amendment to the Constitution does not protect obscenity, which he characterized as being 'utterly without redeeming social importance'. However, Brennan made clear that the First Amendment's protection of freedom of speech and press extends to the arts, and that, accordingly, 'portrayal of sex, e.g., in art, literature and scientific works is not itself sufficient reason to deny material the constitutional protection of freedom of speech and press ...' Against this background, Brennan's opinion ended the reign of *Hicklin* as a matter of constitutional law, thereby extending the reach of the *Ulysses* decisions to every court in the country. Citing the Second Circuit's *Ulysses* opinion as reflecting the constitutionally required standard for determining obscenity, Brennan held that the 'Hicklin test, judging obscenity by the effect of isolated passages upon the most susceptible persons, might well encompass material legitimately treating with sex, and so it must be rejected as unconstitutionally restrictive of the freedoms of speech and press.' A permissible test of obscenity, Brennan wrote, was 'whether to the average person, applying contemporary community standards, the dominant theme of the material taken as a whole appeals to prurient interest.'

Seven years later, in *Jacobellis v. Ohio*, 378 U.S. 184 (1964), Justice Brennan, writing for a plurality, but less than a majority, glossed his opinion in *Roth* by saying that it recognized

> that obscenity is excluded from the constitutional protection only because it is 'utterly without redeeming social importance,' and that ... [it] follows that material dealing with sex in a manner that advocates ideas ... or that has literary or scientific or artistic value or any other form of social importance, may not be branded as obscenity and denied the constitutional protection.

In short, so long as a book has an iota of literary value, it cannot be obscene. This formulation approximates Anderson and Heap's position that literature cannot be obscene.

In 1966, in *A Book Named 'John Cleland's Memoirs of a Woman of Pleasure' v. Attorney General*, 383 U.S. 413 (1966), Justice Brennan, again writing for a plurality of the Court, restated and clarified the evolving constitutional law of obscenity, holding that three elements must be satisfied in order to characterize a work as obscene: '(a) the dominant theme of the material taken as a whole appeals to a prurient interest in sex; (b) the material is patently offensive because it affronts contemporary community standards relating to the description or representation of sexual matters; and (c) the material is utterly without redeeming social value.' After enunciating this three-part test, the Court held that the Supreme Judicial Court of Massachusetts had erred by finding that the book at issue was obscene even though it possessed some social value. Brennan's plurality opinion for the United States Supreme Court held:

> The Supreme Judicial Court erred in holding that a book need not be 'unqualifiedly worthless before it can be deemed obscene.' A book cannot be proscribed unless it is found to be utterly without redeeming social value. This is so even though the book is found to possess the requisite prurient appeal and to be patently offensive. Each of the three federal constitutional criteria is to be applied independently; the social value of the book can neither be weighed against nor canceled by its prurient appeal or patent offensiveness.

Brennan's opinions in *Jacobellis* and *Memoirs* vindicated the views of Anderson, Heap, and John Butler Yeats that literature, by definition, was not obscene. Since literature has some social merit, a work of literature could not be said to be utterly without social merit, and thus could not be obscene. However, this vindication was limited by the fact that neither of Brennan's opinions spoke for a majority of the justices. In *Miller v. California*, 413 U.S. 15 (1973), a majority of justices forged a common definition of obscenity for the first time since *Roth*, and the definition was less protective of literature than Brennan's opinions in *Jacobellis* and *Memoirs*. The majority opinion by Chief Justice Burger traced the evolution of the test from

Roth to *Memoirs*, and after quoting the standard as announced in *Memoirs*, noted 'the sharpness of the break with Roth ... represented by the third element of the Memoirs test ...' Burger explained the difference between *Roth* and *Memoirs*, noting that while *Roth*

> presumed 'obscenity' to be 'utterly without redeeming social importance,' *Memoirs* required that to prove obscenity it must be affirmatively established that the material is 'utterly without redeeming social value.'

Burger concluded that even as the *Memoirs* plurality

> repeated the words of Roth, [it] produced a drastically altered test that called on the prosecution to prove a negative, i.e. that the material was 'utterly without redeeming social value' – a burden virtually impossible to discharge under our criminal standards of proof.

Burger's opinion formulated a new test for obscenity:

> (a) whether 'the average person, applying contemporary community standards' would find that the work, taken as a whole, appeals to the prurient interest [citation omitted], (b) whether the work depicts or describes, in a patently offensive way, sexual conduct specifically defined by the applicable state law, and (c) whether the work, taken as a whole, lacks serious literary, artistic, political, or scientific value.

This approach was later reaffirmed in *Ashcroft v. American Civil Liberties Union*, 535 U.S. 564 (2002).

In fashioning the definition of obscenity in this way, *Miller* re-affirmed the prurience and patent offensiveness elements of *Roth*, but explicitly disclaimed *Memoirs'* added requirement that the work be utterly without redeeming social value. In its place, *Miller* substituted a more lenient requirement that the entire work lack serious value. Thus, under *Miller*, even if a work has some – but short of 'serious' – social value, it may still be excluded from First Amendment protection, even though the original rationale in *Roth* for excluding obscenity from the scope of the First Amendment was that it lacked any redeeming social importance.

With respect to the first two elements of the test, *Miller* explained that the contemporary community standards were to be evaluated at the local level. The Court noted that

> these are essentially questions of fact, and our Nation is simply too big and too diverse for this Court to reasonably expect that such standards could be articulated for all 50 States in a single formulation, even assuming the prerequisite consensus exists ... It is neither realistic nor constitutionally sound to read the First Amendment as requiring that the people of Maine or Mississippi accept public depiction of conduct found tolerable in Las Vegas or New York City.

The implication that *Ulysses* could be obscene in some states is a reminder that the battle against censorship has not been finally won. Even so, the principles of the *Ulysses* decisions are still vibrant in *Miller*'s requirement that these standards are to be fashioned according to the average person, and the Court's later clarification that the third prong of the *Miller* test is governed by an objective standard (i.e. whether a reasonable person would find the work taken as a whole to have serious value).[3]

Even as modified by *Miller*, the constitutional law of obscenity continues to reflect the legacy of the *Ulysses* decisions by distinguishing literature from obscenity. This conceptual link among the *Ulysses*, *Roth* and *Miller* decisions is parallelled by the intriguing factual link arising out of the fact that both Samuel Roth and Marvin Miller, the defendants in these two classic obscenity cases, had, during the course of their careers, published unauthorized editions of *Ulysses*.[4]

Interestingly, none of the lawyers in the *Ulysses* case had cited the First Amendment as a limitation on the government's power to prosecute or seize allegedly obscene literature. Ernst had raised the point in the *Married Love* and *Contraception* cases, but did not assert it in *Ulysses*. Ezra Pound had urged on Quinn his view that obscenity statutes were 'unconstitutional from a Jeffersonian angle', but acceded to Quinn's disingenuous assertion that the New York City Municipal Court was not the place to raise a constitutional issue. As an experienced lawyer, Quinn had to know that it was necessary to raise the issue in the trial court in order to preserve it for appellate review. His preemptive decision that there would be no appeal took Pound's innovative argument off the table – and denied Anderson and Heap a hearing on their shared conviction that literature should not be subjected to regulation by courts, the core of the rationale that prevailed in the federal decisions in *Ulysses* – and thereby fundamentally altered the relationship between law and literature.

The *Ulysses* decisions had far-reaching practical consequences. The fact of *Ulysses'* publication itself caused powerful reverberations in the world of publishing. Joyce's novel was published in New York on 17 January 1934, just in time for Bennett Cerf to dispatch six copies to reach Joyce for his 2 February birthday,[5] much as copies of the Shakespeare and Company edition had been rushed from Dijon to Paris for his birthday in 1922.

Cerf was well aware of the copyright problem presented by Joyce's publication of *Ulysses* in 1922 without seeking copyright protection in the United States. He had written in 1931 that the text of *Ulysses* could not qualify for copyright in the United States.[6] Nonetheless, he was willing to trust in the continuing effectiveness of the 'trade courtesy' customs pursuant to which established publishers would not compete with the first publisher to make an arrangement to compensate a foreign author whose work was in the public domain in the United States.[7] Although renegade publishers could easily print a competing edition of *Ulysses*, Cerf had confidence in the traditional tactic of ostracizing the renegade with public shaming. His 26 December 1933 letter reminded a would-be competing publisher of *Ulysses* that when Roth reprinted Joyce's novel without authorization 'the wrath of all the critics and authors in America descended upon his head'.[8]

Copyright was not Cerf's only potential pitfall. Obscenity charges remained a very real possibility. Nonetheless, Cerf plunged ahead with publication immediately following the district court's judgment, even though the government had ninety days within which to appeal. He may have made the decision to go ahead at a time when it was thought that the government would not appeal, or he may simply have been willing to run the risk of a reversal in the Court of Appeals or in the Supreme Court. The risk of criminal prosecution was likely thought to be minimal, given the difficulty of proving intent to distribute an obscene book when the book at issue had been judicially determined not to be obscene. To capitalize on that fact, Cerf obtained Woolsey's concurrence in printing his opinion as a sort of preface to Joyce's novel. Cerf suggested to Woolsey that including the opinion would 'impress a number of self-appointed smut-hounds in various states sufficiently to keep them from taking any action against the book, and causing us petty annoyance for an indefinite period of time'.[9] In addition, there could be civil law consequences of unpredictable dimension, including the possibility of a recall, but even a final affirmance by the Second Circuit Court of Appeals would not remove the risk of legal action in any state court and in federal courts outside of the geographical boundaries of the Second Circuit, which is comprised of the New York, Connecticut and Vermont federal district courts. Waiting was unappealing from a business standpoint. Plunging ahead paid: Random House sold 35,000 copies in the interval between Woolsey's decision and its affirmance.[10]

The Second Circuit's affirmance paved the way to publication in England. Joyce had anticipated this cascading impact of a favourable decision in the United States. 'I suppose', he had written to Harriet Shaw Weaver of possible vindication in the United States, 'England will follow suit as usual a few years later. And Ireland 1000 years hence.'[11] In the same vein, when Joyce learned of Woolsey's decision in December 1933, he observed, 'Thus one half of the English speaking world surrenders. The other half will follow.'[12]

In fact, England did follow suit, but not without difficulty. Although T.S. Eliot, the Faber director who dealt with Joyce, was eager to publish a series of episodes in the *Criterion Miscellany*, he feared that publication of the entire book, as Joyce wanted, would result in prosecution.[13] Eliot's timidity in 1932 underscores the courage of Anderson and Heap in publishing unexpurgated Joyce beginning in 1918. Joyce responded to Eliot that he would not permit 'any authorities in either of Bull's islands to dictate to me what and how I am to write'.[14] Joyce's rationale for resisting expurgation was true to the principle that guided the favourable federal court decisions. As he explained to Sisley Huddleston:

> To consent would be an admission that the expurgated parts are not indispensable. The whole point about them is that they cannot be omitted. Either they are put in gratuitously without reference to my general purpose; or they are an integral part of my book. If they are mere interpolations, my book is inartistic; and if they are strictly in their place, they cannot be left out.[15]

After negotiating with several publishers, Joyce finally reached agreement with The Bodley Head for publication in 1936 of a deluxe edition of a thousand copies, which included Woolsey's decision. The British government obtained copies of the District Court and Court of Appeals decisions in the *Ulysses* case, and relied on them in deciding not to prosecute The Bodley Head for publishing *Ulysses*.[16] It is difficult to calculate with precision just when it became apparent that Joyce was wrong in predicting that it would take a thousand years for a change of *Ulysses*' status in Ireland. When the Irish Free State was established in 1922, the same year *Ulysses* was published in Paris, the new government carried over most English statutory law, including the Obscene Publications Act of 1857, which was glossed by the *Hicklin* definition of obscenity, and Section 42 of the Customs Consolidation Act of 1876, which authorized customs officials to seize and destroy obscene material.[17] Seven years into its existence, the new state adopted the Censorship of Publications Act of 1929, which, among other things, created a Censorship of Publications Board with power to prohibit the distribution of indecent publications in Ireland.[18] Although the introduction of censorship was a matter of concern to many Irish writers, Joyce, with typical aloofness, declined to involve himself.

W.B. Yeats tried unsuccessfully to persuade Joyce to become a member of the Irish Academy of Letters that he founded with George Bernard Shaw in 1932 to protect Irish writers from censorship. Knowing his quarry, Yeats invoked the name of Dante, whom JBY had identified as Joyce's master. Playing on Dante's reputed response to a request that he head a diplomatic delegation, Yeats entreated Joyce, 'Of course, the first name that seemed essential both to Shaw and myself was your own, indeed you might say of yourself as Dante said "if I stay, who goes, if I go who stays?" Which means that if you go out of our list it is an empty sack indeed.'[19] Joyce, while observing that 'it is now thirty years since you first held out to me your helping hand', declined. It was important to Joyce's concept of himself throughout his life that he was an exile from the Dublin that dominated his imagination. Thus, he loftily staked out his separate place: 'My case, however, being as it was and probably will be I see no reason why my name should have arisen at all in connection with such an Academy …'[20.] As it happened, *Ulysses* was never on the list of proscribed books maintained by the Censorship Board, probably because it was subject to a customs bar. Although the bar was allowed to lapse in the 1930s,[21] *Ulysses* remained a difficult commodity to purchase in Ireland for many years.[22]

In England, the reach of the ideas that powered the *Ulysses* decisions was not limited to the publication of Joyce's novel and the Home Office decision not to prosecute it. Parliament altered the law of obscenity in ways that made English law similar to the doctrines articulated in the *Ulysses* decisions. The Obscene Publications Act of 1959 eliminated the core of the *Hicklin* test by providing that obscenity must be determined by considering the work 'taken as a whole', rather than on the basis of isolated passages. Moreover, the

Act established a defence of 'public good' based on proof 'that publication of the article in question is justified as being for the public good on the ground that it is in the interest of science, literature, art or learning, or other objects of general concern'. The statute further provided that the 'opinion of experts as to the literary, artistic, scientific or other merits of an article may be admitted' to establish or negate the defence. The English statute thus approaches the question somewhat differently from the *Ulysses* decisions but reaches a similar result. Rather than declaring that literature is qualifiedly immune from the law of obscenity, it provides that a work may be obscene, but nonetheless publishable because it is literature. The statute is in accord with the *Ulysses* decisions in admitting expert opinion on the literary value of a work.

The change in English law, and the acceptance of the *Ulysses* decision in other American cases, had a profoundly liberating effect on English publishing. Allen Lane thought that 'if ever there was a test book' for the new English statute, it was *Lady Chatterley's Lover*, but hesitated to risk imprisonment. As his biographer recounts, the publication of *Chatterley* in America – which was declared not to be obscene in decisions that relied heavily on the *Ulysses* case – encouraged him to go forward: 'His decision to press ahead received a welcome boost' when *Chatterley* was published in New York; 'and, as with *Ulysses*, where America led, Lane might safely follow'.[23] Lane later testified that, 'the fact that the new Act was now on the Statute Book and that there had been a trial in America decided us this was a book we should now do'.[24]

The American trial to which Lane referred was the determination by the federal district court in New York that *Chatterley* could not be excluded from the US mails. In affirming the trial court's *Chatterley* decision, the Second Circuit Court of Appeals, in *Grove Press, Inc. v. Christenberry*, 276 F.2d 433 (2d Cir. 1960), characterized Judge Hand's *Ulysses* decision as 'probably the leading case on the subject' prior to the then-recent decisions of the Supreme Court, such as the *Roth* case. Reflecting the practical impact of Judge Hand's authorization of reliance on expert opinion in his *Ulysses* decision, the Second Circuit's opinion in the *Chatterley* case took pains to note at the outset that the book contains a 'prefatory letter of commendation by Archibald MacLeish, poet, playwright and Boylston Professor of Rhetoric and Oratory at Harvard University', and added that it also featured 'an extensive Introduction and a concluding Bibliographical Note by Mark Schorer, Professor of English Literature at the University of California and a Lawrence scholar'. The court accepted the Postmaster's findings that the book was 'replete with descriptions in minute detail of sexual acts' and that such 'descriptions utilize filthy, offensive and degrading words and terms', but disagreed with the Postmaster's approach of weighing such matter against the literary qualities of the book. Rather, the court followed and reiterated the approach of the two *Ulysses* opinions that the author's judgment as to how to carry out his or her artistic plan should not be the subject of judicial review. Pointedly, the court recognized that 'Lawrence could have omitted some of the passages found "smutty" by the Postmaster General and yet have produced an effective work of literature. But clearly it would not have been the book he planned, because for what he had in mind his selection was most effective, as the agitation and success of the book over the years have proven.'

The English trial that exonerated *Chatterley* on the other side of the Atlantic was a remarkable illustration of the impact of the change in the law that admitted literary criticism on the questions presented by the Obscene Publications Act. Indeed, the role of literary criticism was so central that the trial was described as 'probably the most thorough and expensive seminar on Lawrence's work ever given'.[25] As a reviewer of Penguin's publication of the trial transcript put it, such a seminar 'is precisely what the testimony was: a brilliant, provocative, highly sophisticated series of statements on the meaning of the book, its symbolism, Lawrence's intentions in writing it, its merit as a work of art, its place in English literature and in Lawrence's writings, and so on'.[26]

The *Chatterley* trial also put another, although hardly the final, nail in the coffin of John Quinn's patronizing view that what was permissible for upper-class males was not suitable for a broader public. The jury rejected the approach of the prosecutor's question in opening the case – 'Is it a book that you would even wish your wife or your servants to read?'[27]

At least initially, the *Ulysses* decision had more effect on law than literature. One of the most interesting features of *Ulysses*' encounter with the law is that the robust critical assessment of Joyce's achievement by Woolsey and the Hands was more enthusiastic than the reaction of many contemporary writers. Virginia Woolf, for example, famously found *Ulysses* 'underbred … the book of a self taught working man …' Later, before she herself adopted the idea of describing Mrs Dalloway's consciousness on a single day in June, she tepidly conceded that Joyce's novel had 'genius but of the inferior water'.[28] In her famous 1924 essay, 'Mr. Bennett and Mrs. Brown', Woolf qualified the application to Joyce of her declaration that a spectacular change occurred in human nature in December 1910 that required novelists to discard established tools and conventions of writing. While insisting that 'for us those conventions are ruin, those tools are death', she drew the line at what she regarded as Joyce's indecency. *Ulysses*, she said, 'seems to me the conscious and calculated indecency of a desperate man who feels that in order to breathe he must break the windows. At moments, when the window is broken, he is magnificent. But what a waste of energy!'[29]

Edmund Gosse thought Joyce 'a literary charlatan of the extremest order' and *Ulysses* 'infamous in taste, in style, in everything'.[30] Katherine Mansfield couldn't 'get over the feeling of wet linoleum and unemptied pails and far worse horrors in the house of his mind …'[31] Shaw called *Ulysses* 'a revolting record of a disgusting phase of civilization', albeit 'a truthful one'.[32] Edith Wharton branded it 'a welter of pornography (the rudest school-boy kind), and unformed and unimportant drivel'.[33]

D.H. Lawrence thought Molly Bloom's monologue 'the dirtiest, most indecent, obscene thing ever written'.[34] Lawrence's view of *Ulysses* arose out of his conviction that sex and excrement should not be mixed in literature. In his essay 'Pornography and Obscenity' he maintained that '[t]he sex functions and the excrementory functions in the human body' work closely together, yet are 'utterly different in direction', sex being 'a creative flow', whereas the excrementory tends toward 'dissolution, decreation ...'[35] Lawrence maintained that, '[I]n the really healthy human being the distinction between the two is instant' but 'in the degraded human being ... the two flows have become identical', with the result that 'sex is dirt and dirt is sex, and sexual excitement becomes a playing with dirt, ... [a]nd this is the source of all pornography'.[36] Compton Mackenzie, who sent Lawrence the portions of *Ulysses* that had appeared in *The Little Review*, reported that Lawrence was 'horrified by it' and said, 'This *Ulysses* muck is more disgusting than Casanova. I *must* show that it can be done without muck.'[37] Mackenzie wondered if Lady Chatterley and her lover were conceived at that moment – a thought perhaps suggested by the parallels between Molly's relationship with Bloom and Connie Chatterley's with Clifford.

In one way or another, Lawrence, Woolf, Gosse and Mansfield stood at different points along the continuum that W.B. Yeats had defined in an unpublished fragment probably written in 1913 as he thought about reactions of the public to various plays, including his own and those of John Synge: 'Great art, great poetic drama is the utmost of nobility and the utmost of reality ... If there is too much of the first all becomes sentimental, too much of the second all becomes sordid. Nobility struggles with reality, the eagle and the snake ...'[38] *Ulysses* had too much reality, particularly relating to the excretory functions of the human body, for many of Joyce's contemporaries, and certainly for Lawrence. This was probably the aspect of *Ulysses* that caused Judge Woolsey to find its effect 'somewhat emetic'. Judge Hand likely had this same aspect in mind when, using W.B. Yeats's word 'sordid', he wrote that '[t]he book depicts the souls of men and women that are by turn bewildered and keenly apprehensive, sordid and aspiring, ugly and beautiful, hateful and loving.' Hand's insight that the law should protect expression of the hateful and the sordid, as well as the loving and the aspiring, recognizes literature's duty, as Yeats put it in his 1907 address to the British Academy, to 'name and number the passions and motives of men', no matter how terrible.[39] There was no room in Yeats's aesthetic for Lawrence's fastidious abhorrence of excrement.

Given Yeats's broad understanding of the spectrum from the noble to the sordid, it is not surprising that he was an exception to the antipathy to *Ulysses* manifested by many other writers.[40] His comments on *Ulysses* show one capacious mind grasping the genius of another, despite a different view as to the proper balance between the noble and the sordid, and the obstacles presented by the formal novelty of Joyce's prose. For example, Yeats's letter of 27 July 1922 to Ezra Pound reports that

> I have read a great part of "Ulysses" and then gave myself a course of Trollope for a change and then just as I wanted to take up Ulysses again which I admire immensely, found my eyes out of sorts; this does not mean that I do not see the immense importance of the book, and it has been Trollope not it that destroyed my eyes. I read a few pages of Ulysses at a time as if he [*sic*] were a poem. Some passages have great beauty, lyric beauty, even in the fashion of my generation, and the whole book incites to philosophy.[41]

Thus Joyce found his way into the first edition of Yeats's philosophical book, *A Vision*, which, as Ellmann put it, relates *Ulysses* to the 'seemingly dissimilar writings of Pound, Eliot, and Pirandello' by identifying their shared characteristic of 'fragmenting an earlier unity of consciousness'.[42] Yeats identified Joyce's contribution to this dissociation as breaking up 'the logical processes of thought by flooding them with associated ideas or words that seem to drift into the mind by chance' throughout 'the vulgarity of a single Dublin day prolonged through 700 pages ...'[43]

Yeats was a vigorous defender of Joyce in public. Speaking for himself and the other judges when he awarded the literary prize at the Tailteann Games in Dublin in 1924, he said that, although Joyce as a non-resident was ineligible, 'we feel ... that it is our duty to say that Mr. James Joyce's book, though as obscene as Rabelais, and therefore forbidden by law in England and the United States, is more indubitably a work of genius than any prose written by an Irishman since the death of Synge.'[44] Three years later, speaking in the Irish Senate during a debate on copyright law, Yeats confessed, 'I do not know whether Joyce's Ulysses is a great work of literature, I have puzzled a good deal over that question ... All I will say is that it is the work of an heroic mind.'[45]

Trailing behind Yeats, much of the literary establishment only gradually recognized the fullness of Joyce's achievement. The warm critical approbation of the judiciary contributed to that process, influencing Joyce's reception by other writers and the reading public. Indeed, because Woolsey's decision was printed as a sort of preface in the Random House edition of *Ulysses* until 1986, and in The Bodley Head edition until 1960, countless readers first saw Joyce's novel through the lens of Woolsey's legal decision, which may be the most widely read judicial opinion in history. The encounter of law and literature in the trials of *Ulysses* thus had profound implications for both law and literature.

Ironically, and more than a little surprisingly, some literary scholars, writing long after the *Ulysses* decisions had altered the law of obscenity and the practice of publishers, began to criticize the *Ulysses* opinions, especially Judge Woolsey's, for being too deferential to literature and literary critics. The process began with the distinguished scholar Leslie Fiedler's contention that Woolsey's decision was based on two 'well-intentioned lies'. [46] The first 'lie' wasn't anything Woolsey said. Rather it was what Fiedler thought was 'the assumption' behind Woolsey's statement that Joyce was seeking 'to make a serious experiment in a new literary genre'. The underlying assumption perceived by Fiedler was that 'whatever is truly literature' cannot be obscene.[47] Fiedler maintains that this assumption – so dear to Margaret Anderson's heart – is 'palpably false as criticism'. Since Woolsey was writing a judicial opinion rather than literary criticism, and gave great deference to *Ulysses'* quality as literature without adopting the absolutism of the challenged assumption as a legal principle, Fiedler's criticism seems misplaced.

The other 'lie' claimed by Fiedler is what he describes as Woolsey's finding that the novel 'did not tend to excite sexual impulses or lustful thoughts' and that 'though perhaps "somewhat emetic", it was "nowhere aphrodisiac"'. Fiedler omits to say that Woolsey's finding that *Ulysses* did not excite sexual impulses or lustful thoughts was qualified by his statement that such was the 'net effect' of reading the book 'in its entirety'. Although Woolsey's 'nowhere aphrodisiac' statement was not explicitly so qualified, his opinion is susceptible to a reading that accommodates the notion that, as the Second Circuit later explicitly said, certain passages of the novel could excite lustful thoughts. The ambiguity of Woolsey's opinion is best understood in the context in which it was written: Woolsey was a trial court judge bound to adhere to the decision of the Second Circuit in the *Bennett* case that any excitation of sexual desire rendered the entire work obscene. As a trial judge, he lacked the power, exercised by the Second Circuit when the government appealed his decision, to overrule *Bennett* and grant literature a qualified immunity from the law of obscenity.

Paul Vanderham's *James Joyce and Censorship* builds on Fiedler's critique, but addresses Woolsey's opinion as a judicial decision, rather than as literary criticism. Vanderham argues that the opinion is based on an erroneous theory about literature and thus fails 'to provide a lasting foundation for freedom of speech' and encourages 'a dangerous indifferentism'.[48] The erroneous theory of literature that Woolsey's opinion assertedly 'embraces and elaborates' is what Vanderham calls the 'esthetic theory', which he defines as the idea that 'art affects nothing', that 'people are not influenced by what they read'.[49] Vanderham points to no place where Woolsey says this. Rather, he asserts that the 'theory' or 'logic' of Woolsey's decision is that books do not affect readers.[50] Vanderham's assertion is flatly contrary to the opinion's elaborate effort to measure the effect of the book on '*l'homme moyen sensuel*' and its finding that the book is more emetic than aphrodisiac. A finding that the book tends to induce vomit rather than lust cannot fairly be said to be based on the theory that books have no effect on readers.

Given the absence of any reference to the esthetic theory in the text of Woolsey's opinion, Vanderham seeks support for his argument in two minor aspects of Ernst's brief. The first is a reference in a footnote to pages of Stuart Gilbert's *James Joyce's* Ulysses in which Gilbert quotes the passage from *A Portrait of the Artist as a Young Man* that, as recounted in Chapter 3, JBY had recommended to Quinn in 1920. In that passage, Stephen Dedalus espouses the theory that beauty induces stasis rather than the kinetic reactions of desire or loathing.[51] The second is the assertion that Ernst argued that 'people are not influenced by what they read'.[52] In fact, Ernst's brief merely expresses doubt that people are influenced by what they read, and then proceeds on the assumption that they are.[53] But Ernst's brief is a side issue. The important point is that Woolsey's opinion neither quotes Stephen Dedalus's theory nor asserts that readers are not affected by what they read. The fact that a judge rules in favour of an advocate's client does not necessarily mean that the judge has accepted all – or even any – of the advocate's arguments. The judge's opinion must be evaluated on its own terms.

Vanderham repackages his 'esthetic theory' critique by referring to 'Woolsey's characterization of [*l'homme moyen sensuel*] as a sophisticated reader who experiences only esthetic emotion when reading literary works and upon whom *Ulysses* can have no kinetic effect whatsoever'.[54] Woolsey said no such thing. He defined *l'homme moyen sensuel* as 'a person of average sex instincts', the equivalent in obscenity law of the reasonable man in the law of negligence. Vanderham's impression of Woolsey's reaction to *Ulysses* as a reader is not a 'characterization' by Woolsey. This misnomer may result from failing to distinguish between the two roles performed by Woolsey. He was deciding a legal question when he determined that the proper test of obscenity was the book's effect on a person of average sex instincts. This was an important – if implicit – determination and the Second Circuit's explicit affirmance on this point fundamentally changed the law of obscenity. Vanderham seems to have no quarrel with this aspect of Woolsey's decision. Rather, he objects to the fact that Woolsey, as trier of fact, i.e., in the role normally performed by the jury, found that the 'net effect' of the particular book at issue was not to excite sexual impulses. But this is simply a finding of fact about a particular reader's experience of a particular book – not a statement of law.

Joseph Kelly's book *Our Joyce: From Outcast to Icon*, like Vanderham's, focuses on Woolsey's application of the law in his role as finder of fact, rather than on his and the Second Circuit's rulings as to the proper legal standards to be applied by the finder of fact.[55] Although Kelly allies himself with what he describes as Judge Manton's position that 'the testimony of literary experts should not take the place of the Hicklin rule',[56] he does not explicitly argue that critical opinion should be inadmissible in obscenity cases. Rather, he argues that Ernst's reliance on experts implicitly suggested to Woolsey that the average reader of *Ulysses* was equivalent to the experts, and thus the book 'was not obscene because only those at the top of the social ladder would read it'.[57] According to Kelly, Woolsey 'subscribed to the prejudice that Ernst was exploiting' and did not gauge the effect of *Ulysses* on 'the lower classes and the uneducated ...'[58]

There is no prejudice in Woolsey's opinion. He cites experts to establish the literary quality and importance of Joyce's writing, rather than to narrow the scope of his readership. Kelly's argument concerning expert opinion is really not with Ernst or Woolsey, but with the legal principle articulated by the Court of Appeals that the quality of a work as literature gives it a qualified immunity from the law of obscenity, even though the work might have 'a tendency to corrupt' those 'most susceptible to such influences'. To the extent Kelly is arguing that Woolsey, as the finder of fact, was required to consider the effect of *Ulysses* on those most susceptible to being corrupted, he is quarrelling with the law declared by the Court of Appeals. Manton advanced the contrary view, and did not succeed.

Kelly re-frames his argument by faulting Ernst for asserting that *Ulysses* was a 'classic', which, in Kelly's view, implied that it would be 'read only by a narrow audience in a rarefied atmosphere'. Confusing one of Ernst's arguments with what the Court of Appeals actually decided, Kelly argues that Ernst's 'victory was pyrrhic, since it depended so heavily on establishing that the book was a classic'. It was good advocacy for Ernst to try to take advantage of the exception for 'classics', but, as discussed above, the Court of Appeals rejected that jerry-built structure in favour of a broad 'dominant effect' test that applied to all literature. Hand's decision did not limit its holding to books targeted to a rarefied readership. 'The importation of obscene books is prohibited generally,' Hand wrote, 'and no provision is made permitting such importation because of the character of those to whom they are sold.' Hand explicitly contemplated that the doctrine he articulated would apply to all literature. Moreover, he specifically eschewed reliance on the notion that *Ulysses* was equivalent to the time-tested classics. 'We may discount the laudation of *Ulysses* by some of its admirers', he wrote, 'and reject the notion that it will permanently stand among the great works of literature ...' That it was literature was sufficient. Repeating the point later in the opinion to emphasize the breadth of his ruling, Hand wrote, 'It may be that Ulysses will not last as a substantial contribution to literature', but noted that the same was true of many serious efforts of the mind that deserve immunity from the stifling effects of the law of obscenity.

Although Fiedler, Vanderham and Kelly do not fully engage with the import of the *Ulysses* decisions, their energetic critique is a reminder that the issues addressed in the groundbreaking opinions by Judges Woolsey and Hand are still very much alive.[59] More dialogue between the realms of law and literature is necessary to clarify misunderstandings about the significance of the *Ulysses* decisions and fortify the societal commitment to the importance of literature's truth and beauty that is the foundation of authorial freedom.[60]

NOTES

1 Phillip Brooks, 'Notes on Rare Books', *New York Times* (12 May 1935); Morris L. Ernst, 'Reflections on the Ulysses Trial and Censorship', *James Joyce Quarterly* (Fall 1965) (Documents 44 at 51–2).

2 Boyer 267.

3 *Pope v. Illinois*, 481 U.S. 497 (1987).

4 Spoo describes Marvin Miller's edition at 257–8.

5 Letter of 17 January 1934 from Bennett Cerf to Paul Leon (Documents 357).

6 Letter to Margaret Kastor of 30 December 1931, in Spoo at 239.

7 As noted above, Spoo traces the development of the practice of trade courtesy in his authoritative *Without Copyrights*.

8 Letter of 26 December 1933 from Bennett Cerf to John Holroyd-Reece. James Joyce-Paul Leon Papers, National Library of Ireland, quoted in Spoo at 249–50.

9 Letter of 20 December 1933, contained in the John Munro Woolsey papers, Yale Law School, New Haven, Connecticut. Robert Spoo generously drew this letter to the author's attention.

10 Statement by Random House representative Saxe Commins, quoted in *New York World Telegram* (16 May 1934) (Documents 444). See also Jeremy Lewis, *Penguin Special: The Life and Times of Allen Lane* (London: Penguin, 2005) ('Lewis') 63.

11 Letter of 27 October 1931, JLIII, 232–3.

12   Letter to Constantine P. Curran. JLI, 338.

13   Letter from Harriet Shaw Weaver to Joyce, 13 May 1932, cited by Ellmann at 653.

14   Letter to T.S. Eliot, 22 February 1932, JLI, 314–15.

15   Sisley Huddleston, *Back to Montparnasse* (Philadelphia: J.P. Lippincott, 1931) 195.

16   BNA, H.O. 144/20071. Birmingham discusses the Home Office file at 335–6.

17   Michael Adams, *Censorship: The Irish Experience* (Tuscaloosa: University of Alabama Press, 1968) ('Adams') 13–15.

18   *Id.* at 39–63.

19   Letter of 2 September 1932, *CL InteLex* 5725.

20   Letter of 5 October 1932, JLI, 325.

21   Adams, 31; 171–2.

22   Joseph Brooker, *Joyce's Critics* (Madison: University of Wisconsin Press, 2004) 186–7.

23   Lewis 319.

24   C.H. Rolph, ed., *The Trial of Lady Chatterley* (London: Penguin, 1961) ('Rolph') 142.

25   Statement of Penguin Books, quoted in John Sparrow, *Regina v. Penguin Books Ltd.*, 18 Encounter 35 (February 1962).

26   Abe Krash, *The Trial of Lady Chatterley*, a review, *Yale Law Journal*, 71 (1962) 1351, 1359.

27   Rolph 17.

28   Anne Olivier Bell, ed., *The Diary of Virginia Woolf, Vol. 2* (New York: Harcourt Brace Jovanovich, 1977–84) 189, 199 (16 August and 6 September 1922). Woolf and her husband declined to publish *Ulysses* at their Hogarth Press. (Ellmann 443)

29   Virginia Woolf, 'Mr. Bennett and Mrs. Brown', 1924, reprinted in Woolf, *The Captain's Death Bed and Other Essays* (London: The Hogarth Press, 1950).

30   Letter of 7 June 1924 to Louis Gillet, in Louis Gillet, trans. by Georges Markow-Totevy, *Claybook for James Joyce* (New York: Abelard-Schuman, 1958) 31–2.

31   Letter of 15 January 1922 to Sydney Schiff in John Middleton Murry, ed., *The Letters of Katherine Mansfield, Vol. II* (New York: Knopf, 1929) 434.

32   Letter of 11 June 1921 to Sylvia Beach, quoted in JLIII, 50.

33 Quoted in Fitch 124.

34 Dorothy Brett, *Lawrence and Brett: A Friendship* (London: Martin Secker, 1933) 79.

35 D.H. Lawrence, 'Pornography and Obscenity', 1929, reprinted in D.H. Lawrence, *Sex, Literature and Censorship* (New York: Twayne, 1953) 76.

36 *Id.*

37 Compton Mackenzie, *My Life and Times, Octave Five* (London: Chatto & Windus, 1966) 167.

38 Quoted in A. Norman Jeffares, *W.B. Yeats: Man and Poet* (2nd edn, London: Routledge & Kegan Paul, 1962) 318 n. 70A.

39 W.B. Yeats, *Samhain 1908*, in *Explorations* (New York: Collier, 1962) 241–3.

40 Nor did he hesitate to praise *Chatterley*. Writing to Olivia Shakespear in 1933, he commented that, unlike Frank Harris's memoirs, in which 'the sexual passages were like holes burned with a match in a piece of old newspaper ... "Lady Chatterley" is noble ... Those two lovers, the gamekeeper & his employers [*sic*] wife, each separated from their class by their love, and by fate, are poignant in their loneliness, & the coarse language of the one, accepted by both becomes a forlorn poetry uniting their solitudes, something ancient, humble & terrible.' (Letter of 22 May 1933, *CL InteLex* 5879)

41 *Id.* at 4152.

42 Richard Ellmann, *Yeats and Joyce* (Dublin: Dolmen Press, 1965) 470.

43 W.B. Yeats, *A Vision* (London: T. Warner Laurie, 1925) 211–12.

44 W.B. Yeats in *The Irish Statesman*, quoted in R.F. Foster, *W.B. Yeats: A Life, Vol. II: The Arch-Poet* (Oxford: Oxford University Press, 2003) 267.

45 W.B. Yeats, Speech in the Irish Senate, 4 May 1907, in Donald R. Pearce, ed., *The Senate Speeches of W.B. Yeats* (London: Faber and Faber, 1960) 148.

46 Leslie Fiedler, 'To Whom Does Joyce Belong?' in Heyward Erlich, ed., *Light Rays: James Joyce and Modernism* (New York: Horizon Press Publishers, 1984) 26 ('Fiedler') 29.

47 *Id.* at 29. Fiedler uses the word pornography rather than obscenity but the context suggests he equates the two terms.

48 Vanderham 11–12, 167.

49 *Id.* at 11, 115, 166.

50 *Id.* at 166.

51   *Id.* at 127–8; 163. See Documents 249 and 270; and Stuart Gilbert, *James Joyce's* Ulysses (1930; New York: Vintage Books, 1955) 19–23.

52   *Id.* at 166.

53   Documents 266.

54   Vanderham 144.

55   Joseph Kelly, *Our Joyce: From Outcast to Icon* (Austin: University of Texas Press, 1998) ('Kelly').

56   *Id.* at 98.

57   *Id.* at 120.

58   *Id.* at 119–20.

59   Birmingham's *The Most Dangerous Book* does not address in detail the way in which the federal *Ulysses* decisions engaged with and transformed the law of obscenity.

60   A notable contribution to this dialogue is Robert Spoo's incisive critique of Judge Woolsey's critics in his 'Judging Woolsey Judging Obscenity: Elitism, Aestheticism, and Reasonable Libido in the *Ulysses* Customs Case', *James Joyce Quarterly*, Vol. 50. No. 4 (Summer 2013) 115.

Postscript: The Afterlives

The afterlives of the actors in the arresting drama of *Ulysses'* voyage through the courts were guided by the same traits that had driven their earlier performances. John Butler Yeats, who was eighty-one when he wrote his powerful defence of Joyce's terrible veracity, enjoyed another two years of conversation in New York, painting and repainting his unfinished self-portrait and attempting to capture the truth of a beautiful and talented woman, Jeanne Robert Foster, whom he had met at Petitpas' and introduced to Quinn. The procrastinating painter wrote Foster on 12 January 1922 beseeching her to 'give me another chance to save my soul and your face. Both are for eternity'.[1] JBY's last day on earth was 2 February 1922, Joyce's fortieth birthday and the day *Ulysses* was published in Paris. W.B. Yeats later wrote that his father 'kept his interest to the end. His last words [to Jeanne Foster] were "Remember you have promised me a sitting in the morning."'[2] Thanks to Jeanne Foster's kindness and Quinn's generous financial and logistical support, JBY is buried in the Foster family plot in Chestertown, New York, in the Adirondacks.

Ezra Pound, John Quinn, Ford Maddox Ford and James Joyce in Paris, 1923.
(The James Joyce Collection, The Poetry Collection of the University Libraries,
University at Buffalo, The State University of New York, Item 4.6)

John Quinn, who had underestimated the nobility of both the
law and Joyce's contribution to literature, never experienced the
shock of learning of the law's vindication of the novel. He had died
of cancer in 1924[3] not long after a meeting in Paris in October 1923
memorialized in a famous photograph of Quinn with three of the
giants of modernism, showing, as characterized by Ellmann, 'Quinn
severe, Ford [Maddox Ford] agape, Pound sinister, Joyce relaxed and
opaque'.[4] On the occasion captured in the photo, Quinn told Joyce
of his intention to dispose of his entire collection of manuscripts
and offered to give Joyce half the sale price of the *Ulysses* manuscript. When Quinn sold the manuscript the following year to Dr
Rosenbach, whose eponymous museum in Philadelphia still houses

it, Joyce thought the $1975 price ($26,000 today) inadequate, and refused Quinn's generous offer of half the proceeds.[5] Joyce's belief that Quinn undervalued the manuscript likely renewed his lingering thought that Quinn's defence in the *Little Review* case had likewise undervalued his work. When Quinn died, Joyce put his irritation aside long enough to cable his 'grateful sympathy in remembrance of his friendship and kindness' to Quinn's relatives, but his letter to Harriet Shaw Weaver suggested that the sale of the manuscript continued to rankle as an indication of a failure to appreciate the significance of the book, even as he granted that Quinn had done 'many things' for the book and had 'many good qualities'.[6]

Quinn's spectacular art collection survived only a little longer than his assemblage of manuscripts. In contrast to contemporaries like Albert Barnes, A.E. Gallatin and the Cones, Quinn took no steps to ensure the continued life of his collection. Except for a specific bequest of Seurat's *Le Cirque* to the Louvre, Quinn's will required that all his artwork be sold within three years and the proceeds distributed to his sister Julia and her heirs. Thus disappeared what the dealer and novelist Henri-Pierre Roché called the 'explosive nucleus' of a museum of modern art.[7] There is today no Quinn Collection; rather, many of its gems have found their way into other collections. Many paintings purchased in the Quinn liquidation can now be seen in great public museums as part of collections named for those who bought them from the Quinn estate. Examples of such transmutation are the Arensberg Collection of the Philadelphia Museum of Art, the Goodyear Collection of Buffalo's Albright-Knox Gallery, and the Howald Collection of the Columbus Gallery of Fine Arts. Each of the Metropolitan Museum of Art, the Cleveland Museum of Art and the Fogg Art Museum owns eight of Quinn's treasures.[8]

Quinn had found great pleasure in acquiring the works in his collection. He loved, he said, 'the rigor of the game'[9] but in the end he followed the narrow and conventional path of converting his daringly acquired collection back into cash for the benefit of the family from which he had so dramatically emerged. The disposition of his collection was the logical consequence of its acquisition. As noted in Chapter 1, Quinn approached art quite differently from Margaret Anderson and Jane Heap. They saw the experience of art and literature as a path to a life lived more fully and intensely. Quinn found his excitement in the chase of acquiring art, and the satisfaction of supporting the artist. Acquisition was the beginning of the end but, whatever his motivation, Quinn had been an extraordinarily generous and discerning patron of both artists and writers.

William Butler Yeats survived Quinn by fifteen years. He wrote to Jeanne Robert Foster upon Quinn's death, noting his 'great cause for gratitude to [Quinn] on my own & on my father's account', which he summed up nobly by saying that 'his benevolence expressed him as a work of art expresses an artist'.[10] Yeats's candid unpublished comment mentions aspects of Quinn's personality that may have undercut his effectiveness as an advocate: he was 'a friend of many years, to whom I could seldom speak, whose swiftly dictated letters, for all their forcible generalization, told me little. I remember his generosity, his audacity, his irascibility ...'[11]

Joyce was deeply moved when Yeats died on 28 January 1939. He sent a wreath to the funeral, and made a unique concession, telling a friend that Yeats was a greater writer than he.[12] Joyce himself would die nearly two years later, having spent the bulk of his post-*Ulysses* life writing a novel that reacts to the struggle of bringing *Ulysses* to the public by doubling down on the combination of sexuality and linguistic innovation that made *Ulysses*, as Joyce said (borrowing a phrase from Yeats's 'The Madness of King Goll'), 'one of the "world-troubling seamen"'.[13] *Finnegans Wake*, begun in 1923 and published in 1939, emerges out of an obscure sexual or scatological misdeed directed at girls who were 'yung and easily freudened', but the novel is immune from charges of obscenity because it is the product, as Fintan O'Toole neatly put it, of 'a state of associative mania in which practically every word that came into [Joyce's] head, in every language he knew, was pulverized, split, and recombined into as many possible meanings as it could be made to bear'.[14] By putting into hyper-drive the stylistic innovations that made *Ulysses* challenging, Joyce created a work whose difficulties put off many readers, but delight the loyal adherents who spend tremendous energy unpacking its linguistic dazzle. Not surprisingly, Joyce was unmoved by the negative reaction when installments of his final work were published under the title *Work in Progress*. Persistence was his defining quality, and it had served him well in his approach to *Ulysses*. Critic Louis Menand focused on this core characteristic, observing that 'by his persistence' Joyce established the principle 'that the artist must have absolute freedom to work with the world he or she has stumbled across, the world as it is. That most of us now take this for granted is largely because of him.'[15] Certainly Joyce's persistence was a necessary condition to establishing the principle of authorial freedom embodied in the *Ulysses* decisions, but gifted, courageous and far-sighted publishers, a creative lawyer and wise and independent judges were needed too.

Margaret Anderson and Jane Heap continued to perform their lives with the same commitment to truth and beauty without which *Ulysses* might never have reached an audience. Anderson's interest in *The Little Review* waned after the struggle over *Ulysses*, and by 1923 she had decided to move to France in search of the beauty and truth of 'the poignant human being', a decision spurred by a conversation with William Butler Yeats, to whom Quinn had introduced her in New York. Finding in Yeats, whom she proudly referred to as 'one of our earliest contributors', the embodiment of 'the poignant human being' she had been seeking through all her work, and entranced by his 'stories about the people in Europe I wanted to know', she resolved to relocate to Paris.[16] Another factor in her decision was her evolving relationship with the opera singer Georgette Leblanc, who invited her to 'begin a pianistic career by playing accompaniments for her on a forthcoming European tour'.[17] In the spring of 1923 Anderson, Heap and Leblanc sailed to Paris, where Pound introduced Anderson and Heap to the author for whom they had sacrificed so much. Anderson 'had been prepared to see a sensitive man' but 'immediately felt Joyce's strata of sensitization as beyond any possibility for immediate appraisal'. He gave Anderson 'the impression of having less escape from suffering about irremediable things than anyone I had ever known' – an 'impression borne out by nothing that he said so much as by the turn of his head, the droop of his wrist, the quiet tension of his face, his quick half-smile'.[18] She recalled Joyce's account of his famous meeting with Proust: 'I regret that I don't know Mr. Joyce's work, said Proust. I have never read Mr. Proust, said Joyce.'[19]

The opening of the Jockey Club in Montparnasse in 1923 brought together central figures in The Little Review*'s publication of* Ulysses*: Margaret Anderson and Jane Heap (centre second row) and Ezra Pound (far right second row).* Little Review *contributors Mina Loy, Tristan Tzara and Jean Cocteau are in the front row to the right of Man Ray, who took the photo. Kiki de Montparnasse is to Anderson's right. (Library of Congress, copyright Man Ray Trust /ADAGP, Paris and IVARO Dublin 2016)*

Jane Heap, Little Review *foreign editor John Rodker, Martha Dennison, who came to France with Heap, Tristan Tzara, and Margaret Anderson in Paris. (Private collection/Bridgeman Images)*

Anderson and Heap both became followers of the mystic George Gurdjieff, who, as Linda Lappin put it, 'proffered a method of self-development and awareness enhancement'. Gurdjieff's teaching, as summarized by Lappin, focused on 'the awakening of a higher self' that had been 'lulled to sleep by the mechanical quality of modern life'.[20] Gurdjieff's approach found a fertile audience in two frustrated believers in the power of art and literature to awaken the soul from the tedium of daily life. Both spent substantial amounts of time at his Institute for the Harmonious Development of Man located outside Paris.

Heap continued to publish *The Little Review*, turning its focus to the visual arts. By the end of the 1920s she had decided to terminate the journal in order to pursue her spiritual studies. She and Anderson worked together in the rue Bonaparte rooms of Janet Flanner and Solita Solano to assemble the last issue in 1929.[21]

The vindication of their ideas by the United States Supreme Court came too late for the pioneering publishers of *The Little Review*. Anderson continued to live and write in France until Leblanc's death in 1942. Anderson then sailed to America, her passage paid for by Ernest Hemingway, whose work had appeared in *The Little Review*. En route, she met Enrico Caruso's widow, Dorothy, who became her companion over the next decade. After Caruso's death in 1955, Anderson returned to France and died there on 19 October 1973. As Flanner's profile put it:

> [Anderson's] demise ... removed the last standing figure from that small early circle of amateur American publishers – oddly enough, all female – whose avant-garde output a half century ago unexpectedly became a new kind of important international literature. Her most remarkable labor was the serialization – over three years, in the famous vanguard magazine *The Little Review*, which she had founded in 1914 – of James Joyce's 'Ulysses,' that masterpiece of verbal shock and emotional repletion which slowly turned into what it immutably remains today: a literary classic and the guidepost marking the new territory of the twentieth-century English-language novel.[22]

She had performed her life to her own satisfaction: 'The blessings I wanted', she wrote at the end of her last memoir, 'were love and music, books and great ideas and beauty of environment. I have had them all, and to a degree beyond my asking, even beyond my imagining.'[23]

Heap, who had gone to London in 1935 to start a new study group at Gurdjieff's request, remained there until her death in 1964.[24] One of her students, the internationally acclaimed theater director Peter Brook, testified to her continuing power as a conversationalist: 'When she spoke,' he wrote, 'taking as her starting point any simple question, she would open great vistas of understanding, linking the tiniest detail of everyday life to the laws and the forces that conditioned humanity.'[25]

Brook's emphasis on Heap's conversation was a fitting finale to her long and productive life, and almost magically evoked the achievement she shared with Anderson. It had been Anderson's insatiable desire for 'inspired conversation' that led her to found *The Little Review* and to join forces with Heap. The free play of ideas in their conversation animated the extraordinarily influential magazine that brought *Ulysses* to the reading public, and forcefully expressed the powerful principles that ultimately vindicated Joyce's masterpiece and reshaped the law of obscenity. They had both thrown away the script handed them at birth and performed their lives with intensity, meaning and satisfaction.

Ezra Pound died in November 1972 at age ninety-two. Following the launch of *Ulysses*, Pound's poetic energies were largely occupied in composing a long series of poems, *The Cantos,* that begin with Homer's Odysseus – a sign of Pound's desire to replicate Homer's achievement in the new era that, in Pound's view, had begun with Joyce's completion of *Ulysses*.[26] Although *The Cantos* are often difficult and frequently maddening, there is no persuasive counter to Hemingway's assertion that, '[t]he best of Pound's writing – and it is in the Cantos – will last as long as there is any literature.'[27] An admirer of Mussolini, and a terrible anti-Semite (a vice shared, to a lesser degree, by Quinn), Pound made radio broadcasts from Italy during World War II for which the United States indicted him on charges of treason. On 13 February 1946 he was found of unsound mind and not competent to stand trial, and committed to St Elizabeth's Hospital in Washington, DC.[28] Twelve years later, on 8 April 1958, the indictment was dismissed, and he was released on the ground that he was incurably insane and no therapeutic purpose was served by his continued confinement.[29] Even in the sordid circumstances of his later years, Pound's sense of the importance of artistic beauty never deserted him. A passage from one of *The Pisan Cantos*, written while he was incarcerated near Pisa by the US Army, hauntingly evoked Pound's years of pursuit of beauty in art. The passage quotes Yeats's account of Aubrey Beardsley's response when Yeats asked 'why he drew horrors'. The answer: 'Beauty is difficult, Yeats ... So very difficult, Yeats, beauty so difficult ...'[30]

John Sumner died at age ninety-four in 1971, a year before Pound.[31] He had declared in the 1934 Annual Report of The New York Society for the Suppression of Vice that the Second Circuit's decision in the *Ulysses* case 'set a precedent that seriously hampers further work by the society'.[32] He was right. Only once after 1933 did Sumner challenge a book offered for general sale, and '[b]y the end of the decade, the once powerful vice-society movement was a mere shadow of its former self'.[33] Sumner retired in 1950, and, as his *New York Times* obituary put it, the Society 'expired' shortly thereafter.[34]

Morris Ernst outlived Sumner by five years, dying in New York at age eighty-seven in 1976. His post-*Ulysses* years were productive, graced by the fruits of his fee agreement with Bennett Cerf, which had called for only a small retainer but a royalty on sales of Joyce's novel, which, according to the *New York Times,* netted him several hundreds of thousands of dollars.[35] He had a number of significant legal victories, including a 1937 Supreme Court decision upholding the constitutionality of the National Labor Relations Act as applied to the press and establishing the right of news reporters to organize and bargain collectively.[36] His role in the *Ulysses* case figured prominently in a lengthy obituary that described him as a 'witty, tweedy, bow-tied man whose friends included judges and jockeys, bankers and barristers, Presidents and precinct politicians'.[37]

Ernst had a posthumous victory over John Quinn that reflected their differing approaches to dissemination of the truth of literature. The unusual case arose out of a combination of Quinn's generosity and his penchant for exercising control. His will, as construed by the New York Surrogate's Court, left copies of letters of literary and artistic interest to the New York Public Library with a proviso that they could not be copied until 1988. The Irish poet Patrick Kavanagh's brother Peter, believing that the public should have access to the letters, performed the prodigious feat of memorizing passages of the letters, and then writing them down on notepads after he had escaped the watchful eyes of the librarians. After thirty-nine sessions at the library, Kavanagh published 160 excerpts of letters in a 52-page book printed on a hand press he constructed out of a sewing machine, an automobile jack, a ship's wheel, a broom handle and other odds and ends found on sidewalks or in back yards.[38] He offered the volume for sale at thirty-five dollars a copy to collectors of verifiable reputation, sent one copy to the British Museum, and transferred nine copies to his friend Patric Farrell.

When the library commenced suit to enforce Quinn's restriction, Kavanagh appeared in court carrying all remaining copies of the book, other than two which he kept for his personal use, and dumped them onto a table, revealing that he had slashed them in half with a cobbler's knife. That ended the case, except for an order to instruct Farrell to turn over the books in his possession. Farrell consulted the redoubtable Morris Ernst. Not one to surrender, or to ignore an interesting legal issue, Ernst took the position that the 'tawdry' confusions of the law respecting the use of material deposited in libraries needed to be clarified. He urged that the library join in a study to resolve such questions as whose permission was needed to copy a letter, and what constituted 'publication'. More broadly, Ernst stressed that the entire field of law in this area 'needed to be cleaned up'. The library wisely decided it had better uses for its time and money than litigating these issues with Ernst. It dropped the suit against Farrell, who was expected to present his copies of the letters to major libraries, such as the Bibliothèque nationale in Paris and the National Library of Ireland. He gave one copy to Ernst, which now resides at the Ransom Center at the University of Texas. Its echoes of Quinn link the beginning of *Ulysses'* long voyage through the courts to its successful conclusion with Ernst at the helm, and thus make the book a tangible reminder that literature needs the protection of vigorous advocacy.

The measure of an advocate is the satisfaction of the client. Whereas Joyce believed that Quinn had, as Ellmann put it, muffed a chance for a brilliant defence of his novel, his view of Ernst's performance appears in a copy of the Bodley Head *Ulysses* inscribed 'To Morris Ernst, valiant and victorious defender of this book in America, in respectful recognition, James Joyce, 5 October 1934.'[39] Quinn and Ernst were both called on to answer Learned Hand's question whether men will believe 'that truth and beauty are too precious to society at large to be mutilated in the interests of those most likely to pervert them to base uses'. Quinn answered, 'No,' or, at best, 'Not now.' Ernst's answer, echoing Molly, was, 'Yes.'

NOTES

1 Foster-Murphy Collection, New York Public Library ('FM').

2 Unpublished inscription on book of JBY letters in the author's possession.

3 MNY 609, 614–30. Quinn had undergone surgery for intestinal cancer in 1918, and, although abstemious, suffered from cirrhosis of the liver in his last months. *Id.*

4 Ellmann 558.

5 MNY 610–12.

6 Cablegram, 5 August 1924, JLI, 219; Letter to Harriet Shaw Weaver, 16 August 1924, *id.*, 219–20.

7 MNY 647.

8 Zilczer 19.

9 MNY 649.

10 Letter of 10 August 1924 (FM).

11 W.B. Yeats, unpublished note, quoted in John Kelly, gen. ed. *The Collected letters of W.B. Yeats, Vol. III* (Oxford: Clarendon Press, 1994) 730.

12 Ellmann 660 n.

13 Letter of 17 November 1920 from Joyce to Quinn (QC).

14 Fintan O'Toole, 'Joyce: Heroic, Comic', *New York Review of Books* (25 October 2012).

15   Louis Menand, 'Silence, Exile, Punning', *The New Yorker* (2 July 2012).
16   TYW 233–4.
17   *Id.*
18   *Id.* at 244–5.
19   *Id.*
20   Linda Lappin, 'Jane Heap and Her Circle', *Prairie Schooner*, Vol. 78, No. 4 (Winter 2004) 5 at 9.
21   Brenda Wineapple, *Genêt: A Biography of Janet Flanner* (New York: Ticknor & Fields, 1989) 92.
22   Flanner 44.
23   TSN 222.
24   *New York Times* (23 June 1964).
25   Peter Brook, *Threads of Time* (Washington: Counterpoint, 1998) 61.
26   A. David Moody, *Ezra Pound: Poet, Vol. II: The Epic Years* (Oxford: Oxford University Press, 2014) 34. See A. David Moody, *Ezra Pound: Poet, Vol. I: The Young Genius* (Oxford: Oxford University Press, 2007) 314.
27   Ernest Hemingway, in *The Cantos of Ezra Pound: Some Testimonies by Ernest Hemingway et al* (New York: Farrar & Rinehart, 1933), quoted in Noel Stock, *The Life of Ezra Pound* (New York: Pantheon, 1970) 304. Birmingham, without explanation, characterizes Pound as a 'mediocre poet'. (Birmingham 36)
28   Humphrey Carpenter, *A Serious Character: The Life of Ezra Pound* (London: Faber and Faber, 1988) ('Carpenter') 744–53; A. David Moody, *Ezra Pound: Poet, Vol. III: The Tragic Years* (Oxford: Oxford University Press, 2015) ('Tragic Years') 190.
29   Carpenter 842–4: Tragic Years 427–8.
30   Ezra Pound, *The Cantos of Ezra Pound* (New York: New Directions, 1972) 511.
31   *New York Times* (22 June 1971).
32   *New York Times* (25 April 1935).
33   Boyer 246.
34   *New York Times* (22 June 1971).
35   *New York Times* (23 May 1976).
36   *Id.*
37   *Id.*
38   *New York Times*, 23 April 1961.
39   The volume is in the University of Texas Library.

ULYSSES

BY

JAMES JOYCE

*After the law halted the periodic progression of Joyce's story, he framed
the 1922 Shakespeare and Company edition of the completed novel in a
blue-green binding that evokes the Greek flag and the sea. He devoted
careful attention to the precise shade of blue on a cover that became an
integral part of readers' experience of the book. (Bridgeman Images)*

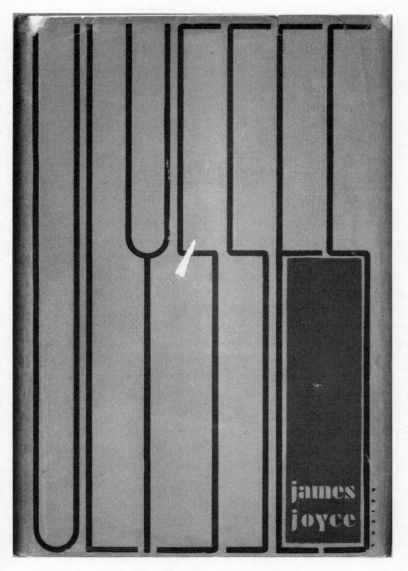

When Judge Woolsey liberated Ulysses, *the novel was heralded by
Ernst Reichl's striking modernist design on the Random House jacket
and introduced by the text of Woolsey's decision. (The James Joyce
Collection, The Poetry Collection of the University Libraries, University
at Buffalo, The State University of New York)*

Abbreviations

The following abbreviations have been adopted for library collections containing material cited in the text.

Berg   The Henry W. and Albert A. Berg Collection, New York Public Library

BNA   British National Archives

BL   British Library

HLS   Harvard Law School

HRC   Harry Ransom Center, University of Texas

NA   United States National Archives

NW   Northwestern University Library

QC   John Quinn Collection, New York Public Library

SUNYB   Poetry Collection, State University of New York at Buffalo

SIUC   University of Southern Illinois Carbondale Special Collections Research Center

UWM   University of Wisconsin-Milwaukee, Archives Department

Acknowledgments

I am deeply grateful to Antony Farrell for his commitment to the book, and to generous friends, named and unnamed, for their essential help: Andrew McNeillie for his unwavering belief in the book, insightful suggestions and energetic support; Roy Foster for his indispensable suggestions; Jim Flannery for his comments and support in the book's early stages; Bob Spoo for generously sharing ideas; Richard Parrino for his very helpful comments; Peter Quinn and Enda O'Doherty for support of early versions; and Eamon Grennan, David Hensler, Joby Ryan, George O'Brien, and Bernard O'Donoghue, for their ideas, support and encouragement. Thanks are gratefully extended to John Vanderham and Kevin Birmingham who each answered a query. I greatly appreciate the assistance of John M. Woolsey III with respect to Judge Woolsey's papers. Many thanks to Djinn von Noorden and Marsha Swan for their care and attention in producing the book. Special thanks to Ger Garland for the beautiful jacket design and Daniel Geist for his generous assistance with respect to the Sidney Geist drawing.

Thanks are gratefully extended to the following unfailingly helpful libraries, archives, and their staffs: John Quinn papers, Manuscripts and Archives Division, The New York Public Library, Astor, Lenox, and Tilden Foundations and the extraordinarily helpful staff, including Tal Nadan and Maurice Klapwald; The Henry W. and Albert A. Berg Collection, New York Public Library and its curator Isaac Gewirtz; the Archives of American Art; the Rosenbach of the Free Library of Philadelphia and Jobi Zink; Papers of James Joyce from the Harley K. Croessmann Collection, Special Collections Research Center, Southern Illinois University Carbondale, and Aaron M. Lisec; Beinecke Rare Book and Manuscript Library, Yale University and June Can; the British Library; the British National Archives and Rodney French; Harvard Law School; Harry Ransom Center, University of Texas, and its director, Stephen Enniss, and Paul Gansky; Georgetown University library; the Library of Congress; United States National Archives, and its able staff, including William Creech and Richard Peuser; Northwestern University Library; Poetry Collection, State University of New York at Buffalo, James Maynard and Marie Elia; and University of Wisconsin-Milwaukee, Archives Department (Abigail Nye) and Special Collections (Alice Ladrick).

Bibliography

Adams, Michael, *Censorship: The Irish Experience* (Tuscaloosa: University of Alabama Press, 1968).

Allt, Peter, and Russell K. Alspach, eds, *The Variorum Edition of the Poems of W.B. Yeats* (New York: Macmillan, 1957).

American Academy of Arts and Sciences, *The Heart of the Matter* (Cambridge: American Academy of Arts and Sciences, 2013).

Anderson, Margaret, 'Announcement', *The Little Review* ('LR') (March 1914) 1–2.

Anderson, Margaret, 'Mr. Comstock and the Resourceful Police', LR (April 1915) 3.

Anderson, Margaret, 'An Obvious Statement (for the millionth time)', LR (September–December 1920) 9.

Anderson, Margaret, 'Mrs. Ellis's Failure', LR (March 1915) 19.

Anderson, Margaret, *My Thirty Years' War* (1930; New York: Horizon Press, 1969).

Anderson, Margaret, *The Strange Necessity* (New York: Horizon Press, 1969).

Baggett, Holly A., *Dear Tiny Heart: The Letters of Jane Heap and Florence Reynolds* (New York: New York University Press, 2000).

Beach, Sylvia, *Shakespeare and Company* (New York: Harcourt, Brace & Company, 1956).

Bell, Anne Olivier, ed., *The Diary of Virginia Woolf, Vol. 2* (New York: Harcourt Brace Jovanovich, 1977–84).

Berman, Avis, '"Creating a New Epoch": American Collectors and Dealers and the Armory Show', in Marilyn Satin Kushner *et al.*, *The Armory Show at 100: Modernism and Revolution* (New York: New York Historical Society, 2013).

Birmingham, Kevin, *The Most Dangerous Book: The Battle for James Joyce's Ulysses* (New York: Penguin, 2014).

Borkin, Joseph, *Corrupt Judge* (New York: Clarkson Potter, 1962).

Bowker, Gordon, *James Joyce* (London: Weidenfeld & Nicholson, 2011).

Boyer, Paul S., *Purity in Print* (2nd edn, Madison: University of Wisconsin Press, 2002).

Brett, Dorothy, *Lawrence and Brett: A Friendship* (London: Martin Secker, 1933).

Brome, Vincent, *H.G. Wells: A Biography* (London: Longmans, Green, & Co., 1951).

Brook, Peter, *Threads of Time* (Washington: Counterpoint, 1998).

Brooker, Joseph, *Joyce's Critics* (Madison: University of Wisconsin Press, 2004).

Bryer, Jackson, 'Joyce, *Ulysses*, and the *Little Review*', *The South Atlantic Quarterly*, 66 (Spring 1967) 148.

Burke, Edmund, *A Philosophical Enquiry into the Origin of our Ideas of the Sublime and Beautiful*, 1757; ed. James T. Boulton (London: Routledge & Kegan Paul, 1958).

Butler, Nicholas M., 'On Permitting Students to Take Studies in Professional School While Pursuing a Regular Undergraduate Course', 3 *Educ. Rev.* 54, 56 (1892).

Cardozo, Benjamin, 'Law and Literature', *Yale Review* (July 1925), in Cardozo, *Law and Literature* (New York: Harcourt Brace, 1931).

Cardozo, Benjamin, 'Modern Trends in Law', Andrew L. Kaufman Papers, Harvard Law School Library.

Carpenter, Humphrey, *A Serious Character: The Life of Ezra Pound* (London: Faber and Faber, 1988).

Carrington, Paul, 'Hail! Langdell!' 20 *Law and Social Inquiry* (1995) 691.

Carrington, Paul, *Stewards of Democracy* (Boulder: Westview Press, 1999).

The Century Association, *List of Members for the Year 1922* (New York: Knickerbocker Press, 1922).

Cerf, Bennett, *At Random* (New York: Random House, 1977).

Cockram, Patricia, *James Joyce & Ezra Pound: A More Than Literary Friendship* (Dublin: National Library of Ireland, 2004).

Colum, Padraic and Margaret Freeman Cabell, *Between Friends: Letters of James Branch Cabell and Others* (New York: Harcourt, Brace & World, 1962).

de Grazia, Edward, *Girls Lean Back Everywhere* (New York: Random House, 1992).

Dell, Floyd, *Homecoming: An Autobiography* (1933; New York: Kennikat Press, 1961).

Deming, Robert H., *James Joyce: The Critical Heritage* (London: Routledge & Kegan Paul, 1970).

Dwight, Theodore W., 'Columbia College Law School, New York', *Greenbag* 1 (1889) 146.

Eliot, Valerie and Hugh Haughton, eds, *The Letters of T.S. Eliot, Vol. 2* (New Haven: Yale University Press, 2011).

Ellmann, Richard, *James Joyce* (rev. edn., New York: Oxford University Press, 1982).

Ellmann, Richard, ed., *The Letters of James Joyce, Vol. II* (New York: Viking, 1967).

Ellmann, Richard, ed., *The Letters of James Joyce, Vol. III* (New York: Viking, 1967).

Ellmann, Richard, ed., *Selected Letters of James Joyce* (New York: Viking, 1975).

Ellmann, Richard, *Yeats and Joyce* (Dublin: Dolmen Press, 1965).

Ernst, Morris, *A Love Affair with the Law* (New York: Macmillan, 1968).

Ernst, Morris and Alexander Lindey, *The Censor Marches On* (New York: Da Capo Press, 1971).

Fiedler, Leslie, 'To Whom Does Joyce Belong?' in Heyward Erlich, ed., *Light Rays: James Joyce and Modernism* (New York: Horizon Press Publishers, 1984) 26.

Fitch, Noel Riley, *Sylvia Beach and the Lost Generation* (New York: W.W. Norton, 1983).

Flanner, Janet, 'A Life on a Cloud', *The New Yorker* (3 June 1974) 44.

Foley, Declan J., ed., *The Only Art of Jack B. Yeats* (Dublin: Lilliput Press, 2009).

Foster, R.F., *W.B. Yeats: A Life, Vol. II: The Arch-Poet* (Oxford: Oxford University Press, 2003).

Gautier, Théophile, *Mademoiselle de Maupin*, 1835, trans. Burton Rascoe (New York: Knopf, 1920).

Georgetown University Law Center, *The First 125 Years: An Illustrated History of the Georgetown University Law Center* (Washington: Georgetown University Law Center, 1995).

Gilbert, Stuart, *James Joyce's Ulysses* (New York: Vintage Books, 1955).

Gilbert, Stuart, ed., *Letters of James Joyce, Vol. I* (New York: Viking, 1957).

Gillers, Stephen, 'A Tendency to Deprave and Corrupt: The Transformation of American Obscenity Law from Hicklin to Ulysses II', *Washington University Law Review*, 85 (2007) 215.

Gillet, Louis, trans. Georges Markow-Totevy, *Claybook for James Joyce* (New York: Abelard-Schuman, 1958).

Goodman, Daniel Carson, *Hagar Revelly* (New York: Macauley, 1913).

Gorman, Herbert, *James Joyce* (New York: Farrar & Rinehart, 1939).

Gregory, Augusta, *Our Irish Theatre* (1913; New York: Capricorn Books, 1965).

Groden, Michael, *Ulysses in Progress* (Princeton: Princeton University Press, 1977).

Gunther, Gerald, *Learned Hand: the Man and the Judge* (New York: Alfred A. Knopf, 1994).

Hand, Learned, 'Sources of Tolerance', in Hand, *The Spirit of Liberty: Papers and Addresses* of *Learned Hand* (New York: Knopf, 1952).

Hapgood, Hutchins, 'Life at the Armory', *New York Globe and Commercial Advertiser* (17 February 1918), 8.

Harvard Law School, *Quinquennial Catalogue of the Law School of Harvard University 1817–1899* (Cambridge: Harvard Law School, 1900).

Heap, Jane, 'Art and the Law' LR (September–December 1920) 5.

Heap, Jane, 'The Episode Continued' LR (November 1918) 35.

Holland, Merlin, ed., *Irish Peacock and Scarlet Marquess* (London: Fourth Estate, 2003).

Hone, Joseph, ed., *John Butler Yeats: Letters to His Son W.B. Yeats and Others* (London: Faber & Faber, 1944).

Huddleston, Sisley, *Back to Montparnasse* (Philadelphia: J.P. Lippincott, 1931).

Jeffares, A. Norman, *W.B. Yeats: Man and Poet* (2nd edn, London: Routledge & Kegan Paul, 1962).

Jepson, Edgar, 'The Western School', LR (September 1918) 4.

Joyce, James, 'Drama and Life', in Ellsworth Mason and Richard Ellmann, eds, *The Critical Writings of James* Joyce (New York: Viking, 1959) 38.

Joyce, James, *A Portrait of the Artist as a Young Man* (New York: Viking, 1962).

Joyce, James, *Stephen Hero* (New York: New Directions, 1963).

Joyce, James, *Ulysses* (New York: Modern Library, 1934).

Kaufman, Andrew L., *Cardozo* (Cambridge: Harvard University Press, 1998).

Kelly, John, ed., *The Collected Letters of W.B. Yeats, Vol. III* (Oxford: Clarendon Press, 1994).

Kelly, John, ed., *The Collected Letters of W.B. Yeats*, Oxford University Press (InteLex Electronic Edition, 2002).

Kelly, John and Ronald Schuchard, eds, *The Collected Letters of W.B. Yeats, Vol. IV* (Oxford: Oxford University Press, 2005).

Kelly, Joseph, *Our Joyce: From Outcast to Icon* (Austin: University of Texas Press, 1998).

Killeen, Terence, *Ulysses Unbound* (Dublin: Worldwell, 2005).

Kilroy, James, *The Playboy Riots* (Dublin: Dolmen, 1971).

Kohfeldt, Mary Lou, *Lady Gregory* (New York: Atheneum, 1985).

Krash, Abe, *The Trial of Lady Chatterley*, a review, *Yale Law Journal* 71 (1962) 1351.

LaPiana, William P., *Logic and Experience: The Origin of Modern Legal Education* (New York: Oxford University Press, 1994).

Lappin, Linda, 'Jane Heap and Her Circle', *Prairie Schooner*, Vol. 78, No. 4 (Winter 2004) 5.

Larrabee, Eric, 'The Cultural Context of Sex Censorship', *Law and Contemporary Problems* 20 (Fall 1955) 672, at 675.

Latham, Sean, *Joyce's Modernism* (Dublin: National Library of Ireland, 2005).

Lawrence, D.H., 'Pornography and Obscenity', 1929, in D.H. Lawrence, *Sex, Literature and Censorship* (New York: Twayne, 1953) 76.

Londraiville, Richard and Janice Londraville, *Dear Yeats, Dear Pound, Dear Ford: Jeanne Robert Foster and Her Circle of Friends* (Syracuse: Syracuse University Press, 2001).

Macaulay, Thomas Babington, *Essay On Milton*, 1825, in Herbert Augustine Smith, ed., *Macaulay's Essays on Addison and Milton* (Boston: Athenaeum Press, 1902) 60.

Mackenzie, Compton, *My Life and Times, Octave Five* (London: Chatto & Windus, 1966).

Martin, Augustine, 'Sin and Secrecy in Joyce's Fiction', in S. Bushrui and B. Benstock, eds, *James Joyce: An International Perspective* (Gerrard's Cross: Colin Smythe, 1982) 143.

Materer, Timothy, ed., *The Selected Letters of Ezra Pound to John Quinn 1914–1924* (Durham: Duke University Press, 1991).

Medina, Harold R., 'Some Phases of the New York Civil Practice Act and Rules', *Columbia Law Review*, XXI, No. 2 (February 1921).

Mill, J.S., *On Liberty* (1859; London: Penguin, 1985).

Monroe, Harriett, 'An International Episode', *Poetry* (November 1918) 34.

Moody, A. David, *Ezra Pound: Poet, Vol. I: The Young Genius* (Oxford: Oxford University Press, 2007).

Moody, A. David, *Ezra Pound: Poet, Vol. II: The Epic Years* (Oxford: Oxford University Press, 2014).

Moody, A. David, *Ezra Pound: Poet, Vol. III: The Tragic Years* (Oxford: Oxford University Press, 2015).

Morison, Samuel Eliot, *Three Centuries of Harvard, 1636–1936* (Cambridge: Harvard University Press, 1936).

Moscato, Michael, and Leslie LeBlanc, eds, *The United States of America v. One Book Entitled Ulysses By James Joyce, Documents and Commentary – A 50-year Retrospective* (Frederick: University Publications of America, 1984).

Murphy, William M., *Prodigal Father* (Ithaca: Cornell University Press, 1978).

Murry, John Middleton, ed., *The Letters of Katherine Mansfield, Vol. II* (London: Constable, 1929).

Nabokov, Vladimir, *Lectures on Literature* (New York: Harcourt Brace Jovanovitch, 1980).

Nowlin, Christopher, *Judging Obscenity: A Critical History of Expert Evidence* (Montreal & Kingston: McGill–Queen's University Press, 2003).

Nussbaum, Martha C., *The Fragility of Goodness* (Cambridge: Cambridge University Press, 1986).

Nussbaum, Martha C., *Love's Knowledge: Essays on Philosophy and Law* (New: York: Oxford University Press, 1990).

Paige, D.D., ed., *The Letters of Ezra Pound* (New York: Harcourt Brace, 1950).

Partridge, M.H., 'The Feminist Discussion', LR (March 1914) 22.

Pater, Walter, *The Renaissance* (1873; New York: Modern Library, 1919).

Pearce, Donald R., ed., *The Senate Speeches of W.B. Yeats* (London: Faber and Faber, 1960).

Plato, *The Republic*, trans. Benjamin Jowett (New York: Modern Library, 1982).

Posner, Richard A., *Law and Literature* (3rd edn, Cambridge: Harvard University Press, 2009).

Pound, Ezra, 'The Classics "Escape"', LR (March 1918) 32.

Pound, Ezra, 'At Last the Novel Appears,' *Egoist*, iv, No. 2 (February 1917) 21.

Quinn, John, review, *Vanity Fair* (May 1917).

Reid, B.L., *The Man from New York: John Quinn and His Friends* (New York: Oxford University Press, 1965).

Roberts, W. Rhys, and Ingram Bywater, translators, *The Rhetoric and the Poetics of Aristotle* (New York: Modern Library, 1954).

Rolph, C.H., ed., *The Trial of Lady Chatterley* (London: Penguin, 1961).

Russell, George, Introduction to *John Butler Yeats, Essays Irish and American* (Dublin: Talbot Press, 1918).

Saarinen, Aline B., *The Proud Possessors* (New York: Random House, 1958).

Shaw, George Bernard, *The Doctor's Dilemma*, 1911, in George Bernard Shaw, *Complete Plays with Prefaces* (New York: Dodd, Mead & Co., 1963) I, 110.

Shesol, Jeff, *Supreme Power* (New York: W.W. Norton, 2010).

Sparrow, John, '*Regina v. Penguin Books Ltd.*', 18 *Encounter* 35 (February 1962).

Spoo, Robert, 'Judging Woolsey Judging Obscenity: Elitism, Aestheticism, and Reasonable Libido in the *Ulysses* Customs Case', *James Joyce Quarterly*, Vol. 50. No. 4 (Summer 2013) 115.

Spoo, Robert, *Without Copyrights: Piracy, Publishing, and the Public Domain* (New York: Oxford University Press, 2013).

Stock, Noel, *The Life of Ezra Pound* (New York: Pantheon, 1970).

Sullivan, Mark C.N., 'Never on Sunday', *University of New Hampshire Magazine* (Spring 1912).

Sultan, Stanley, *Eliot, Joyce and Company* (New York: Oxford University Press, 1987).

Sumner, John, 'The Truth About Literary Lynching', *The Dial*, 71:1 (July 1921) 66.

Tietjens, Eunice, *The World at My Shoulder* (New York: Macmillan, 1938).

Torchiana, Donald J. and Glenn O'Malley, eds, 'A Letter: J.B. Yeats on James Joyce', *Tri-Quarterly* (Fall 1964) 70–6.

Trilling, Lionel, *Sincerity and Authenticity* (Cambridge: Harvard University Press, 1972).

Vanderham, Paul, *James Joyce and Censorship* (New York: New York University Press, 1998).

Walsh, Keri, ed., *The Letters of Sylvia Beach* (New York: Columbia University Press, 2010).

Wilde, Oscar, 'The Decay of Lying', 1891, in *The Prose of Oscar Wilde* (New York: Bonibooks, 1935) 25.

Wilde, Oscar, *The Picture of Dorian Gray*, 1891, in Joseph Bristow, ed., *The Complete Works of Oscar Wilde* (Oxford: Oxford University Press, 2005), Vol. 3, 167.

Wineapple, Brenda, *Genêt: A Biography of Janet Flanner* (New York: Ticknor & Fields, 1989).

Woolf, Virginia, 'Mr. Bennett and Mrs. Brown', 1924, in Woolf, *The Captain's Death Bed and Other Essays* (London: The Hogarth Press, 1950).

Wooten, James A., *Law School: The Establishment of New York Law School, 1891–1897*, N.Y.L. SCH. L. REV. 36 (1991) 337; and 'Must the Law School Go', *New York Times* (4 March 1891) 8.

Yale University, *Catalogue of the Officers and Graduates of Yale University 1701–1910* (New Haven: Tuttle, Morehouse and Taylor, 1910).

Yale University Library, *Guide to Henry Seidel Canby Papers*.

Yeats, John Butler, *An Address Delivered Before the Law Students' Debating Society of Dublin at the Opening Meeting of the Fourteenth Session, in the Lecture Hall, King's Inns, on Tuesday Evening, 21 November 1865, By the Auditor John Butler Yeats A.B., Student of the King's Inns, Dublin, and of the Middle Temple, London* (Dublin: Joseph Dollard, 9 Dame St, 1865).

Yeats, John Butler, *Early Memories: Some Chapters of an Autobiography* (Dundrum: Cuala Press, 1923).

Yeats, John Butler, 'Ireland Out of the Dock', *United Irishman*, 10, No. 241 (10 October 1903).

Yeats, John Butler, 'The Irish National Theatre', *United Irishman*, 10, No. 244 (31 October 1903).

Yeats, W.B., *Autobiographies* (London: Macmillan, 1955).

Yeats, W.B., 'Samhain 1908' in *Explorations* (New York: Collier, 1962) 241.

Yeats, W. B., 'Swedenborg, Mediums and The Desolate Places', 1914, in *Explorations* (New York: Collier, 1962) 31.

Yeats, W.B., *A Vision* (London: T. Warner Laurie, 1925).

Yeats, W.B., *A Vision* (New York: Macmillan, 1938).

Zilczer, Judith, 'The Dispersal of the John Quinn Collection', Archives of American Art Journal, Vol. 30, No. 3 (1979).

Zilczer, Judith, '*The Noble Buyer': John Quinn, Patron of the Avant-Garde*, Exh. Cat. Hirshhorn Museum (Washington, 1978).

Index

Figures in italic denote illustrations.

Abbey Theatre 23, 83, 90
Aesthetic Movement 8
Albright-Knox Gallery 191
Alexander & Colby 18
American Academy of Arts and
  Sciences 156
American Civil Liberties Union 126
American Committee for Relief in
  Ireland 56, 57
American Irish Historical Society 24
Anderson, Margaret: background
  7–8; and beauty 10–11; blank
  pages protest 16; conviction
  and fine 2, 100; cuts *Ulysses*
  62; death 196; education 8;
  feminism 11; first editorial 9–10;
  founds, finances *Little Review* 8,
  11–12; hooked by *Ulysses* 7, 51;
  immortality of books vii, 10;
  inspired conversation 8–9;
  Jockey Club, Paris *194*; Leblanc
  relationship 193–4; lesbianism 29;
  life as performance 9; meets
  Joyce 194; moves to Paris
  193; on Quinn 103; opposes
  discrimination against
  homosexuals and lesbians 11;
  photos *13*, *112*, *195*; prosecution
  76; publishes *Ulysses* extracts vii;

Quinn introduces her to
  W.B. Yeats 193; relationship with
  Heap 15; spirit of *Little Review*
  10–11; supports birth control 52;
  tent dwelling 11–12; trial report
  102; vindication 152, 168
Anderson, Sherwood 9
Andrews, Judge William 102–3
Aquinas, St Thomas 72, 86
Arensberg Collection 191
Art Institute of Chicago 12

Barnes, Albert 191
Beach, Sylvia: captivated by *Ulysses*
  106; 118; cedes *Ulysses* rights 129;
  contract with Joyce 128; Joyce's
  'representative' 128; Joyce visits
  bookstore 108; meets Cerf 128;
  offers to publish *Ulysses* 112–13,
  118; photo with Joyce *107*
Beardsley, Aubrey 198
Bennett, Arnold 135
Bibliothèque nationale, Paris 199
Biggs, James Crawford 144,
  153, 154
Birmingham, Kevin 109
Blackwell's Island 118
Bodley Head 3, 173, 180
Boni & Liveright 118

Bowker, Gordon 108
Boyd, Ernest 135
Brâncuşi, Constantin 20, *21*, 29, *112*
Brennan, Justice William 167, 168
British Academy 179
British Museum 199
Brook, Peter 196–7
Broun, Heywood 78
Browne, Maurice 8
Bryer, Jackson 155
Burger, Chief Justice Warren 169
Butler, Nicholas M. 158, 159

Cabell, James Branch 77, 78, 136
California, University of 176
Canby, Henry Seidel 142–3
Cardozo, Judge Benjamin 158–9
Carson, Sir Edward 82
Censorship of Publications
   Board 173–4
Century Association 129, 143
Cerf, Bennett 128, 171–2
Civil War, US 37
Clean Books Committee 56
Cleveland Museum of Art 191
Coates, Dorothy 27, 28
Cockran, Bourke 56, 57
Cocteau, Jean 112, *194*
Colahan, Judge Daniel 19, 56
Colum, Padraic 129
Columbia Law School 129,
   145, 157–8
Columbia University 96
Columbus Gallery of Fine Arts 191
Committee for Relief in Ireland
   145
Comstock Act 37, 50
Comstock, Anthony 37, 50

Comte, Auguste 85
Conboy, Martin 56–7, 143–4,
   145, 153
Conrad, Joseph 19, 23
Coolidge, Calvin 41
Copyright Office, US 118–19, 120
Corrigan, Archbishop Michael 96
Corrigan, Joseph E. 56, 95, 96, 104
Cowper, William 8
Cros, Guy Charles 112
Cyrus McCormick 8

Davies, Arthur B. 29
Davy Byrne's pub 60
Dean, Harriet 12
de Bosschère, Jean 16
Dell, Floyd 9, 22
de Montparnasse, Kiki *194*
Dennett, Mary 130
Dennis, Holly 126
Dennison, Martha *195*
Dignam, Paddy 60
Dreiser, Theodore 9
Dwight, Theodore 158

Einstein, Albert 122
Eliot, Charles W. 18, 41
Eliot, T.S.: *Little Review* 17,
   29; Quinn buys MSS 19–20;
   reluctant to publish *Ulysses*
   172–3; signs protest against Roth
   122; *Ulysses* on course reading
   list 135
Ellis, Havelock 11, 130
Ellmann, Richard 108, 179, 190, 200
Equitable Life Assurance Society
   18, 56
Ernst, Morris: aesthetic arguments

viii; background 125–6; burned books exhibition 166; censorship 126; defends Farrell 199; freedom of expression 155–6; Joyce dedicates *Ulysses* copy to 200; obituary 198; seeks publisher for *Ulysses* 127–8; structure of *Ulysses* 135; *Ulysses* royalties 198

Farr, Florence 24
Farrell, Patric 199
Fiedler, Leslie 180–1
Fitzgerald, F. Scott 11
Flanner, Janet 10, 16, 196
Fogg Art Museum 191
Ford, Ford Maddox 190
Foster, Jeanne Robert *21, 27,* 189
Frost, Robert 125

Gallatin, A.E. 191
Gautier, Théophile 47, 102–3
Georgetown University 157, 159
Georg, Victor 15
Gilbert, Stuart 135, 182
Goebbels, Joseph 76
Goldman, Emma 11, 46
Gonzaga, St Aloysius 65
Goodman, Daniel Carson 36, 37, 39
Goodyear Collection 191
Gorman, Herbert 135
Gosse, Edmund 177
Gregory, Lady Augusta 23, 27
Gurdjieff, George 195

Hall, Radclyffe 126
Hand, Judge Augustus 40, 87, 130
Hand, Judge Learned: literary judges ix; obscenity definition

viii, 146; on Woolsey 147; photo *147;* Kennerley trial 38, 41–2, 46, 96, 110, 111
Hapgood, Hutchins 22
Harvard Law School 18, 41, 144, 146
Harvard University 41, 176
Heaney, Seamus viii, 59
Heap, Jane: background 12; commitment to beauty 12; conversation 15, 196–7; conviction and fine 2, 100; death 196; defends *Ulysses* 101; Jockey Club, Paris *194;* photos *14, 112, 195;* prosecution 76; publishes *Ulysses* episodes vii; skewers Pound 58; vindication 152, 168; writings 12–13, 15
Hemingway, Ernest 196, 197
Hesiod 48
Hirshhorn Museum 20
Holmes, Justice Oliver Wendell 4
Homer 38, 48
Hoppé, E.O. 15
Horace Mann School 125
Houghton Mifflin 11
Howald Collection 191
Howth Head 61
Huebsch, B.W.: *Finnegans Wake* rights 126; gives up on *Ulysses* 128; meets Ernst 127; negotiates with Quinn 117–18; publishes Joyce's work 116
Hugo, Jean 112

Institute for the Harmonious Development of Man 195
Irish Academy of Letters 174

Jackson, Holbrook 138
James, Henry 103
James, William 41
Jepson, Edgar 57, 58
Jockey Club, Montparnasse *194*
John, Augustus 20
Joyce, James: advised to withdraw *Ulysses* 105; declines to pay lawyers 126; high opinion of W.B. Yeats 192; Irish Academy of Letters invitation 174; meets Proust 194; Paris photos *107, 190*; poetry 17; on *Playboy of Western World* 84; reads about Quinn's defence of *Ulysses* 108; reaction to manuscript sale 191; sends partial manuscript of *Ulysses* to Pound 50; teaches in Trieste 17; UCD L&H 90; uses trial material in *Ulysses* 111

Kavanagh, Peter 199
Keenan, Joseph B. 144, 153, 154, 183–5
Kennerley, Mitchell 36–7, 40
Keough, Judge Martin 19, 56
Killeen, Terence 60
Kuhn, Walt 29

Lamar, W.H. 39
Lane, Allen 175
Langdell, Christopher Columbus 18, 158
Lappin, Linda 195
Larbaud, Valery 132
Law Students' Debating Society of Dublin 85
Lawrence, D.H. 56, 178

Leslie, Shane 65, 96, 97
Lewis Institute 12
Lewis, Ted 125
Lewis, Wyndham 17, 30, 39, 42, 65
Library of Congress 119
Light, James 64
Linati, Carlo 71, 132
Lindey, Alexander 126–7
Lindsay, Vachel 57
Literary & Historical Society, UCD 90
Little Review, The: burning 65; cover March 1918 *54–5*; founding of 2; *Ulysses* extracts vii, 58; protest issue about trial 111–12; supports Emma Goldman 46; visual arts focus 196
Little Theatre 8, 12
Liveright, Horace 118, 120–1
Low, Seth 158
Loy, Mina *112, 194*

Macaulay, Thomas 85, 138
Mackenzie, Compton 178
Mansfield, Katherine 177
Manton, Judge Martin 56, 145–6, 148, 151–2
Martin, Gus 141
Medalie, George 130, 143
Menand, Louis 193
Merrill Jr, Charles E. 142–3
Metropolitan Museum of Art 191
Mill, John Stuart 85–6, 126, 138
Miller, Marvin 170, 171
Moeller, Phillip 100, 111
Monroe, Harriet 16, 57–8
Morand, Paul 112
Morris, May 27

Murphy, William 108
Murry, J. Middleton 135

Nabokov, Vladimir 72–3, 74
National Library of Ireland 62, 199
Nazi book-burnings 75
New York Armory Show 20, 22, 29
New York Law School 126, 157,
    158, 159
New York Public Library 199
New York Society for the
    Suppression of Vice: book-
    burning 75; expiry 198; officers
    143; powers 74–6, 78; prosecutes
    publishers 56; seal 76; sues Roth
    123; sued by Halsey 102
New York University School of
    Law 157

O'Toole, Fintan 192–3
Odyssey, The 103

Pater, Walter 8–9
Petitpas boarding house 24–5
Philadelphia Museum of Art 191
Phillips Academy 129
Picabia, Francis 112
Picasso, Mme 21
Pinker, James 125. 128
Plato: banishes writers 1, 49;
    dangers of language 38; function
    of writers 46
Posner, Judge Richard 4, 156
Pound, Ezra: anti-semitism 197;
    committal to St Elizabeth's
    Hospital 197; final years 197–8;
    Jockey Club, Paris 194; Little
    Review foreign editor 29, 57–8;

on Ulysses 120; Paris photo 190;
    protest over trial 102; reading
    the classics 50–1; reviews Joyce
    36; supports Joyce's work 17;
    supports Little Review 16–7;
    treason charges 197; urges Joyce
    to go to Paris 106
Powys, John Cowper 8, 100, 134–5
Proust, Marcel 194

Queensberry, Marquess of 82
Quinn, John: Anderson and
    Heap's lesbianism 81; art and
    manuscript collector 19–20,
    25–6, 191–2; art collection sale
    191–2; background 17–18; bias
    against Anderson and Heap
    109; biographer 109–10, 155;
    buys Jack Yeats paintings 23;
    buys Ulysses manuscript 20;
    copyright advice 119; arranges
    W.B. Yeats lecture tour 23–4;
    correspondence bequeathed
    in will, 198–9; death 122, 190;
    defends 'Cantleman's Spring-
    Mate' 35, 39–40, 45–6, 50–2;
    defends Kennerley 36–9; defends
    Ulysses 94–6, 97–8; discourages
    US Ulysses edition 121; drawn
    by J.B. Yeats 43; endows Little
    Review 30, 57; and Florence Farr
    24; Joyce's incomprehensibility
    97–8; and Lady Gregory, 23, 27;
    legal approach 2, 156–7; legal
    training, practice 18–19, 156–7,
    159; letter transcripts for sale 199;
    lunches with Picasso 20; meets
    Ezra Pound 25–6; modernism

22; non-communication with Joyce 105; opposes court appeal 46, 99–100, 103, 171; opposes serialization 80–1; Paris photo *190*; patron of Anderson 29; poor defence 109–10; puritanism viii, 77, 81; photos *21, 28*; represents Anderson and Heap 77; reviews Joyce 35–6, 88; rift with W.B. Yeats 27–8; seeks publisher for *Ulysses* 116, 118; sells *Ulysses* manuscript 190–1; sexual secrecy viii, 27–8, 52; sketch *89*; supports J.B. Yeats in New York 24–5, 189; supports Pound 30, 57; thinks *Little Review* case unwinnable 4; writers' and artists' patron 20

Random House: copyright issues viii; Woolsey preface 3, 146, 180; *Ulysses* sales 172
Ransom Center, University of Texas 199
Rascoe, Burton 78
Ray, Man *194*
Reichl, Ernst 203
Reid, B.L. 109–10
Ridgely, Harry S. 153
Roché, Henri-Pierre *21*, 191
Rodker, John 58, *195*
Roosevelt, Theodore 24, 143, 144
Rosenbach Museum 190
Roth, Samuel 121, 122, 166, 170, 171
Royce, Josiah 41
Russell, Bertrand 122
Ryan, Thomas Fortune 18, 56

Saarinen, Aline *21*, 22

Sandburg, Carl 57
Sandymount Strand 59, 72–4, 101
Sanger, Margaret 52
Santayana, George 41
Schorer, Mark 176
Scott, Walter 85
Scribner's Publishers 11
Seton Hall College 96
Shakespeare and Company 106, *107*, 118
Shakespeare, William 62
Shaw, George Bernard 174, 177
Sheehan, Daniel T. 84
Sloan, John 25
Smith, Ada 27
Smith, Paul Jordan 135
Solano, Solita 196
Sophocles 38
Spoo, Robert 119, 120
Star of the Sea church 72, 74
St Elizabeth's Hospital, Washington, DC 197
Stopes, Marie 128, 130, 131
Sultan, Stanley 20
Sumner, John: book burning 74–6, 166; final years 198; *Jurgen* 78; New York Society for the Suppression of Vice 198; Woolsey's opinion 143–4
Swift, Jonathan 88
Symons, Arthur 77
Synge, John Millington 83

Taft, William Howard 41
Tailteann Games 180
Tammany Hall 19
Tarbell, Ida 39, 99
Thayer, Scofield 104, 120